The Home Guard

The
Home Guard

A Military and Political History

S. P. MACKENZIE

OXFORD UNIVERSITY PRESS · 1995

Oxford University Press, Walton Street, Oxford OX2 6DP
Oxford New York
Athens Auckland Bangkok Bombay
Calcutta Cape Town Dar es Salaam Delhi
Florence Hong Kong Istanbul Karachi
Kuala Lumpur Madras Madrid Melbourne
Mexico City Nairobi Paris Singapore
Taipei Tokyo Toronto
and asspociated companies in
Berlin Ibadan

Oxford is a trade mark of Oxford University Press

Published in the United States
by Oxford University Press Inc., New York

British Library Cataloguing in Publication Data
Data available

Library of Congress Cataloging-in-Publication Data
Mackenzie, S. P.
    The home guard : a military and political history / S.P.
Mackenzie.
      p. cm.
    Includes bibliographical references.
    1. Great Britain—History, Military—20th century.   2. Great
Britain—Politics and government—20th century.   3. World War,
1939–1945—War work—Great Britain.   4. Great Britain.   Home Guard—
History.   5. Militia—Great Britain—History.   I. Title.
DA69.M33   1995
941.084—dc20   94-43350
    ISBN 0-19-820577-5

10 9 8 7 6 5 4 3 2 1

Typeset by Best-set Typesetter Ltd., Hong Kong
Printed in Great Britain
on acid-free paper by
Biddles Ltd., Guildford & Hing's Lynn

*For William and Pamela MacKenzie and
Michael and Barbara Richards*

Acknowledgements

This book would not have been possible without the patient assistance of staff from the following libraries and archives: the Berkshire Record Office; the Birmingham Reference Library; Birmingham University Library; the Bodleian Library, Oxford; the British Library; the Buckinghamshire Record Office; the *Bundesarchiv-Militärarchiv*, Freiburg; the Carmarthen County Record Office; the Cheshire Record Office; the Chester City Record Office; the Chesterfield Public Library; the archives of Churchill College, Cambridge; the Gloucestershire Record Office; the Greater London Record Office; the Guildhall Library; the Hampshire Record Office; the Imperial War Museum; the Leicestershire Record Office; the Liddell Hart Centre for Military Archives, King's College London; the Liddle Collection, Leeds University; the Ministry of Defence Library, Whitehall; the Modern Records Centre, University of Warwick; the National Library of Scotland; the Northamptonshire Record Office; the Public Archives of Canada; the Public Archives of Newfoundland; the Public Record Office, Kew; the Public Record Office of Northern Ireland; the Royal Archives; the Scottish Record Office; the Shropshire Record Office; the Suffolk Record Office (Ipswich); the Tom Harrisson Mass-Observation Archive, University of Sussex; the West Yorkshire Archive Service; and the Wiltshire Record Office.

I owe thanks to those who have kindly granted permission to quote from or reproduce copyright material: Her Majesty the Queen for the papers of her father, King George VI; the Controller of Her Majesty's Stationery Office for official papers in the Public Record Office and other archives; the Avon Trustees for the correspondence of Sir Anthony Eden, 1st Earl Avon; the present Lord Croft for the papers of his father, 1st Baron Croft; Mr Michael J. Dible for the papers of his father, Professor J. H. Dible; the County Archivist, Berkshire Record Office for the papers of Lord Glyn; Mr D. C. Grigg for the papers of his uncle, Sir Percy James Grigg; the Clerk of the Beaverbrook Foundation for the diary of Sir Percy Harris and the Beaverbrook correspondence; Mrs D. Bagnall-Oakley for the papers of her father, Major-General L. A.

Hawes; the Imperial War Museum for official photographs; the Trustees of the Liddell Hart Centre for Military Archives for the diary of General Sir Henry Pownall and the papers of Field-Marshal Lord Alanbrooke, General Sir Ronald Adam, General Sir Walter Kirke, General Sir John Burnett-Stuart, and Sir Basil Liddell Hart; the Central Librarian, Chesterfield Library, for the papers of Mr A. E. Slack; the Trades Union Congress for TUC papers; and Mr Peter Liddle for the papers of Mr J. Walker. Efforts have been made to contact all relevant copyright holders, and any omissions from the above list are purely unintentional.

I am also most grateful to David Hall and Andrew Parsons, both of whom offered stimulating comment on the subject of the Home Guard and pointed me to sources I might otherwise have missed. Shawn Spiers, an expert on the career of Tom Wintringham, was kind enough to show me a very useful unpublished paper on his subject which appears in the bibliography. I must also acknowledge the moral support and encouragement provided by my editors, Tony Morris and Anne Gelling, by my desk-editor, Dorothy McCarthy, and by their respective readers.

All opinions expressed in the following pages are, of course, my own responsibility, and do not necessarily reflect the views of the many people who have been of assistance.

Contents

List of Illustrations

List of Abbreviations

AA	Anti-Aircraft (or Ack Ack)
AC	Army Council
ADGB	Air Defence of Great Britain
ARP	Air Raid Precautions [organization]
BEF	British Expeditionary Force
Berks. RO	Berkshire Record Office
Bn	Battalion
BRL	Birmingham Reference Library
BUL	Birmingham University Library
Bod. L.	Bodleian Library, Oxford
Bucks. RO	Buckinghamshire Record Office
CCC	Churchill College, Cambridge
CCRO	Carmarthen County Record Office
CGS	Chief of General Staff
Chester City RO	Chester City Record Office
CIGS	Chief of the Imperial General Staff
C-in-C	Commander-in-Chief
Cmd[r{s}]	Command[er{s}]
CO	Commanding Officer
COS	Chiefs of Staff [committee]
Coy	Company
CPL	Chesterfield Public Library
CRO	Cheshire Record Office
DCIGS	Deputy Chief of the Imperial General Staff
D-G	Director-General
D-GHG	Director-General Home Guard
Div	Division
DMO	Directorate of Military Organization
DPR	Directorate of Public Relations
DSD	Directorate of Staff Duties
GHQ	General Headquarters
Glos. RO	Gloucestershire Record Office

GL	Guildhall Library
GLRO	Greater London Record Office
GOC	General Officer Commanding
GS	General Staff
GSO	General Staff Officer
Hants RO	Hampshire Record Office
HF	Home Forces
HG	Home Guard
IWM	Imperial War Museum
JIC	Joint Intelligence Committee
LCC	London County Council
LDV	Local Defence Volunteers
Leics. RO	Leicestershire Record Office
LHC	Liddell Hart Centre, King's College London
MA	Military Assistant
MAP	Ministry of Aircraft Production
MGGS	Major-General, General Staff
M-O	Tom Harrisson Mass-Observation Archive, University of Sussex
MRC	Modern Records Centre, University of Warwick
NCO	Non-Commissioned Officer
NLS	National Library of Scotland
Northants RO	Northamptonshire Record Office
NUR	National Union of Railwaymen
OKW	*Oberkommando der Wehrmacht* [German Armed Forces High Command]
Ops	Operations
PM	Prime Minister
PRO	Public Record Office
PRONI	Public Record Office of Northern Ireland
RA	Royal Archives
RIIA	Royal Institute of International Affairs
RVC	Rifle Volunteer Corps
Shropshire RO	Shropshire Record Office
SIP	Self-Igniting Phosphorous [bomb]
SMLE	Short Model Lee Enfield
S of S	Secretary of State

SOHG	Staff Officer, Home Guard
SRO	Scottish Record Office
Suffolk RO	Suffolk Record Office (Ipswich)
TA	Territorial Army
TAA	Territorial Army Association
Trg	Training
TUC	Trades Union Congress
UTP	Upper Thames Patrol
VCIGS	Vice-Chief of the Imperial General Staff
VTC	Volunteer Training Corps
WYAS(B)	West Yorkshire Archive Service (Bradford)
WYAS(H)	West Yorkshire Archive Service (Huddersfield)
Wilts. RO	Wiltshire Record Office

Introduction

> . . . anyone who supposes that Captain Mainwaring of Dad's Army is
> a latter-day caricature can rest assured that Mainwaring was there,
> in his hundreds of thousands.
>
> George Macdonald Fraser[1]

Like many others of my generation, the sons and daughters of those who
grew up in the Second World War, my first exposure to the Home Guard
was through the BBC television series *Dad's Army*, which first appeared
in 1967. As my research progressed, I came to suspect that in some ways
at least the fictional platoon of Walmington-on-Sea was not as far off the
mark as I had once thought: full of exaggeration, of course, emphasizing
the absurd, but nevertheless not that distant from reality in at least some
respects.

I cannot, however, claim *Dad's Army* as the inspiration for writing this
book. Conversations with a number of fellow scholars interested in the
political aspects of defence policy formulation stimulated my interest in
the force, but what really made the Home Guard appear a suitable
subject of study was the curiously small amount that had been written on
the subject.

During the war itself a journalist in the Home Guard, Charles Graves,
was given permission to correspond with other units in order to write a
history of the force for the third anniversary. Though containing many
interesting reports and still the most substantial work written on the
subject, *The Home Guard of Britain*, published in the summer of 1943,
was written rather hurriedly and is not always very well organized.
Graves wrote without benefit of access to all the relevant War Office
files, and potentially embarrassing episodes such as the confusion surrounding the decision to raise the force were edited out by military

censors.[2] Moreover, the book was written while the force was still in existence and still evolving.

Graves's book was followed at the end of the war by a much slimmer work by another writer in the force, John Brophy. Published in 1945, *The Home Guard: A Character Study*, is a subjective, rather impressionistic account of life in the Home Guard. With supporting portraits by Eric Kennington, RA, emphasizing the nobility of volunteers, the book is essentially an evocation of what might be termed the Home Guard self-image or ethos: the long, reflective night watches in the countryside, the old men doing their bit, the tendency to improvise and muddle through. Brophy's work, though dealing in generalizations, can best be situated among the dozens of local Home Guard unit histories written by former members that were appearing around the same time and which celebrated their comrades' outlook and activities.[3]

There is no evidence to suggest that Brophy's rather innocuous work was blue-pencilled by censors, but it is worth noting that even after the war there was a distinct reluctance within the military establishment to encourage discussion of the rather chaotic first days of the Home Guard. An article entitled 'Birth Pangs of the Home Guard' by Brigadier William Carden Roe, an officer involved in the planning of the force, was turned down by *Army Quarterly* due to concerns that certain revelations would be embarrassing. 'It would not do, I think,' the editor wrote in February 1946, 'to disclose that co-operation between Home Forces and the War Office was not quite as cordial as one would have liked.'[4]

Perhaps because the force never actually fought off an invasion, for the next thirty years the Home Guard was virtually ignored by military and other historians. An attempt at a volume on the force in the Official History of the Second World War was abandoned in the early 1950s after the proposed author died.[5] Indeed, it was only in the wake of the success of *Dad's Army* that a new book appeared. Written by another writer who had served in the force, Norman Longmate, *The Real Dad's Army*, which came out in 1974, was designed to give people who knew the television series a broader perspective on the Home Guard. It is a good narrative account of how the force developed and what it looked like, but is based exclusively on published sources (mostly Graves's book and a number of unit histories) and the author's personal experience, and does not attempt much in the way of analysis. Furthermore *The Real*

Dad's Army does not deal at all with the brief resurrection of the force in the 1950s.

More recently, Sandhurst historian Ian Beckett has written a typically meticulous study of volunteer forces as part of a new Manchester University Press series on the history of the British Army. This book, *The Amateur Military Tradition*, helps put the Home Guard in proper historical perspective, but—understandably in view of its scope—does not deal in great detail with the Home Guard as an entity unto itself.[6] With the files of the War Office and other relevant government departments nearly all open for inspection at the Public Record Office but as yet untapped, and a growing collection of unit papers surfacing in the county record offices and other local archives in the 1980s, again not previously used, a new history of the Home Guard from the perspective of one not involved in the force seemed worthwhile.

This book is not, I hasten to add, by any means an attempt at a definitive history of the Home Guard, particularly in the social context. Rather, it sets out to explain and analyse the origins, nature, and significance of the Home Guard as a military and a political phenomenon.

The central theme is straightforward. From first to last, for reasons which I hope will become evident in the following chapters, the evolution of the Home Guard was influenced as much by a desire on the part of the government and military authorities to keep the force happy through catering to their perceived wishes as it was by specifically military considerations.

Instead of Home Guard policy being formulated in Whitehall and General Headquarters purely on the basis of defence needs and then sent down the chain of command to be unquestioningly implemented— as was the case with the Regular Army—ministers both junior and senior, civil service mandarins, and even field-rank officers found themselves time and again dancing to a tune set by influential members of the Home Guard. Indeed, it was only through learning to deal with the Home Guard in political terms—not least the gentle art of appearing to follow one policy line while pursuing another—that those who walked the corridors of power were able to assert real control over the force.

This is not to suggest that the Home Guard was lacking in military significance: rather that its military functions were, to a considerable extent, conditioned by what volunteers and (later on) conscripts thought they ought to be doing. Despite the popular image of the force as a collection of old men and teenagers merely playing at soldiers, and by implication not taken seriously by either the public or the authorities, the Home Guard, often as large as the wartime British Army, was in fact an astonishingly strong political force in its own right. As I hope to show, it was able for the most part to pressure the government into addressing its demands as to role and equipment on the basis of its being—quite literally—the people in arms.

To understand this phenomenon fully, however, it is first necessary to examine its ancestry. References during the Second World War to earlier manifestations of the desire to organize the population to repel an imminent invasion were highly romanticized and often historically inaccurate.[7] Distortions and myths aside, however, the Home Guard did have antecedents; and many of the attitudes and actions characteristic of the force and the authorities it dealt with were manifestations of an outlook on the relationship between government and home defence in time of peril which dated back at least to the middle of the nineteenth century and probably earlier. In short, as Ian Beckett has suggested, in order to explain the Home Guard it is first necessary to examine the historical context.

Prologue:
The Amateur Tradition
1558–1939

Form, riflemen, form!

Alfred Lord Tennyson, 1859[1]

'Who shot the dog?'

Popular cry, 1860[2]

At various times over the past 400 years threats of invasion and foreign-inspired revolution, both real and imagined, have haunted the public imagination in England. Each time an invasion or subversion scare developed, moreover, so in most cases did volunteer forces, designed to augment what were considered inadequate defensive measures taken by the government of the day. The combination of circumstances that produced the Home Guard in 1940—the prospect of invasion and an upsurge in the desire of citizens to take personal action—was by no means entirely unique.

The amateur military tradition in England is deep-rooted.[3] Its origins date back to the formation of trained bands in the sixteenth century and even, in certain respects, to the raising of the Saxon *fyrd*. Long-standing suspicions among the gentry that a professional army under central authority would lead to despotism (apparently confirmed by the English Civil War and its aftermath[4]) meant that even after the establishment of the first true standing army in 1689, there remained strong support for the continuation of amateur forces under some degree of local control. Hence the continued existence of part-time forces, and the evolution of various forms of legal obligation for citizens to serve in or contribute to militias when called upon to do so.

The militia, however, in its various forms, suffered from numerous organizational, administrative, and other problems related to spheres of authority and financial responsibility. Especially in time of peace any obligation to serve in or contribute to the militia was considered onerous, and few units had much in the way of arms, training, or *esprit de corps*. The militia smacked too much of imposed obligation rather than appearing a true manifestation of local patriotism. When danger threatened, local notables and even the government might bypass or augment the militia by helping raise special volunteer forces to deal with the emergency at hand.

In 1690, for example, after the defeat of the English fleet by the French off Beachy Head, local volunteer units began hastily to form, both with and without official sanction. Similarly, in 1744–5, when the threat of a Jacobite invasion of England from Scotland seemed great, volunteers came forward to defend their land and liberties. However, it was during the long wars against Revolutionary France and Bonaparte that the volunteer movement came into its own.

Within weeks of war breaking out with the French Republic in February 1793, the Home Secretary, Henry Dundas, found himself deluged with letters from patriotic persons, many living along the south coast of England, proclaiming their willingness to form local defence forces and asking for government help in the way of arms. Volunteers were motivated by two related patriotic aims: to thwart any French invasion attempt and to guard against Jacobin-inspired subversion within the country.

By the following year, 1794, the local gentry and aristocracy had also begun to organize mounted patrols made up of themselves and their tenant farmers—the yeomanry—to watch for possible French landings and guard against republicanism. In the same year an act of parliament was passed to encourage and regulate the raising of volunteer companies.[5] French successes on the Continent and the rise of Napoleon Bonaparte did little to calm the public mood. In 1803, as Napoleon concentrated an army of 150,000 at Boulogne and assembled a transport fleet at ports along the Channel coast, new local volunteer units were raised with official encouragement. By January 1804, there were 342,000 enrolled volunteers, not including officers.[6]

As the likelihood of invasion faded, so too did government and public enthusiasm for the volunteers, who by 1808 were down to 189,000 officers and men. Once the war ended in 1815, only the yeomanry, whose establishment was steadily reduced, were allowed to remain in being to any meaningful extent—chiefly as a means of supplementing the Army in maintaining public order. The incompetent involvement of the Manchester and Salford Yeomanry in the Peterloo Massacre in 1819 heavily eroded public confidence in the force, and successive governments were themselves so lacking in faith that by 1838 the yeomanry establishment had been cut to 14,000 (though they remained one of the few means of curbing riots). When the Chartist demonstrations of the 1840s led to calls from the more affluent sections of society for volunteer units to be raised to keep the peace, the Home Office concluded that the risks outweighed the potential benefits.[7]

The prospect of war, however, and more particularly invasion, could still produce calls for officially sanctioned but locally raised volunteer defence forces. A French invasion scare in 1852, as well as the Crimean War and Indian Mutiny later in the decade, gave rise to talk of re-establishing the volunteers. Suggestions to this effect, from whatever quarter, were rejected by the government of the day. By 1859, however, public suspicions that Louis Napoleon, the new Emperor of France, was planning an invasion, had generated sufficient anxiety to induce widespread support for the formation of rifle volunteer corps.[8] In April 1859, coinciding with French intervention in Italy, public enthusiasm reached a crescendo, *The Times* opining that 'a large and permanent volunteer force' was the only way to keep the country safe.[9]

The Tory government of Lord Derby responded somewhat reluctantly to public pressure by authorizing the War Office to grant official recognition to local rifle volunteer corps raised, armed, and equipped by sufficiently prosperous commanding officers. In June 1859 a new ministry headed by Lord Palmerston sanctioned the issue of twenty-five rifles for every hundred volunteers; and in 1863 a new Volunteer Act was passed, providing government financial support for corps on a per caput basis. With popular enthusiasm running high, recruiting boomed. In 1861 there were over 160,000 volunteers enrolled in the various corps; by 1868 the total had risen to almost 200,000.[10]

The demise of any threat from France in the near future as a result of the defeat of Napoleon III at the hands of the Prussians in 1870 did not, as had been the case after the Napoleonic Wars, signal the rapid decline of the volunteer forces. The rank and file, and even the officers, tended to be less exclusively bourgeois and more working-class in background. But there were still enough commanding officers of influence to form what by the end of the 1880s had become a potent lobby group within the Conservative Party. This group was able to protect the interests of rifle volunteer corps to the same extent as the social importance of the yeomanry and militia officers protected the other two amateur forces.[11]

As manifestations of a popular desire to act locally in defence of the country, the volunteers and yeomanry were a great success.[12] Their actual effectiveness in the event of war, however, was open to serious question. Training was necessarily more limited than in the regular forces, and funding—a mixture of private sponsorship and government grants—often was not entirely adequate to arm and properly equip the volunteers who came forward. Doubts were often expressed over the competence of volunteer units by regular officers, and while professional narrow-mindedness and social snobbery coloured official perceptions in some cases, there can be little doubt that the efficiency of many units left much to be desired.

This gap in efficiency became increasingly evident as changes in weapons, communication and transportation technology emphasized the need for clearly thought-out structures of command and control to make best use of well-trained soldiers and junior officers conversant with the latest tactical developments. As the Prussians had demonstrated against the French to devastating effect in 1870–1, and the British Army was to learn in the South African War with the Boers at the start of the new century, bravery was no substitute for a clear command structure, well-trained infantry, and adequate tactical knowledge.[13] Military forms and attitudes which were appropriate at the beginning of the nineteenth century,[14] in short, were singularly inappropriate by the start of the twentieth.

Through the course of the nineteenth century and on into the first decade of the twentieth century, the regular army, in fits and starts, had undergone a series of reforms (usually in response to major military disasters).[15] The volunteer forces, in contrast, had changed very little. Both the yeomanry and volunteers still functioned largely on a local basis into the first decade of the twentieth century, lacked any administrative or logistical staff beyond individual unit level, were poorly armed and trained, and were almost totally devoid of support services such as transport and medical aid; all at a cost of £4 million per annum.

By the first decade of the twentieth century the yawning gap between the nature of the British volunteer forces and the reserves of Continental armies had become too wide to ignore. But the first efforts at limited reform were thwarted by a barrage of vocal and politically effective obstructionism by volunteer COs and their many Conservative friends in parliament. Anything which might diminish the size or alter the fundamentally individualist and amateur character of the force seemed doomed to failure. In the General Election of 1906, however, the Conservative Party suffered a disastrous defeat, losing over 100 seats. The ranks of volunteer MPs were much reduced, thereby opening the way for radical reform under the direction of a new Liberal war minister, Richard Haldane.[16]

The plan, as Haldane explained in a lengthy memorandum, was to create a new Territorial Force, drawn from the same pool of men as the existing voluntary forces but fundamentally different from its disparate and parochial predecessors. Administration would be taken out of the hands of individual commanding officers and vested in new Territorial Associations in each county. Territorial units would receive standard uniforms and training, and would be organized such that they could take to the field beside the regulars within six months of the outbreak of war. The Territorials, in short, were to be a true second-line national army, based on voluntary part-time service but in other respects similar to the regulars as far as possible. By June 1907 the Territorial and Reserve Forces Bill has passed its third reading, and within ten months 240,000 men had enrolled.[17]

The birth of the Territorial Force appeared to mark the demise of the amateur tradition. Instead of spontaneously generated local corps of men, quite willing to accept government aid when needed but nevertheless seeing themselves as essentially independent entities, there was from 1908 onward to be (in theory at least) a truly national and professionally administered part-time reserve force. The days of the volunteer corps, a more or less satisfactory method of local defence in time of emergency up to the mid-nineteenth century but now anachronistic, seemed over for good. Yet when war broke out in Europe six years later, the idea of rallying and organizing local armed units against invasion was to stage a remarkable come-back.

Official strategic thinking in Britain in the early twentieth century minimized the threat of a German invasion. Sub-committees of the Committee of Imperial Defence (CID) set up in 1903, 1907, and 1913 to assess the potential danger all reported that the problems of shipping enough men across the North Sea, and the likelihood of interception by the Royal Navy, made it unlikely that any full-scale invasion attempt would be made. The most that could be expected, the final CID sub-committee report stated with considerable prescience, were coastal raids which would necessitate the upgrading of certain harbour defences.[18]

Popular opinion in Britain, however, had by this point been thoroughly imbued with the idea that the country was full of German spies and saboteurs, and that with their help the German fleet was preparing to launch a 'bolt from the blue', a lightning invasion of England. In part this was the result of the steady growth of the German navy in the first decade of the new century, and in particular the way in which this expansion was portrayed by lobby groups keen to see the size of the Royal Navy or the British Army increased. Why, they asked, did a Continental power like Germany need to build an increasingly formidable battle fleet, if not ultimately to challenge British naval hegemony and directly threaten the British Isles?[19]

With help from the popular press, organizations such as the Navy League and National Service League quickly succeeded in generating widespread public alarm over the prospect of a German attack. In 1905 the novelist William le Quex was commissioned by Lord Harmsworth to write a blow-by-blow account of how, five years hence, a German force would evade detection and land in England with the help of spies and saboteurs, creating havoc among the unprepared and inadequately defended population until finally brought to book. Serialized in the *Daily Mail* from March 1906 in the wake of a crude but effective advance publicity campaign, *The Invasion of 1910* was an immediate success. Copies of the book were sold in large numbers to a public both fascinated and frightened at the thought of bloodthirsty Uhlans galloping their way into peaceful English towns. Amid continued warnings about the potentially or actually parlous state of British arms, similar fictional accounts followed, including the popular play *An Englishman's Home* by Guy de Maurier, staged in early 1909 at the height of concern over the German naval building programme.[20]

The degree to which talk of a lack of preparedness to meet an invasion attempt, once taken up and sensationalized in the popular press, created a climate of opinion where fiction tended to blend with fact, is illustrated by the spy mania which gripped the country in the years leading up to the outbreak of war. *The Invasion of 1910* had been based on the premiss that a well-organized Fifth Column and spy network would prepare the way for a German invasion, and newspapers continued to feature articles and letters detailing suspicious behaviour by German waiters and spurious plots involving armed risings by German reservists in England as a prelude to invasion.[21]

Thus when war did break out in 1914, there was widespread concern that with their agents in place the Germans would seize the opportunity offered by the dispatch of the British Expeditionary Force to the Continent and attempt a landing on the east coast of England. As one might expect, public anxiety manifested itself, in part, through pressure in parliament and in the press for the government to intern all enemy aliens at once.[22] But it also showed in the spontaneous desire to form new volunteer corps.[23]

For those unable to join up for reasons of health, age, occupation, location, or personal circumstance, a new volunteer force seemed an ideal way to do their bit in defending their country in what appeared to be its hour of peril. With the interventionist state yet to come, and the nineteenth-century self-help ethic still prevalent, it seemed quite natural for many patriotic citizens to begin to organize local anti-invasion forces while calling on the government to provide arms.

As early as 6 August 1914, two days after the British declaration of war, *The Times* was printing a letter from Percy Harris, a Liberal member of the London County Council writing on behalf of a group of similarly minded individuals who were already forming a patriotic committee, suggesting that a volunteer defence force be set up in the capital. Two days later letters appeared from Arthur Conan Doyle, the creator of Sherlock Holmes, and H. G. Wells, among other things the most imaginative of the invasion novelists. They too proposed the raising of local defence forces, Wells talking of 'corps of local volunteers' and Conan Doyle of 'civilian companies'.[24] Around the country there were local notables with similar ideas, as the appreciative correspondence these letters generated shows; and within days local 'Town Guards' and dozens of other similarly named groups were making an appearance in a variety of locations.[25]

The War Office, meanwhile, was not very impressed by all this spontaneous activity. Lord Kitchener in particular, suspicious enough of the effectiveness of the Territorials, was not about to allow untrained civilians to take up arms to no good purpose while diverting recruits and resources away from his New Armies. Consequently in mid-August 1914 a notice was circulated in the national press forbidding the formation of voluntary local defence corps.[26]

In London, however, the patriotic committee of which Percy Harris was a leading member had enlisted significant backing in the persons of Lord Desborough (appointed President) and General Sir O'Moore Creagh (former C-in-C India and now military adviser), and was not about to take this instruction as the final word. In the second half of August, Harris, now honorary secretary of the association, in concert with Lord Desborough, managed through sheer persistence to persuade H. J. Tennant (Under-Secretary of State for War), and finally even Lord Kitchener himself, to allow the committee to organize drill and musketry instruction for those interested.[27]

This compromise, though, did not suit those who wanted a true local defence force, and as fears of invasion grew in the autumn of 1914, fanned by the Northcliffe press, pressure for a more militant role continued to build. 'We want', H. G. Wells explained in a letter printed in *The Times* at the end of October 1914, 'the military status that is conferred by a specific enrolment and some sort of uniform. We want accessible arms.'[28]

The War Office, its position made more difficult by the dispatch of the remaining regular troops to join the BEF on the Continent, finally caved in to this pressure in November 1914. The Army Council were now prepared to grant official recognition to both the Central Association and the various affiliated corps, the former serving, on behalf of the War Office, as the training and administrative headquarters for the latter. There were, however, qualifications. Nobody was to be enrolled in a

Volunteer Training Corps if able to serve in the Regular or Territorial Army; those who might in future be eligible for military service would have to sign an undertaking to enlist if their circumstances changed; uniforms and ranks would be allowed, but only if they did not match those of the Army and a special red armlet with the letters 'GR' sewn on in black were added. No oaths were to be taken. Arms, ammunition, and clothing would have to come from private sources rather than out of public funds.[29]

Such partial recognition did not agree with those who wanted War Office arms as well as a more enthusiastic form of recognition, and though some resigned in disgust many stayed on to work towards making the VTCs as professional as possible.[30] Members of various corps and their supporters, MPs ranging from John Annan Bryce (Liberal MP for Inverness) to Walter Long (Tory MP for the Strand), also put down questions for the Under-Secretary of State for War concerning the future intentions of the War Office. Tennant replied only that the combatant status of the VTCs was 'under consideration' and that all arms and equipment being produced were needed for the Army.[31]

There were, however, signs that by late 1915 the military authorities were beginning to have a change of heart over the VTC issue. The growing manpower demands of the BEF in France were creating considerable difficulties for home commands, and some commanders had already begun to take up offers of help from individual Volunteer Training Corps. By the end of the year, without official status, volunteers were being employed to guard ammunition stores and other vulnerable points, were digging trenches, and were acting as an *ad hoc* Army Service Corps.[32]

Observing this and impressed by the enthusiasm of these volunteers, Field-Marshal Lord French (C-in-C Home Forces since the end of 1915) became a vocal proponent of fully incorporating the volunteer movement into the armed forces of the Crown. GOCs were also keen to put arrangements on a more formal footing, and supporters were keeping up the pressure in the House of Commons.[33] By early 1916 military necessity and political expediency were combining to force the government to take the initiative on the VTC question.

At the end of February 1916, David Lloyd George, then Minister of Munitions, announced in the Commons that the government planned to revive the Volunteer Act of 1863. This would give full recognition to the Volunteer Training Corps as an integral part of the armed forces of the state, and would place them under the jurisdiction of the War Office and the administration of the Lords Lieutenant at the county level.[34] In May, regulations were issued laying down the dimensions of new, standardized volunteer battalions, 229 of which were in the process of forming out of the old corps by June. The War Office conceded that arms and equipment would be provided, when available, to supplement what the volunteers had already come up with through private means. As for the Central Association, it too was drawn into the new order of things when in July 1916 its status was changed to that of an advisory body to the new administrative chief, Lieutenant-General Sir E. C. Bethume, Director-General of the Territorial Force and now also of the volunteers.[35]

The authorities were, in effect, taking over the voluntary movement, the revival of the 1863 Act being one among a number of new measures—the most obvious of these being the introduction of conscription in January and May 1916—designed to mobilize the nation for total war. The enthusiasm with which the War Office now seemed to be taking control of the volunteer movement disturbed some of the original lobbyists, men who had always wanted weapons and equipment from the central authorities but who otherwise viewed the volunteer corps as a locally controlled defence effort by, and for, the local inhabitants.[36]

But by this time it was becoming quite clear to those directing the national war effort that to carry on the fight Britain would have to coherently mobilize and direct all its resources, both material and human. Volunteers could serve a useful function as general auxiliaries. Their efforts, however, had to be centrally organized and deployed to best advantage, avoiding wasteful duplication of function. The traditional concept of the volunteer unit as essentially self-generated and locally controlled was once again proving to be anachronistic.

The extent of the official embrace was evident in December 1916, when the somewhat *laissez faire* Act of 1863—which had among other things stipulated that volunteers could resign on two weeks notice—was replaced by legislation more tailored to the times. Henceforth volunteers were in for the duration unless they could persuade the military authorities that they were incapable of serving. Men were to be divided into five categories, depending on age and occupational circumstance, a certain number of drills per month were required, and all volunteers became subject to military law at all times. Finally, there was a change in uniform. In 1914–15 every effort had been made by the War Office to distinguish the volunteer from the ordinary soldier. Now it was announced that khaki uniforms, the purchase of which would be subsidized by the War Office, were to be worn by the volunteers instead of distinctive green tunics. Volunteer battalions were also getting a full-time regular adjutant, sergeant-major, and musketry instructor, and their officers and NCOs were given the opportunity to train under regular auspices at command training schools.[37]

Put into effect in 1917, the new Act did not in fact prove a success. Neither the Territorial Associations, made responsible for administration at county level, nor all senior Army officers were as enamoured of the force as Field-Marshal Lord French and other VTC proponents. The way in which conscription tribunals were allowing men in certain key occupations to avoid service in the Army on condition they joined the volunteers led to heightened suspicions—probably unjustified—that volunteer units were serving as a haven for men needed at the front. Lieutenant-General Sir Nevil Macready, the Adjutant-General, argued in June 1917 that the Army had lost 100,000 men to the volunteers.[38]

Even more disturbing was the accumulating evidence that the volunteers could not, despite the new Act, take the place of full-time troops in home defence. Though two-month Special Service Companies were created in early 1918 to replace garrison troops needed on the Western Front, the numbers of men with the requisite fitness or time to spare turned out to be only 8,261 rather than the anticipated 13,224.[39] The erratic distribution of volunteer units, their part-time, local nature, the increasing average age of volunteers (as conscription was extended), and finally the limited resources the Army could employ to train and equip them, all militated against success in a more than secondary capacity as guards and general labourers.

As early as December 1917, the War Office had come to the conclusion that the force ought to be trimmed down to 267,150 of the more able volunteers;[40] but volunteer influence in parliament remained strong, and in consequence attempts in early 1918 by Macready and a number of other senior War Office figures to close down the volunteer regiments entirely were unsuccessful.[41]

The armistice of November 1918 spelled doom for the volunteer regiments. The nation was exhausted, and public opinion, viewing the volunteers with a certain cynicism even at the best of times—'George's Wrecks' and 'Genuine Relics' were some of the less charitable interpretations of the 'GR' armband[42]—was in favour of disbandment. The Cabinet quickly suspended the 1916 Volunteer Act, thus ending compulsory service. In February 1919 stand-down orders were issued, and in October 1920 the force—that 'curious amalgamation of martial, moral, and middle-class mentalities', as John Osborne has aptly described it—was formally disbanded.[43]

All in all, the revival of the volunteer movement in 1914, and the ideals of self-help and local patriotism it represented, must have seemed rather quixotic to most senior soldiers and statesmen by the time the First World War had ended four years later. No enemy invasion or raid had been staged, while effort and manpower, despite a certain amount of official discouragement, had been diverted away from the more important needs of the Army. Even after 1916, when the volunteer movement was essentially taken over by the War Office and integrated into the national war effort, the positive contribution of the volunteer battalions to victory as a military force was, to say the least, rather limited.

Thus in the mid-1930s, when the aggressive intentions of Nazi Germany, Fascist Italy, and Imperial Japan forced governments to begin rearming the regular forces, isolated calls in parliament for the revival of some sort of volunteer force met with little official interest or enthusiasm.[44] When small National Defence Companies were organized in 1936 on the premiss that older ex-servicemen might be willing to guard vulnerable points in the event of war, no public funds were expended, the units existed on paper only, and only a few thousand volunteers signed on.

The one or two supporters of a less tokenistic volunteer force were ignored in parliament, and even Basil Liddell Hart, at the height of his influence within the War Office in 1938, was unable to convince anyone that the companies—still two thousand men short of the 1936 target strength of 8,500 and never embodied for even the briefest period of training until 1939—ought to be given a higher profile so that they could 'take over the responsibility for guarding this country against internal dislocation, including the risks of the new type of [aerial] invasion'.[45]

Not even a new war, apparently, could generate sufficient enthusiasm to keep the game alive. In October 1939, one month into the Second World War, recruitment for the companies was discontinued, and in the following months the small number of active volunteers faded entirely from the consciousness of ministers and public alike.[46]

The old volunteer tradition, it seemed, was finally dead beyond re-suscitation. What place was there for Tennyson's call to 'Form, Rifle-men, Form!' in an age of tanks, bombers, and other sophisticated and destructive engines of war? Yet, to an even greater extent than in the First World War, events were to take an unexpected turn. Within nine months a volunteer force appeared so urgently necessary that it rapidly came to dwarf all previous popular efforts in size and scope.

2 Invasion Scare
1939–40

> Telegraph and telephone lines might be cut. Road and rail bridges might be blown up . . .
>
> Basil Liddell Hart, 1939[1]

> We cannot really consider putting against a first class enemy a formation armed with obsolete weapons which we do not consider suitable for modern warfare, except, perhaps, as a last resort . . .
>
> Leslie Hore-Belisha, 1939[2]

Over the twenty years that separated the scuttling of the High Seas Fleet at Scapa Flow and the German attack on Poland, the prospect of invasion had receded from public and official consciousness in Britain.[3] Even after Hitler had begun to rearm Germany in the 1930s, the Royal Navy clearly remained the paramount naval force in European waters. The overriding anxiety in the minds of the public and ministers alike in these years was the new spectre of mass aerial bombardment. It was German bombs raining down on London, rather than bloodthirsty Uhlans in the streets of Dorking, that exercised the popular imagination.[4]

As in 1914, however, the reality of war in 1939 proved rather different than popularly expected. The wailing air-raid sirens that had sent people scurrying for cover within minutes of the British declaration of war on Germany had been a false alarm; and while Warsaw was being razed by the Luftwaffe, the cities of Britain were left alone. The war, it seemed, would not after all begin with a knock-out blow from the air.

That left open the question of what the Germans *did* intend to do against Britain. If the enemy was not about to strike through bombing, in what form could a threat come? It was at this point that invasion fears began to resurface in official circles. In the first weeks of the war a spate of diplomatic and Secret Intelligence Service reports seemed to point to an imminent German seaborne assault on Britain, and the possibility of a small airborne landing was also mooted.[5] Despite the inherent improbability of such moves—the surface units of the German navy, tiny in comparison to its Wilhelmine predecessor, were vastly outnumbered by the ships of the Home Fleet, and a few thousand paratroopers would have been unable to accomplish much by themselves—these intelligence reports were taken seriously enough for the War Cabinet to consider what action might be taken.

The C-in-C Home Forces, General Sir Walter Kirke, thought the threat exaggerated, and some ministers were equally sceptical; but the newly installed First Lord of the Admiralty, Winston Churchill, was convinced that the possibility of German troops being landed on the east coast of England should not be overlooked.[6] Even if—as the War Cabinet eventually concluded—the real risk of attack in the autumn of 1939 was slight, the First Lord argued that forming a home defence force from those who could not be accommodated within the regular armed forces but who were keen to play their part would be popular and would free soldiers from garrison duty.

Writing to Sir Samuel Hoare, the Lord Privy Seal, on 8 October 1939, Churchill waxed enthusiastic:

Why do we not form a Home Guard of half-a-million men over forty (if they like to volunteer) and put all our elder stars at the head and in the structure of these new formations. Let these five hundred thousand men come along and push the young and active out of all their home billets. If uniforms are lacking, a brassard would suffice, and I am assured there are plenty of rifles at any rate.[7]

Meanwhile, without any official encouragement, a very similar idea was being put into effect in Essex, where volunteers not liable for call-up into the services were coming forward to join the self-styled 'Legion of Frontiersmen'. The Adjutant-General, Sir Robert Gordon-Finlayson, was enthusiastic when told of this development in November, and argued that 'if encouragement were given to the creation of a voluntary force of this nature, it was likely to meet with a very ready response all over the United Kingdom'. War Office files on the VTC were suddenly dusted off for reference purposes.[8]

The initial enthusiasm, however, quickly waned. With the Chiefs of Staff concluding that the danger of invasion or raids was slight as long as sufficient naval and air forces were protecting the sea approaches to Britain, nothing came of Churchill's suggestion, while the Legion of Frontiersmen appears to have died a natural death. As the belligerents settled into the months of the Phoney War, that apparently bloodless stalemate after the German conquest of Poland had been completed, the novelty of enemy inactivity *vis-à-vis* Britain began to wear off.[9] By the end of 1939 the mini-invasion scare was over.

The Phoney War, of course, was merely the calm before the storm. An eventual clash of arms between the main armies on the Continent had been expected. What had not been expected was the speed and over-whelming success of the first enemy thrusts. Acting with the boldness and masterly co-operation of arms that would soon make *Blitzkrieg* a household word, German units occupied Denmark and most of the key cities and ports of Norway within hours of their first assaults on 9 April. The shocked Allies responded with weak, ill-prepared, and ultimately futile expeditions to re-take Trondheim in central Norway and Narvik in the north.

Barely a month later, as the Allies were still scrambling to respond to events in Scandinavia, the main attack in the West began as German units moved into the Netherlands and Belgium. On 14 May, four days into the fighting, the situation in Holland became so hopeless that the Dutch army was forced to surrender. Two days later an even more alarming development occurred as the bulk of the German armoured force, after forty-eight hours' fighting, smashed through weak French defences in the Sedan area and drove rapidly westward, threatening to cut off the main Allied field armies fighting in Belgium. By 20 May the Germans had reached the sea, and eight days later the Belgian army capitulated.

These developments transformed both the strategic situation and the public mood. In the wake of the demonstrated ability of the German armed forces to carry out a large-scale combined operation in Norway, and in the knowledge that most, if not all, of the Channel coast would soon be occupied, the prospect of a German invasion of England sud-denly seemed alarmingly real. The public apathy characteristic of the Phoney War rapidly dissolved into general concern and alarm.[10] Two threats in particular came to haunt both the public and the government: the likelihood of a Fifth Column and airborne landings.

As the news from the Continent went from bad to worse, questions began to be raised as to how the Germans could have overcome Allied resistance with such apparent ease. With verifiable facts hard to come by, rumours began to multiply. Nazi sympathizers, it was said, had engaged in a co-ordinated campaign of espionage and sabotage which had gravely weakened local defences. Though a Fifth Column of sorts did exist in Norway and the Low Countries, its impact on the fighting was in reality quite minimal; but as the Norwegians, then the Dutch, and finally (and most shockingly for those who remembered the grim defiance of King Albert in 1914) King Leopold of the Belgians made terms with the Germans—thereby apparently leaving the BEF and French forces in the lurch—Fifth Column suspicion continued to grow.[11]

Moreover, if the presence of enemy agents was such a central feature of German strategy against allies, who was to say that there was not an active Fifth Column in England too? The papers were soon full of such speculation, and by late May 1940 the intelligence division of the Ministry of Information, set up to monitor civilian opinion and morale, was noting that public fears concerning the Fifth Column were reaching alarming proportions. Indeed, 'the situation in a few places has become slightly hysterical'.[12]

The authorities were almost as worried as the public. A widely circulated report from Sir Neville Bland, the former British minister in the Hague, painted a nervous picture of 'the enemy in our midst' based on supposedly hard evidence he had gathered in Holland. 'I have not the least doubt', Bland argued, 'that when the signal [by Hitler to invade] is given . . . there will be satellites of the monster *all over the country* who will at once embark on widespread sabotage.'[13] On 27 May the Chiefs of Staff argued in a paper presented to the War Cabinet that 'ruthless action should be taken to eliminate any chances of "Fifth Column" activities'.[14]

Of even greater concern was the likelihood of parachute landings. The daring glider and parachute assaults on the forts at Eben Emael in Belgium and other important sites had quickly led, through enemy propaganda and rumour, to the strong belief that the Germans could and would use large numbers of airborne troops in an attack on Britain.

This threat was bound up with Fifth Column fears, in that it was generally expected that spies and traitors would help German parachutists and glider troops find their landing areas and guide them to important targets. Enemy parachutists, moreover, could themselves be in disguise: after all, had not that been the case in Holland? (German paratroopers were said to have been seen in nuns' habits and other unlikely costumes: Virginia Woolf, living in Monks House, Rodmell, near the Sussex coast, found herself being 'warned of clergymen in parachutes'.[15]) Even the normally rather staid *Times* was caught up in the mood of alarm, running an editorial on 11 May which categorically stated that enemy parachutists 'might speak English quite well. Some might be sent over in civilian dress to act as spies. The general public must be alert.'[16]

Whitehall was just as alarmed. On 10 May the Air Ministry circulated a rather bizarre memorandum to other government departments warning that the reason enemy parachutists held their arms aloft while floating to the ground was to lull defenders into thinking they were surrendering; whereas in fact they held a grenade in each hand, ready to hurl down on unsuspecting troops. The Home Office, meanwhile, was distributing a circular to the public explaining that 'German parachutists may land disguised as British policemen and Air Raid Wardens'.[17] Lord Croft, who had been appointed Under-Secretary of State for War when Churchill became Prime Minister on 10 May, estimated with some alarm that the Germans could land up to 100,000 troops from the air.[18] Five days after the issue of the Air Ministry memorandum a 'parachutist scare' in London led to the instant recall of officers to Wellington Barracks.[19]

The parachute threat, like the danger of sabotage and espionage, was in reality less great than was feared. Sympathy for National Socialism had always been confined to a small minority in Britain, and Sir Oswald Mosley as leader of the British Union of Fascists made it clear that while he opposed the war, if England was actually attacked he and his men would fight against rather than aid any invader.[20] Alien residents of Austrian or German origin were for the most part political refugees even more hostile to National Socialism than the locals. Enemy agents could indeed be landed by parachute, but due to the vigilance of the population and the nascent double-cross system MI5 found it comparatively easy to pick them up before they could do any harm.[21] As for a full-scale airborne assault, the German armed forces had only 7,000 fully trained paratroopers in the spring of 1940, and had suffered quite severe losses in men and transports during operations in Holland. When an invasion plan was finally drawn up in the summer, it called for the landing by parachute and glider of only one-tenth the number of troops Lord Croft had feared could be used.[22]

Subjective impressions, however, can be just as influential as objective reality, bearing in mind that even supposedly well-informed figures had little to go on beyond the undoubted reality that the Germans were sweeping all before them. As Allied fortunes went from bad to worse, and rumour-fed speculation hardened into the certainty that the enemy could strike anywhere at any time through combined operations by airborne assault forces, spies, and local traitors, fears that the country was inadequately protected began to be voiced. The BEF was across the Channel fighting for its life, and few localities had the reassurance of troops nearby. What use would the village constable be against ruthless saboteurs and parachutists?

Within days of the German offensive in the West getting under way, the government found itself under pressure in parliament and in the press to take two courses of action. First, suspect aliens should be interned as a security measure. Second, the government should take steps to allow the people to take up arms in defence of their homes against the invader.

Sections of the Rothermere press, it has been suggested, were rather more strident in their demands for the internment of enemy aliens than public concern justified.[23] Whatever the truth of the matter, the campaign was strong enough as early as 23 April for the calmer *Times* to complain of undue 'hysterics'. Parliament was also soon in on the act, seventy Conservative MPs meeting on 19 April to discuss the Fifth Column threat. Five days later Sir John Anderson (Home Secretary) found himself having to explain the government's position before the 1922 Committee. 'It is very easy in wartime', as Anderson put it in a letter to his father, 'to start a scare.'[24]

Despite such pressure, and the rather alarmist reports of Bland and others, there was resistance within the Home Office to the idea of depriving German refugees and others of their liberty without evidence of actual wrongdoing. But with the War Cabinet JIC (Joint Intelligence

Committee) and MI5 clamouring for action, Anderson was forced to give way. On 12 May, orders were issued for the internment of German and Austrian nationals in coastal areas, but letters continued to stream in to Anderson's office calling for wholesale incarceration. The *Manchester Guardian* summed up the general reaction by stating that 'no half measures will do'. On 16 May most of the remaining male aliens were rounded up, and on 21 June the decision was taken to intern even those aliens, men or women, previously considered harmless.[25]

The internment of aliens, however, was only one aspect of popular concerns over invasion. Just as strident were calls for the government to allow people to take up arms. After all, even if every German refugee was behind barbed wire, enemy agents could still be landed by parachute along with actual parachute troops as a precursor to seaborne invasion. People were eager to do their bit.

As early as 22 April, the Scottish press baron Lord Kemsley was privately proposing to the War Office that rifle clubs be formed to serve as the nucleus for a home defence force. Kemsley thought the need for such a force so 'urgently necessary' that he was prepared to organize and finance such an effort himself.[26] The deteriorating military situation only served to make such ideas more attractive, and by 8 May Lord Mottistone was proposing in the House of Lords that 'local levies armed with rifles might be found from among the older men to guard isolated places of importance'.[27] Two days later, as public concern mounted even further, Josiah Wedgwood, the maverick Labour MP for Newcastle-under-Lyme, wrote to the Prime Minister and to the War Office urging that the entire adult civilian population be trained in the use of arms and given weapons with which to repel the invader. Wedgwood then decided to prod the government further by tabling a question for the Secretary of State for War asking if 'plans had now been made for effective civilian defence against invasion' and stressing that within the civilian population there existed 'a great demand for instructors, training, rifles and organization, as well as a willingness to take their part efficiently, without pay, especially against parachutists'.[28] Sir Percy Harris, meanwhile, the Liberal MP who had played a central role in pressuring the Asquith government to support the VTC in the First World War, was being urged by friends to renew his lobbying efforts.[29]

Newspaper columnists employed by many of the major papers were also enthusiastic about the raising of local defence forces. In the 12 May issue of the *Sunday Express*, for example, Brigadier E. L. Spears suggested that the government should 'issue free arms licences and permits to buy ammunition to men possessing revolvers, rifles, or guns who are judged trustworthy by the police'. On the same day the *Sunday Pictorial* was asking (apparently in all seriousness) 'whether the Government has taken steps to train golfers in rifle shooting, so that they can deal with stray parachute descenders'. Two days later G. Ward Price argued in the *Daily Mail* that a volunteer 'national militia', composed of veterans too old to join up again, should be formed to combat parachutists. 'The middle-aged man', Price concluded in ringing tones, 'is entitled to demand the right to defend his country against the new danger that threatens us.'[30]

The British Legion, meanwhile, was formulating its own plan for a home defence force. At the annual conference of Legion representatives, the Legion President, Major-General (retd.) Sir Frederick Maurice, introduced a motion on Whitsun urging the War Office 'to consider the immediate formation of Local Defence Rifle Units with the co-operation of British Legion Branches'.[31] The motion was passed enthusiastically, and on 15 May it, along with a summary of Legion resources, was passed on to the War Office by the National Chairman with the support of sympathetic MPs such as Sir A. R. J. Southby (Tory Member for Epsom, Surrey).

Letters poured in to editorial offices, military headquarters, and the offices of MPs and the Prime Minister supporting such ideas or proposing similar organizations.[32] A letter printed in *The Times* on 12 May typified the general expectations and fears of many concerned citizens throughout the country. Roderick Jones explained how

I have spent this Sunday in my village in Sussex. An air troop carrier landing on the Downes—indeed a handful of German parachutists—could take possession of the village and of the look-out posts on the cliffs. . . . Some dozens of able-bodied men and myself, armed with rifles, could handle this situation with at least some measure of success. But as things are we should be obliged to stand by helpless and do nothing. A similar situation might arise in hundreds of other villages and towns from Land's End to John o' Groats within the next few months. Ought we not to anticipate it by arming—and swiftly?[33]

The attitude of the authorities to such calls to arm the people was more ambivalent than it was on the connected issue of the internment of enemy aliens. It was true that the possibility of a secret espionage network unaffected by internment efforts was regarded with some concern in security circles.[34] The threat of airborne attack was also a source of continual worry, ministers agreeing that there was serious cause for concern in 'the lack of defensive measures against attack by parachute troops'.[35] At the same time, however, both the Home Office and the War Office were concerned that arming the people (unlike interning aliens) would give rise to more problems than it solved.

The prospect of citizens being allowed to take matters into their own hands, rather than relying on the traditional forces of security and public order—the Army and the police—raised some disquiet. Who knew what chaos might ensue if, as the journalist John Langdon-Davies was advocating in a soon-to-be-published paperback on the parachute menace, 'every householder, every head of family', took up arms 'to protect his own homestead'?[36] If every Tom, Dick, and Harry started carrying a loaded weapon around and thinking of himself as an independent or local patriotic fighter, the potential for mayhem and manslaughter would be incalculable.

In the second week of May, the Home Office issued a press release explaining what the public should and should not do in the event of an enemy landing. 'It would not be correct', *The Times* paraphrased the key passage, 'for country gentlemen to carry their guns with them on their walks and take flying or running shots as opportunity offered.' It was the task of the Army to deal with enemy parachutists; civilians who offered armed resistance would only put themselves in the position of *francs-tireurs* and be shot out of hand if captured.[37]

Senior military authorities also had reservations, foreseeing residents forming 'private defence bands' which the Army would not be able to control properly. Early representations by a well-connected former VTC member calling for the revival of the Corps met with no evident enthusiasm in the War Office, and Lord Kemsley's proposal, while acknowledged as a 'generous and patriotic offer', was, like other written representations by civilians, politely turned down.[38] Similarly, when GHQ Home Forces received an unsolicited plan dated 6 May for an independent local defence organization from an unemployed colonel in the TA Reserve, the assistant military secretary replied by suggesting that such a plan was really a matter for the Home Office rather than the

Army (the implication being that any such organization could only be considered viable as a branch of civil defence—i.e. that civilians should not bear arms).[39] As the then Chief of the Imperial General Staff (shortly to become C-in-C Home Forces), General Sir Edmund Ironside, later argued for the benefit of the Cabinet, 'armed civilians acting independently might well upset the plans of a Military Commander by their unexpected and unorganized activities'.[40]

On the other hand, to ignore or sidestep the calls for local defence bands to be organized would place the new government in an awkward situation at a time when many Conservative MPs were still deeply uneasy at the thought of Churchill as Prime Minister.[41] It was true that many of those lobbying for action could appear rather shrill. ('He gives the impression', Harold Nicolson noted of Josiah Wedgwood after his first call to arms in the Commons, 'of being a little off his head.'[42]) But there were enough such people in and out of parliament to make some placatory action appear politically judicious. What was more, it was becoming clear to both the government and the military authorities that people were already beginning to take matters into their own hands.

In Deptford, an attempt was underway by the municipal government and the local Labour MP, W. H. Green, to organize a local force armed with revolvers and cudgels which would guard 'vital points' such as the ARP control room against attempts at sabotage. In Herefordshire, Lady Helena Gleichen was organizing eighty of her staff and tenantry into irregular observation bands around the ancestral home of Much Marcle, and felt no hesitation in approaching a nearby battalion of King's Shropshire Light Infantry to ask for the loan of rifles, ammunition, and 'a couple of machine guns if you have any'.[43] In Northamptonshire, G. Drummond was described by an observer as 'inciting villagers [of Walgrave] to form into a defence force'.[41] In Essex, the Territorial Association, devoid of function since the merging of the part-time Territorial Army with the Regular Army at the start of the war, became involved in another unauthorized attempt to create a local force, initially labelled in this case the 'County of Essex Volunteer Corps'.[45]

Similar efforts were taking place in other parts of Northamptonshire, in Worcestershire, Cambridgeshire, and in East Anglia. There were reports that all along the east coast 'farmers are oiling up their fowling pieces, preparing to receive what they call "those umbrella men"'.[46] By midnight, 12 May, the Ministry of Home Security was alarmed enough to send out a teleprinter message to all regions requesting confirmation that 'bands of civilians were forming all over the country and arming themselves with shotguns, etc., for the purpose of detecting and dealing with German parachutists'.[47]

Faced with this alarming prospect and the continuing lobbying efforts of MPs and others, the military authorities and their political masters began to reconsider their position. An officially sponsored paramilitary body would allow for a degree of control over people's patriotic urges, and would also allow for extra security around vulnerable points ranging from aerodromes to munitions factories—a task from which General Kirke had for many months wanted regular troops withdrawn.[48] Time, however, was at a premium by the second week of May. The situation on the Continent was daily changing for the worse, the public mood of impending crisis was evolving at the same brisk pace, and all planning had to be done in conditions of considerable alarm and great administrative confusion—so much so that in the wake of a War Office query to Home Commands on 7 May concerning the potential merits of a 'Volunteer Home Army' two separate schemes for an official local volunteer defence force were inadvertently begun.[49]

On 9 May, just before the fall of the Chamberlain government, Lord Halifax, the Foreign Secretary, had suggested to the War Cabinet that, in response to Lord Mottistone's call, 'local levies armed with rifles might be found among the older men to guard places of importance'.[50] By 11 May, with the approval of a new War Cabinet even more anxious to respond, the Chiefs of Staff were considering a provisional War Office plan put forward by the Adjutant-General, Major-General Sir Robert Gordon-Finlayson. Anxious to keep any new force as controllable as possible, Finlayson envisaged small groups of British Legion volunteers being attached to searchlight companies—the only regular units to be found just about everywhere in the country. The volunteers, once they had spotted the invader, would enable the regulars to report the landing area to higher authority and take appropriate action.[51]

Meanwhile, in a manner typical of the last-minute improvisation that characterized home defence measures in this period, the C-in-C Home Forces had gained the impression on the evening of 10 May after conversations in London that GHQ Home Forces, rather than the War

Office, was to produce a plan. For some weeks General Kirke had been discussing with General Sir Guy Williams (GOC Eastern Command) what the C-in-C's GSOI described as 'the burning problem' of what action to take 'before civilian residents on the East Coast took the law into their own hands and formed their own private defence bands'.[52] Hence even before the decision to raise a force had been taken in Cabinet, a rough outline for a volunteer organization had been prepared by the staff at GHQ Home Forces in consultation with Eastern Command, a plan which Kirke believed had been accepted on 10 May as the basis for future action.

The GHQ plan was different in certain key respects from the outline drawn up by Gordon-Finlayson. Less worried at the prospect of volunteers running amok if not under direct supervision by the Army, the GHQ staff envisioned a loosely organized force raised in villages and towns for the defence of the immediate locality. Units would begin as sections of a dozen or so men, expanding to form platoons, companies, and eventually battalions as more recruits came forward. The Lords Lieutenant, meanwhile, would be called on to organize things at the county level and appoint suitable district organizers.

Harking back to the days when the Lords Lieutenant had played an active military role and striking a strong note of aristocratic *noblesse oblige*, the organizational aspect of the plan was less a matter of class bias than the logical consequence of the severe shortage of trained staff officers within Home Forces. Given that GSOs could not be spared for new duties, the only alternative was to bring into play the existing social hierarchy of the countryside for administrative purposes. In operational terms, however, Kirke's plan was more radical than reactionary, envisioning local sections and platoons acting as independent reconnaissance bands 'on the principle of the Boer Commando'.[53]

The existence of two separate plans for a volunteer force came to light on Sunday, 12 May, at a hastily arranged meeting at the War Office. Gordon-Finlayson was understandably nonplussed to hear a comparatively junior representative from Home Forces point out that his ideas did not at all accord with what General Kirke understood to be his sphere of responsibility. Worse yet, the man responsible for searchlight units, General Sir Frederick Pile (C-in-C ADGB) voiced his concern that the RAF would take a dim view of any scheme which threatened to disrupt the smooth operation of the air defence system. In a rather embarrassing scene, the C-in-C Home Forces himself had to be called in to thrash the matter out with the Adjutant-General. With time at a premium, Gordon-Finlayson eventually agreed that Kirke's plan should go forward.[54]

A whirlwind of *ad hoc* decisions were made the following day at the War Office, normal procedure giving way before the urgent need to get things started as quickly as possible. A representative from the Adjutant-General's directorate shrank from the use of the word 'commando' in the Army Council instruction being drafted on the new force, but otherwise an impromptu group of three or four GHQ and War Office staff officers, all colonels or below in rank, simply made up the details concerning recruitment, uniform, and (a very bold departure from normal Whitehall practice) financial liability as they went along. All seemed to be moving briskly, if not always smoothly. 'Little did they realise', as Brigadier W. Carden Roe, then serving as Kirke's GSOI, later noted, 'the enormities which they were committing.'[55]

By 8 p.m. on 13 May the essential details had been worked out and instructions prepared for dispatch to Army commands and the police (it had been decided that the constabulary would be best able to handle enrolment through the presence of police stations throughout the country). The necessary instructions were duly signed by the nearest available senior officer, Major-General L. K. H. Finch (Director of Recruiting and Organization), and the message sent out by word of mouth to GHQ Home Forces and Eastern Command that a green light had been given for the raising of Local Defence Volunteers.

Given that the details had been thought up and finalized in the space of a single day (13 May 1940), it was inevitable that the LDV would suffer from a certain number of administrative and logistical teething problems. There was, for instance, the not inconsequential fact that the War Office 'operations group' had given no consideration to arming the volunteers who signed on. (Perhaps the result of an implicit belief that the key thing was to get people involved in an official organization, however lacking in logistical support, before they became *de facto* vigilantes.) This omission, along with others, would lead to trouble. But confusion was worsened by the intervention of higher authority.

The original idea had been for General Kirke to make a broadcast on 13 or 14 May calling for volunteers. Anthony Eden, however, the newly appointed Secretary of State for War, made it clear that as the minister concerned it was he, and not Kirke, who should speak to the people. It would be a chance for a new minister working in the shadow of Churchill to impress himself upon the public mind, and, as an inside observer wrote, he 'seized the opportunity' with alacrity.[56] 'I decided', Eden himself later explained in a rather high-minded tone, 'to talk to the nation on this subject.'[57] This caused a certain amount of last-minute revision in the script before Eden was on the air after the BBC nine o'clock evening news on 14 May. In the end this delay may have been a blessing in disguise, given the problems staff officers were having in coming up with suitable instructions to issue to home commands ex- plaining the new plan.

While Carden Roe and the others involved in the *ad hoc* group of 13 May had been making decisions, they had worked with a consciousness of the need to avoid unnecessary delay. On the morning of 14 May, however, a sudden halt was called by a senior civil servant, probably P. J. Grigg, the Permanent Under-Secretary and the man in charge of War Office finance. Did Carden Roe realize that out-of-pocket expenses had been promised without Treasury approval? Who was he to say that the civilians enrolled in the LDV would be granted combatant status under international law? No legal officer had been over the plans. All in all the plan appeared slapdash and ill-thought-out in the extreme. 'Did I realise', Carden Roe paraphrased Grigg's final words of rebuke, 'that it had taken years of forethought and an Act of Parliament to inaugurate the Territorial Army?'[58]

The result was a further delay in the issue of the official Army Council instruction while at least some of the relevant authorities were con- sulted. Hence while in Eastern Command matters had been set in train on 13 May, the other home commands and chief constables did not receive instructions until 15 May. In effect much of the civil and military command structure was quite unaware of what the LDV was supposed to look like beyond what every citizen knew from Eden's broadcast on the evening of the 14th.[59] It was only on 16 May that GHQ Home Forces felt able to issue general instructions on the subject.[60]

In spite of confusion and delays, however, it must have appeared to those most immediately involved with the genesis of the Local Defence Volunteers that matters were more or less unfolding as they should. After all, the central point of announcing the formation of the LDV was to curb spontaneous public action and show that the authorities were responsive to parliament and the press.

It could hardly be denied that the whole thing had been put together, as Lieutenant-General Sir Henry Pownall dryly wrote, 'without sufficient time for previous thought and organization by the War Office or G.H.Q. Home Forces'.[61] But given that the primary objective was simply to meet public demands for action, it was not so important that no thought had been given to weapons (or indeed anything much beyond the announcement that a force was to be raised). The authorities would be seen to be on the move, and technical problems could be sorted out as they arose. 'Perhaps', Carden Roe noted while reflecting on the public enthusiasm for the LDV idea and his own *faux pas* with the civil service, 'it did not matter much after all.'[62] Unfortunately this would prove not to be the case.

3 Local Defence Volunteers

Spring 1940

LDV: 'Can I have a rifle yet?'
Officer: 'I'm afraid not. Your rifle is coming.'
LDV: 'Humm, so's Jerry.'

Joke, 1st Bn (Cambs) HG[1]

In a voluntary organization such as the Home Guard, public opinion
can never be entirely ignored without disastrous consequences.

T. H. Bisgood, HG Bn Commander, 1940[2]

On the night of 14 May 1940, just after the BBC news, Anthony Eden
made his first speech to the nation as Secretary of State for War. Hundreds of thousands were listening.

'I want to speak to you tonight', Eden began in earnest tones, 'about
the form of warfare which the Germans have been employing so suc-
cessfully against Holland and Belgium—namely, the dropping of troops
by parachute behind the main defence lines.' This much was known to
his listeners, who were well aware of the parachutist menace. The real
news was to come.

'In order to leave nothing to chance,' Eden continued after describing
German tactics, 'and to supplement resources as yet untapped and the
means of defence already arranged, we are going to ask you to help us in
a manner which I hope will be welcome to thousands of you.' Referring
to the countless ordinary citizens—especially those not eligible to enrol
in the regular forces—who had asked to be allowed to serve in defence
of their country in its hour of peril, Eden dramatically announced: 'Well,
now is your opportunity.'

We want large numbers of such men in Great Britain who are British subjects,
between the ages of seventeen and sixty-five, to come forward now and offer
their services in order to make assurance [that an invasion would be repelled]

doubly sure. The name of the new force which is now to be raised will be the Local Defence Volunteers. This name describes its duties in three words. You will not be paid, but you will receive uniforms and will be armed. In order to volunteer, what you have to do is give your name at your local police station, and then, when we want you, we will let you know . . .[3]

The announcement met with an almost instantaneous reaction. In the third and fourth weeks of May and on into June, public concern at the prospect of a Fifth Column and invasion—first aerial and then, as the enemy seized the Channel ports, seaborne—continued to mount, as did the desire to 'do something'. The English Channel, as an American observer put it on 24 May, 'has suddenly shrunk in most people's minds to something no bigger than the Thames'.[4]

Hence, even before Eden had finished speaking, police stations up and down the country—some of which had not been warned of what they were expected to do—were being contacted by eager volunteers. Long lines formed outside the police stations next morning, and within twenty-four hours of the broadcast around 250,000 men had put down their names.[5]

The level of enthusiasm for what the press initially called 'the parashots' was quite astounding. Without waiting for instructions, volunteers in various localities were from the evening of 15 May onward going out on patrol, eager to spot any suspicious activity or sign of the enemy landing. In a manner strongly reminiscent of Kitchener's armies, social organizations—everything from cricket clubs to local hunts—began to form parashot patrols. There was even an 'Eton College Anti-Parachutist Observer Corps'. Civil defence and civil service officers grew alarmed at the number of wardens and office workers who wanted to switch their allegiance.[6]

Nor was the response confined to people living in rural areas, as the War Office planners had assumed would be the case. In towns and cities volunteers signed on in even greater numbers, and a significant number of concerned captains of industry began with the support of the workers to organize special LDV factory defence units.[7] Lord Beaverbrook, as Minister of Aircraft Production, took great pains to sponsor such groups in all 'his' factories in order to boost morale.[8]

By the end of May the total number of volunteers had climbed to between 300,000 and 400,000, and showed no signs of levelling off.[9]

Some in the War Office had apparently been anticipating a maximum of about 150,000 recruits, others perhaps 200,000; even Lord Croft, given to exaggeration, thought that at most 500,000 men would come forward. By the end of June 1940 there were 1,456,000 registered volunteers. 'My expectations', Eden ruefully admitted in August, 'have been far exceeded.'[10]

The War Office, meanwhile, was scrambling to lay down the administrative structure and logistical foundations for a force whose nature had only been sketched out at the time of the 14 May broadcast. On 15 May the help of the Lords Lieutenant was sought in a telegram signed by Eden, and, as already noted, the first telegrams went out from the War Office explaining how the LDV—as conceived by Carden Roe and his group—was to be organized. Military areas would form the basis of administration, with a GSOIII, in consultation with the (civilian) regional commissioner, dividing each area into zones and groups, and with the help of the Lord Lieutenant choosing suitable men to organize these zones and groups.[11] The Home Office, on learning that regional commissioners were to be involved, suggested to them on 16 May that they divide areas into zones on police district lines, which was to be the case in London.[12]

On 17 May, the LDV—in some areas already active—achieved legal status with the passing of a Defence (Local Defence Volunteers) Order in Council.[13] The following day further War Office instructions were issued to Command and Area HQs explaining that volunteers, organized into sections, platoons, and companies (the latter commanded by appointees chosen by area and zone organizers, the company commanders appointing the platoon and section leaders) would not be paid. LDV organizers and leaders, moreover, would not hold commissions or have the power to command regular forces.[14]

Carrying out these instructions in the military crisis surrounding the evacuation of the BEF from Dunkirk (27 May to 4 June) was often a less than orderly process. GHQ Home Forces and home commands were desperately trying to organize their very meagre resources to deal with what seemed like an imminent invasion, and did not have much time to devote to getting the LDV organized.[15] The County Territorial Army Associations, which were soon called on to help administer funds for the LDV, were almost overwhelmed by the task of trying to interpret and process sometimes contradictory but always urgent orders from higher authority while keeping impatient local LDVs at bay. The contrast with the more orderly days of peacetime TAA work was striking. As Colonel (retd.) Sir Francis Metford, chairman of the Gloucestershire TA Association finance sub-committee, later lamented:

In place of T.A. Regulations which run to over 500 closely printed pages and gives [*sic*] full information and instruction on every conceivable subject connected with the Territorial Army, the Association is expected to administer the [Local Defence Volunteers] on instructions contained in an Army Council Instruction of 29 paragraphs together with a few non-committal letters from the War Office.

'Problems arise almost daily which cannot be solved without reference to Military Authority or to the War Office,' Metford complained, 'and often it is doubtful which should be the addressee.'[16]

To make matters even more difficult, more than one Lord Lieutenant proved obstructive due to fears that volunteers would be treated as *francs-tireurs* in an invasion, and some of the junior appointments were causing disgruntlement. In Northamptonshire, for example, Major (retd.) T. C. Shillito, a group organizer, felt it urgently necessary to go round villages to try and gain acceptance for his choices, as some of those passed over were 'disgusted'.[17] In a few cases the local volunteers had already elected their officers; in others, especially in rural areas, the job had already fallen to what one observer characterized as 'the local feudal overlord'.[18] Either way, there was potential for friction with the evolving county administrative hierarchy.

Meanwhile, as the War Office, GHQ Home Forces, subsidiary commands, regional commissioners and Lords Lieutenant scrambled to put together an administrative structure for the LDV, many volunteers were becoming impatient. Eden's dramatic announcement had raised their spirits immensely, but as the days passed and nothing seemed to be happening beyond the taking down of names by the police, a sense of let-down became evident. Eden had stated that the LDV would 'receive uniform and will be armed'; but on 15 May the War Office had let it be known that for the time being only arm-bands with 'L.D.V.' stencilled on them would be available until khaki denim two-piece overalls and extra service caps could be manufactured in sufficient quantity. As for role, all that was said was that it would vary according to local circumstances. Nothing at all was said about the issue of weapons.[19]

Some units, as already noted, responded by simply organizing patrols without waiting for instructions from higher authority, and arming themselves with shotguns and whatever else they could lay their hands on (meaning everything from bags of pepper and cutlasses to ancient muskets and cannon ransacked from museums).[20] But even these volunteers seem to have been troubled by the lack of clear instructions as to training and role, and above all by the absence of arms and equipment. The sense of let-down and resentment increased as more and more people began to get what one zone organizer described as 'a nasty feeling that the Government was not in earnest'.[21] What was more, they were far from reticent about their concerns.

This was in large part a function of the makeup of the force. As the authorities had expected, a large number of volunteers were veterans— though exactly how many was the subject of a variety of estimates. Lloyd George, in a speech in July 1940, stated that 40 per cent of volunteers were Great War veterans, a figure which matched a War Office estimate in early 1941; Churchill spoke in parliament in November 1940 of half the force having seen service in the First World War; while the *Sunday Graphic* later stated that around 75 per cent of the volunteers were ex-servicemen.[22] The latter estimate as an average for the force as a whole is certainly too high, though possible in particular units.

Ex-officers, it is worth noting, appear to have made up a good proportion of the junior command appointments and, in some cases, the ranks. In Peterborough, for example, of the 400 enrolled in the LDV by 16 May, former officers and NCOs numbered twenty-six and fifty-two respectively.[23] Ex-officers also made up a notable proportion of junior appointments in Northamptonshire, where of fifty-five platoon commanders twenty-seven had previously held commissions.[24]

Veterans could also make up a fair proportion of the rank and file. In Westbury, forty-three of the eighty-three volunteers were ex-servicemen. The percentage did, however, vary from unit to unit; in a platoon based in Singleton and Charlton, only seven out of thirty-odd volunteers had previously served in the army.[25] The number of veterans, in short, could vary; but in the summer of 1940 it was on average somewhere in the region of 35 per cent. Not surprisingly in view of the fact that they generally could not join the regular forces, volunteers tended to be either in their teens, middle-aged, or older; though celebrated cases such as Thomas Walton, who lied about his age and joined the LDV at the age of 84 and had served in the Sudan, were the exception rather than the rule. The mean age in 1940 was probably in the region of 35 years.[26]

The administrative appointments were, as might be expected in light of the need to use men of experience, weighted toward retired middle- and senior-ranking officers. *Picture Post* did a survey of one command which reveals that about 37 per cent of the group organizers, 58 per cent of the zone organizers, and all of the area organizers were retired generals, mostly over 60 years of age.[27] Of the ten central London zones, four were run by retired lieutenant-colonels, one by a retired full colonel, two by retired brigadiers, and one each by a major-general, lieutenant-general, and full general.[28] Not all retired generals, however, served in higher appointments. An East Sussex company had six in the ranks, while in exclusive Kensington-Belgravia one squad was made up of eight field-rank officers (plus a token civilian).[29]

There were two important consequences of this veteran-laden composition. First, Great War citizen-soldier veterans tended to think they already knew their job, and as self-styled 'old sweats' were not averse to communicating their frustrations over lack of action to their commanders, the press, or MPs. Second, many of the more senior retired officers, whether serving in the ranks or as organizers and commanders, were men of influence. Either behind the scenes or in public, they were quite prepared to dispute and complain about how the LDV was being handled. As one War Office observer put it, there was bound to be trouble caused by 'the masses of retired officers who have joined up, who are all registering hard and say they know much better than anyone else how everything should be done'.[30]

The real nexus of what can best be described as an unofficial LDV lobby, however, was the Houses of Parliament, wherein sat a large number of ex-service MPs and peers who were either in or had some family or constituency connection with the Local Defence Volunteers. The Palace of Westminster unit included the impressive total of 95 MPs and 17 peers; figures which do not include those MPs who served in other units and as organizers, ex-MPs of influence like Colonel John

Colville, former Secretary of State for Scotland and now an LDV liaison officer at Scottish Command HQ, or Lord Beaverbrook (self-appointed overlord of LDV units in MAP factories).[31]

The government therefore soon found itself under pressure to act more swiftly in the face of volunteer disillusionment. In the Commons, for example, Sir Alfred Knox (Conservative MP for Wycombe), a retired major-general and current member of the Westminster LDV, pointedly told Eden on 21 May that the public was still waiting for something concrete to be done about the force beyond the taking down of names.[32] The following day, Sir Ralph Glyn (Tory MP for Abingdon) began to pressure the Secretary of State for War to sponsor a river-borne version of the LDV to patrol the Thames.[33] Area organizers, meanwhile, were talking to the press, and letters complaining of the delay were being received by Eden daily.[34]

Within the War Office, every effort was being made to keep abreast of events. A relatively small number of .303 SMLE rifles were issued to some LDV units, but there were never enough to go round: a far from atypical company in Caernarvonshire received a grand total of six Lee-Enfields for 400 men.[35] Moreover, in the wake of Dunkirk it was recognized that the re-equipping of the Army (which had left most of its equipment on the beaches) would have to take precedence. Instead, instructions were issued as to how to make molotov cocktails, emergency orders were placed for the shipment of 75,000 First-World-War-vintage Ross Rifles from Canada, and 100,000 mothballed .300 Springfield and Remington P14 and P17 rifles were hastily purchased in the United States.

On 23 May, in recognition that it would take until July for these weapons to arrive in England and that no more Lee-Enfields could be spared, Richard Law (Financial Secretary to the War Office and Conservative MP for Hull West) announced that an appeal was being made to all persons possessing shotguns and rifles to hand them in at police stations so that they could be distributed to needy LDVs.[36] At the end of the month Ralph Glyn, still agitating furiously, was given permission to form the LDV Upper Thames Patrol.[37]

In the first days of the LDV, with little planning done and far more volunteers than expected coming forward at a time when the staff resources of the War Office and home commands were increasingly stretched by the task of building up Home Forces, it was inevitable that the War Office should delegate as much responsibility as it could to the Lords Lieutenant and others for the raising of the force. On 18 May, the Adjutant-General's office had stressed to home commands that the 'outstanding features [of the LDV] should be simplicity, elasticity, and decentralized control'.[18] This resulted, as already noted, in a good deal of confusion and uncertainty, and with over 100 MPs about to meet to make a formal protest in June, the War Office thought it prudent to appoint an Inspector-General for the LDV, Lieutenant-General Sir Henry Pownall (formally Chief of Staff to the BEF). By the end of the month the War Office was also finally able to begin to issue denim overalls and service caps to serve as uniforms.[39]

Such measures did not, unfortunately, entirely alleviate popular anxiety. The overalls often took until July to arrive at unit level, and some volunteers were anxious that with only an armband to identify them, they might be shot by invading Germans as *francs-tireurs*.[40] Moreover, when the overalls were delivered lack of a variety of sizes caused irritation (and much secret mirth among observers). 'If a prize had been offered for the designer of garments that would caricature the human form and present it in its sloppiest and most slovenly aspect,' wrote the historian of the 4th Buckinghamshire battalion, 'the artist who conceived the [LDV] denim was in a class apart.'[41] A rather more substantial cause of continuing concern was the shortage of rifles. Even with private sporting rifles and shotguns supplementing the very small number of issued Lee-Enfields, there were never enough guns to go round. After the arrival of the first batch of Ross Rifles from Canada in the third week of June, Pownall estimated that there was still only one rifle for every six men.[42]

The historian of the Exeter LDV paints a rather alarming picture of what such deficiencies could mean in practice.

The volunteers on patrols and observation posts [in June 1940] were still in civilian clothes and carrying anything they could get hold of. Shotguns, many and weird varieties of revolvers, usually without ammunition, and last but not least, a good hefty stick.[43]

Sir Ralph Glyn, chairman of the House of Commons weapons committee as well as the champion of the river patrol, noted in a justifiable fit of irritation to Kingsley Martin (editor of the *New Statesman*) that until the American rifles arrived volunteers 'really had nothing to fight with except garden-tools'.[44]

Those dedicated to the force, furthermore, were not always certain that the authorities were doing all they could to arm and equip the LDV. The splendidly named Sir Hereward Wake, area organizer in Northamptonshire and a retired major-general, wrote to the Lord Lieutenant on 22 June that there were only 190 rifles for over 15,000 men in his area, that this was having 'a demoralizing effect', and that he and many volunteers shared a 'growing uneasiness' regarding the authorities' concern for the LDVs' welfare in the event of an invasion.[45] 'I think', General (retd.) Sir Hubert Gough reflected when looking back on his first weeks as organizer of the Chelsea LDV, 'they [in the War Office] were positively frightened of "arming the people".'[46] Whatever the constraints on (and prejudices of) the War Office, the fact remained that the public had little confidence in official handling of the LDV.[47]

Lack of weapons and uniforms was one source of controversy. Another, of equal magnitude, was the question of what role the LDV was to play. In the hectic days prior to 14 May, as we have seen, the formation of a volunteer force had been seen by those involved in its planning as being as much a pre-emptive measure as a positive contribution to national defence. Beyond that, the aim seems to have been to use the LDV to combat the Fifth Column and keep an eye out for parachutists. What this meant in effect, as a staff officer assigned to examine the history of the force wrote, was that the Local Defence Volunteers were supposed to 'resemble an armed special constabulary' rather than a front-line combatant force.[48] This was publicly confirmed by Sir Edward Grigg (joint Under-Secretary of State for War with Lord Croft and the man Eden had designated to handle the day-to-day running of the LDV[49]), who sketched out an observation and security role made more concrete when the War Office issued its first real training instruction to the LDV in June.

The Local Defence Volunteers [the pamphlet stated] are neither trained nor equipped to offer strong prolonged resistance to highly trained German troops, and they will therefore best fulfill their role by observation, by the rapid transmission of information, and by confining the enemy's activities. They will also act as guards at places of tactical or industrial importance.

In addition the LDV were to guide regular troops, serve as sentries where necessary, and look out for spies: 'Local Defence Volunteers will be of the greatest value in counter espionage work. They know the local residents and can keep an eye on strangers. Anything suspicious should be reported to the local police.'[50] The LDV, in short, was to be a relatively passive force, reporting to higher authority on German landings and doing what it could to spot spies and hinder enemy communication. As an internal government memorandum put it later that month, the LDV 'are *not* designed for serious offensive fighting'.[51]

From the perspective of the War Office and GHQ Home Forces, conscious of the lack of arms and training in the LDV, this was both wise and prudent. Many LDV units, indeed, had already been manning observation posts, checking identity cards at road blocks, and going on night patrols either under instructions from higher LDV or Army authority or on their own initiative.[52] There was, however, a good deal of variation in orders issued in the summer of 1940, and therefore some conflict with the official line eventually put forth from GHQ and Whitehall.

Many LDV commanders and organizers had been assuming that the Local Defence Volunteers were meant, as the Rutland LDV were told, 'to attack and harass the enemy' as well as to observe them.[53] In May, after all, although GHQ Home Forces had been promoting a passive role, Eastern Command had produced an instruction explaining that 'the L.D.V. will exist to deal without delay with enemy arriving by whatever means possible', and Aldershot Command had sent out a memorandum which stated in unequivocal terms that beyond serving as guards and observers the LDV were to engage in 'immediate offensive action'.[54] This was a very congenial role for those itching to get at the Hun. 'The Volunteer force is a fighting force,' as an operational order issued to one company in Somerset asserted, 'and every means in our power must be taken to kill and disable the enemy.'[55] An inside observer stressed in a letter to Liddell Hart that there were numerous fire-eaters who believed strongly 'that the L.D.V. can tackle anyone and anything' if led with sufficient aggressiveness.[56]

Some unit commanders, to be sure, accepted that observation really was about the only effective action the LDV could take until enough weapons arrived. They, like the War Office, were opposed to letting volunteers bite off more than they could chew. 'It is clear to me', the commander of the Peterborough LDV wrote to his zone organizer on 27 June, 'that my Group Commanders can undertake no offensive or defensive action of any military value with the limited number of weapons under their control.'[57]

There were, however, many LDVs who yearned for a fighting role and were dead set against allowing the authorities to avoid arming and equipping the force by making it virtually non-combatant. Such men had joined up on the assumption that they were in 'some sort of military formation', as one organizer put it, and had no desire to be glorified policemen whose motto (to quote a widely circulated quip) ought to be 'Look, Duck, and Vanish'.[58] Members of the unofficial LDV lobby, MPs and organizers, suspected that the authorities regarded the force, as Wedgwood put it, as a 'stepchild' worthy of little attention or support; or worse yet, in the words of General Gough, as some sort of 'Frankenstein monster' which ought to be strictly controlled.[59] Men like Gough and Wedgwood much preferred the kind of aggressive, martial note struck by the first operational order issued in the 4th (Cambridgeshire) LDV battalion: 'If anything happens, start shooting.'[60] To meekly accept current limitations, as one very keen platoon leader in Leicestershire wrote to his company commander, would be 'almost treasonable'.[61]

Complaints about War Office attitudes were not slow in coming. On 4 June, the Earl of Breadalbane (a member of the Westminster LDV) rose in the House of Lords to state that 'I feel it is my duty to voice the anxiety and dissatisfaction which exist over a large part of the country as to our preparations for home defence.' In his view the LDV were underequipped, were not being given adequate training facilities by the authorities, and needed transport: sentiments echoed by several other peers.[62] Similar though rather less restrained criticism was voiced in the Commons. On 18 June, during a debate on the war situation, Wedgwood asked

if we could have from any Minister opposite [on the government front bench] some reassurance this afternoon that the Local Defence Force is not a mere stepchild of the War Office but is genuinely intended to act in the service of this country, not as an extra policeman to guard the German soldiers when they march through London, but as an active Defence Force, that this Force, if it cannot get rifles, will at least have hand grenades and that it will not be required to retreat but to hold the country.[63]

In Wedgwood's mind, as he made clear in secret session, not only were the authorities not helping volunteers but also 'everything is done to discourage them'.[64] He was not alone in being suspicious.

Throughout the summer months, indeed, MPs concerned over lack of weapons and equipment—people ranging in political stripe from Lieutenant-Commander Richard Tufnell (Tory MP for Cambridge) to George Griffiths (Labour MP for Hemsworth)—tabled a series of potentially embarrassing questions and made suggestions as to how the War Office should act if it was *really* serious about the LDV.[65] A letter published in *Picture Post* some weeks later captured the mood of disgruntlement. 'I want to become,' George Simpson wrote, 'not a middle-aged bridgewatcher, but a capable fighting man.'[66]

Faced with a sustained barrage of complaint and criticism in parliament, the press, and personal letters to everyone from the Secretary of State for War to the C-in-C Home Forces, the War Office continued its efforts to prove that the LDV was in fact being taken seriously. Already a secret letter had been sent out by GHQ Home Forces to units asking 'that it should be explained to members of L.D.V. that all possible is being done to hasten the issue of arms and clothing to them' and that they should try not to 'become disgruntled' while the BEF was re-equipped.[67]

By the end of the second week of July, 82,878 Ross, Springfield, and Remington rifles had been distributed (albeit irregularly and unevenly), supplementing over 56,000 private sporting rifles and shotguns. By the beginning of August these figures had risen to 483,924 and 63,440 respectively.[68] The War Office also announced in July in response to complaints about the meagreness of LDV clothing and equipment that volunteers would be entitled to steel helmets, service respirators, greatcoats, leather gaiters, boots, leather belts, and haversacks. On 19 July, furthermore, Field-Marshal Lord Gort, former C-in-C of the now defunct BEF, was appointed Inspector of Training for the force (which he rightly suspected was a position with no authority, designed to instil public confidence).[69]

As to role, the War Office quickly began to modify its initial stand. Responding to Lord Breadalbane in the House of Lords, Lord Croft struck a conciliatory note.

I should like to say at once that the Secretary of State and the Army Council regard the Local Defence Volunteers as a really vital part of our essential defences. It is no mere outlet for patriotic emotion that we are trying to create, but a fighting force which may be at death grips with the enemy next week, or even to-morrow.[70]

By early July, Eden himself was implicitly accepting the idea pressed on him by critics that the 'utmost initiative' should be encouraged in the LDV, and that as well as observing and reporting, volunteers should, when possible, 'attack' the enemy.[71]

In August, the function of the volunteers was officially re-defined to include delaying and obstructing the enemy advance 'by any means in their power'. New, more aggressive tactical instructions were also pro- duced by the War Office, including a missive on how to deal with German armour. 'From the moment the enemy tanks are located,' the instruction leaflet read in part, 'they must be harried, hunted, sniped, and ambushed without respite until they are destroyed.'[72]

This was a rather tall order for men armed only with a few rifles and molotov cocktails, but it harmonized well with the belligerent mood of many volunteers (the more optimistic of whom hoped that No. 10 shotgun ammunition would pierce armour plate, and that, as one of their number later explained, 'the occupants [of a tank after a molotov cocktail had ignited on the hull] would be so blinded or choked by smoke and fumes that their despatch by riflemen in ambush would be a compara- tively easy matter').[73]

On the other hand, despite the best efforts of the War Office, growth in the size of the LDV continued to outpace efforts to provide an adequate supply of equipment, clothing, and weapons. On 13 July, the War Office calculated that there were 1,166,212 men enrolled. By 1 August, returns from LDV units indicated that there were now 1,472,505 volunteers on strength around the country.[74] Hence, despite the arrival of tens of thousands of rifles from the USA and Canada, most LDV units continued to be desperately short of weapons (as well as ammunition, which worked out at as little as ten rounds per rifle), and

complaints and criticism continued to be voiced. 'Opinion', as Harold
Nicolson observed of the House of Commons on 20 July, 'slides off into
oblique animosities such as criticism of the Old Gang and rage that
L.D.V. are not better equipped.'[75] It was in this context that the Prime
Minister began to impose his formidable personality on the develop-
ment of the Local Defence Volunteers.

The LDV was, in public-relations terms at least, the creation of
Anthony Eden. It was probably inevitable, however, that Churchill
would eventually make it his business to become involved in the affairs
of the new force. As warrior-premier at a time of constant crisis, Churchill had much else to occupy his mind. On the other hand the Local
Defence Volunteers were tailor-made to stir his imagination. Here were
the people of Britain heeding the call to arms, men of all classes and
backgrounds hastening forth as one to defend their homes and defeat
the invader, as their forefathers had done since the reign of Elizabeth I.
The LDV idea, in short, catered to Churchill's romantic view of war,
society, and history.

When still First Lord of the Admiralty, Churchill had proposed a
'Home Guard' during the invasion scare of the autumn of 1939. Caught
up in the drama of the fall of France, he had not given much attention
to the LDV in its first month or so of existence. As Prime Minister,
however, he was the natural figure to whom those dissatisfied with
the speed of War Office responses would turn when it seemed Eden
and others were not moving fast enough. One of the main conduits for
such appeals to reach Churchill was his long-time friend and personal
assistant, Desmond Morton.

Morton, after hearing from various sources—Sir Ralph Glyn appears
to have been one of them—of the confusion surrounding the organizing
and equipping of the LDV, wrote a note on 13 June suggesting that
Churchill obtain a summary of developments from the War Office so
that he, the Prime Minister, could impose some order on what appeared
to be a rather chaotic situation. The command and administrative structure had yet to sort itself out—'a case has been brought to my notice
where no less than five distinct authorities have demanded reports from
the L.D.V.'—and the more active role being postulated by the force was
being questioned by the more level-headed in view of a quite evident
lack of training.[76]

On 17 June, in a War Cabinet meeting to which he was invited, Eden explained to his colleagues what steps were being taken to improve the training and administration of the LDV. Sir Edward Bridges, one of Churchill's secretaries, suggested that this statement made a War Office memorandum on the state of the LDV redundant, but the Prime Minister thought otherwise. He was now aware of the level of criticism in the press and parliament concerning management of the force—having received, among other things, a series of forceful letters from the indefatigable Jos Wedgwood, who in his own words was engaged in 'waging a private war on the War Office'[77]—and evidently believed that it was his duty to take whatever action was necessary to restore public confidence in such a magnificent organization.[78]

On 22 June, therefore, a note was dispatched from 10 Downing Street to the War Office requesting a concise summary of the current LDV position. 'It would be a great comfort to me', Churchill added to the draft, 'if this could be compressed into one or two sheets of paper.'[79] A two-page memorandum was duly drawn up and delivered, and after some days ruminating on the matter, Churchill decided that one of the main problems with the LDV was its name. Herbert Morrison, the Home Secretary, also thought so, and on 26 June the Prime Minister wrote a note to Eden suggesting that it be changed. 'I don't think much of the name Local Defence Volunteers for your very large new force,' he bluntly stated. 'The word "local" is uninspiring.' Morrison had suggested that a better title would be Town Guard or Civic Guard, but Churchill had thought these names 'too similar to the wild men of the French Revolution'. Instead, Churchill came up with his own title: 'I think "Home Guard" would be better.'[80]

By making this suggestion Churchill was evidently hoping to associate the volunteer movement more closely with his own person. The heroic imagery, the rolling prose, the absolute refusal to admit defeat, had made the Prime Minister almost the living embodiment of all that Britons felt was greatest in themselves. In an opinion poll taken in July 1940 an astonishing 88 per cent of respondents expressed confidence in his leadership—and this in the face of almost unrelieved military disaster.[81] As Lord Woolton, the rather severe Minister of Food, noted in his diary, Churchill possessed 'a quite extraordinary capacity . . . for expressing in Elizabethan English the sentiments of the public'.[82] The

Prime Minister was quite aware of how much the image he projected—or the virtues he was thought to embody—mattered to the public. 'I represent to them', he noted to one of his private secretaries on being cheered by passers-by, 'something which they wholeheartedly support: the determination to win.'[83] To associate himself with the LDV, not least by giving it a Churchillian title, would be good for over a million volunteers' morale.

To Eden, on the other hand, the Prime Minister probably appeared to be taking a hand in matters he did not know enough about, and—not coincidentally—moving his Secretary of State for War out of the spotlight. Eden's star, quite high in the months before the war, had been eclipsed to a great extent by the steady wartime rise in Churchill's public standing, despite efforts to bolster his public image once at the War Office.[84] A hint of wounded pride is detectable in Eden's responses to the Prime Minister's sudden interest in the LDV.

Churchill, meanwhile, became more enthusiastic about the title 'Home Guard' the more he thought about it. On a tour of the south coast on 27 June, he had spotted a group of volunteers and had taken a strong dislike to their 'LDV' armbands. The moment he returned to London the Prime Minister prodded Eden again. 'I hope you liked my suggestion of changing the name "Local Defence Volunteers",' Churchill wrote pointedly, 'which is associated with local government and local option, to "Home Guard". I found everybody liked this on my tour yesterday.'[85] The Secretary of State for War, however, had resolved to resist the idea.

Writing to the Prime Minister on 28 June, Eden pointed out that the term LDV 'has now passed into current military jargon', and that a million armbands with LDV stencilled on them had already been manufactured. 'On the whole,' the War Minister concluded, 'I should prefer to hold by our existing name.'[86]

Facing resistance from Eden, the Prime Minister—still very keen on his Home Guard proposal—decided to circumvent the War Office by getting the volunteers themselves to adopt the new title. If, as he believed, Home Guard was a label 'which many people think much better', then perhaps the press could be co-opted into a publicity effort to sell Home Guard over LDV. 'Do you think', the Prime Minister asked Duff Cooper, then Minister of Information, 'you could inquire of the editors whether they could put the new name across swiftly, and let me know what you advise.'[87] Much to the chagrin of Churchill, the Minister of Information tended to agree with Eden that the acronym 'LDV' had entered people's consciousness and that it would be too costly to substitute H.G. armbands for the million already manufactured (and for the most part distributed) with L.D.V. stencilled on them. Moreover, Cooper added mischievously, an armband with H.G. on it 'would suggest association with the Horse Guards or Mr Wells'.[88]

The PM was not amused. On 6 July, he let the Minister of Information know in no uncertain terms that 'I am going to have the name "Home Guard" adopted, and I hope you will, when notified, get the Press to put it across'. Ten days later, the Prime Minister's Office was enquiring of the War Office 'what steps are being taken to enforce the name "Home Guard" instead of "Local Defence Volunteers" '.[89] The new name, thanks in large part to Churchill's use of 'Home Guard' in parliamentary speeches and radio addresses, was already coming into popular use by mid-July, and—perhaps because the Prime Minister used it—tended to be regarded by the public as superior to LDV.[90]

The War Office, meanwhile, continued to resist the change. General Pownall was opposed, correctly guessing that at an estimated cost of £40,000 the change was a 'pure Winstonian' publicity manoeuvre. '"Home Guard"', he noted privately, 'rolls better off the tongue and makes a better headline.' In his opinion the PM 'could well have left things alone!'.[91] The script of an LDV film drama sponsored by the Ministry of Information in July, in which the protagonists all spoke of 'the Home Guard', was viewed with suspicion within the War Office.[92] Eden himself was also still very much against the change of name, but with waning hope of success. On 22 July, after meeting Churchill, he wrote despairingly in his diary, 'we discussed LDV. He was still determined to change name to Home Guard. I told him that neither officers nor men wanted the change, but he insisted.'[93] The Local Defence Volunteers were now the Home Guard.

From now on, with the title Home Guard associated in the public mind with his own person—it quickly became general knowledge that the Prime Minister was responsible for the change of name—Churchill was to pay special attention to the mood and wishes of the volunteers. Indeed, he was already doing what he could to cater to the wants of the newly baptized force.

At a War Cabinet meeting on 1 July, he had argued for the force to be given a greater sense that it was a valued and essential part of Britain's defences. 'It would be very unfortunate', the Prime Minister warned, 'if there was any failure to make fullest practicable use of the widespread desire for combatant service.'[94] Subsequently he took a very close interest in deliveries of rifles for the Home Guard from the United States, passed on letters of complaint from Wedgwood to the War Office for action, and personally assured Wedgwood that despite his fears the Home Guard in London would in fact be called upon to fight for every house and street when the invader came.[95] On 9 July, the Prime Minister asked the War Office to provide him with weekly reports on the current strength, weapons, and equipment of the Home Guard, and stressed to the War Cabinet secretary on 2 August that it was 'very important to get on with the uniforms for the Home Guard'.[96]

Churchill, furthermore, was not slow to indicate to the public his personal interest in the Home Guard as a fighting force. On the evening of 14 July, he made a radio broadcast to the nation on the state of anti-invasion preparations which included references to the important role the Home Guard—'as they are much better called'—now played. Volunteers, Churchill explained, possessed 'the strongest desire to attack and come to close quarters with the enemy, wherever he may appear', which would mean a hot reception for invaders in every village and city street. The speech was a huge success, confirming in the public mind that the Prime Minister empathized with the desire for an aggressive role.[97]

The Prime Minister also proved sympathetic to personal appeals directed at him by prominent volunteers who evidently did not trust the War Office to get things done. On 11 August, for example, he forwarded to Eden a letter from Lord Wyfold making a case for a special Home Guard badge rather than (as the War Office had announced) using the badges of the local county regiments. 'I am sure you ought to look again at the idea', Churchill noted in a covering letter.[98]

Those within the War Office responsible for the Home Guard were not particularly pleased at the way in which people like Wedgwood and other interested MPs and organizers used every means at their disposal to make the authorities bend to their will. 'The determination of some Members of Parliament to prove that all connected with the War Office, Generals and Politicians, are soft in the head,' Eden wrote in a letter to

Churchill on 22 July, 'is not a heartening experience.'[99] But it was clear even to the irascible General Pownall, who had no great love for his role as Home Guard Inspector-General, which way the wind was blowing. 'The H.G. are voters first and soldiers afterwards,' he reflected privately on 12 August. 'What they think they need, if they say so loudly enough, they will get.'[100] Lord Bridgeman, soon to become Deputy Director-General of the Home Guard, later admitted that the War Office was more often than not dancing to a tune set by the volunteer lobby: 'if ever the War Office let off trying its best to make the Home Guard efficient,' he stated candidly, 'the Home Guard would rise up in its wrath and insist on being taken seriously.'[101] The clearly expressed preference of the Prime Minister to allow this to happen, mostly in the name of keeping up national morale, confirmed the basic truth of these observations.

There were, however, limits to the tolerance of the War Office (and indeed other government bodies, both Whitehall-based and local) toward the assertiveness of the Home Guard. Putting pressure on higher authority through both orthodox and unorthodox channels was one thing; behaving as if authority derived from below rather than above was quite another. In the late summer and early autumn, as the picture of what was actually happening at unit level became clearer, these limits would become apparent.

4 People in Arms

Summer 1940

'Glad to find you Bartle. The Zone Commander's been ringing.'
'Yes?'
'Yes. I'm damned if I can make him out. All he'd say was
"Cromwell".'
'Good Lord. What's he mean by that?'
'That's what I want to know . . .'

5th Bn (Caernarvonshire) HG HQ, 7 Sept. 1940[1]

If the night is a little misty the first big battle on English soil will
probably be fought out between the British Army and the L.D.V.

Army Officer, 6 July 1940[2]

As more than one inside observer noted at the time, the Home Guard
evolved from below more than it derived from higher authority, improvisation and *ad hoc* decision-making by local commanders taking the
place of an overall plan in the early summer months.[3] Under ordinary
circumstances, this would have made the force deeply suspect in the
eyes of professional soldiers. The summer of 1940, though, was not
conducive to normal patterns of thought, even within the traditionally
quite conservative hierarchy of the British Army.

England, it appeared, was bound to be invaded now that France had
fallen, and the means by which to repel such an invasion seemed fright-
eningly inadequate. To defend southern England the C-in-C Home
Forces had at his disposal at the start of June 1940 a total of 22 infantry
divisions and one armoured division. The infantry divisions were on
average only half-strength, had only about one-sixth of the (obsolescent)
artillery they needed, and almost no transport. As for armour, there
were, all told, a total of 463 tanks in the entire country—most of them
obsolete.[4] Ammunition, especially for the artillery, was in such short

supply that little or none could be used for practice.[5] Under conditions like this, any additional men in arms, no matter how badly organized, ill-equipped, and unorthodox to the traditional military mind, simply could not be ignored.

General Ironside, who replaced General Kirke as C-in-C Home Forces in late May 1940 and served until 19 July, privately thought that lacking as the volunteers were in organization, training, and equipment, they would not be able to do much once the balloon went up. As he outlined in a note to the Chief of the Imperial Staff, General Sir John Dill, 'their exact value [in an invasion] is problematical'.[6] Yet he was immensely stirred by their evident patriotic enthusiasm, and on 29 May was moved to write in his diary:

we shall get these L.D.V.'s going. Static defence in every village by blocks . . . And thousands of Molotoff cocktails thrown down from the windows of houses . . . We just want the courage of the men. Nothing else matters. No defence is any good if the men behind it run away. The old L.D.V.s won't do that.[7]

The C-in-C's evident desire to view the LDV in the best possible light and let it enter the fray in the hope of inflicting some damage was reflected to a greater or lesser extent among his subordinate commanders. In the first days of the force, Lieutenant-General Sir Guy Williams (GOC Eastern Command) had issued instructions which simply stated that the LDV was to serve in an anti-invasion role 'by whatever means possible', and Aldershot Command had given orders that LDVs were to 'at once engage and destroy any parachutists known to be hostile'.[8] In Northern Command, the equivalent order was for the LDV to 'take prompt and suitable action against the enemy'.[9] Lieutenant-General Andrew Thorne, appointed GOC 12 Corps, Southern Command, in early June, was impressed by the keenness of the volunteers and at Ironside's urging was giving them his 'wholehearted encouragement and support' in preparing for combat.[10]

Not all generals were so hopeful. 'It is sometimes alleged', *The Times* military correspondent wrote on 24 July, 'that military commanders are inclined to doubt the value of the L.D.V.s, or Home Guard.'[11] Lieutenant-General Sir Alan Brooke (Williams's successor as GOC Southern Command and the man who was to replace Ironside as C-in-C on 20 July), came away from a meeting with LDV organizers on 29 June gloomily asking himself 'why do we in this country turn to all the old men when we require a new volunteer force? Old men spell delay and chaos!'[12] Like Ironside and others, however, he ultimately recognized that the spirit was willing even if the flesh was weak, and that every means of delaying the German advance had to be utilized, no matter how questionable.[13] He therefore made no objection when in September Lieutenant-General Sir Claude Auchinleck (formerly commanding 5 Corps and his successor at Southern Command) issued orders encouraging a local combat role for the Home Guard.[14]

Auchinleck himself had few illusions about the capabilities of the volunteers—'They wouldn't have stopped the Germans, of course, just shot them up and that sort of thing'[15]—but evidently thought that no orders would prevent volunteers from responding furiously when their homes were under attack. So, as Churchill was urging, he made a virtue out of necessity by making what the Home Guard were likely to do anyway their official duty.[16] This appears to have been the one thing Auchinleck's successor at 5 Corps, Bernard Montgomery—who like Brooke was worried about the age factor but wanted to utilize every potential asset at his disposal—could agree on with his superior.[17]

Subordinate commanders were sometimes bemused by the way in which the Home Guard demonstrated that it was rather different from the Army—'There was nothing in our book', the BGGS of 2 Corps later noted, 'telling us how to deal with a strike of troops in protest at the appointment of an unwelcome commander'[18]—but were often, like their superiors, impressed by the sheer enthusiasm of the men. Major-General A. E. Percival, in charge of the 44th Division, thought that the Home Guard was 'a very formidable fighting force', though seriously short of weapons.[19] 'The more I saw of the Home Guard,' the GOC of the 9th Brigade, 3rd Division, later wrote in his memoirs, 'the more I came to respect their keenness.'[20]

There was, in short, a general willingness in Home Forces to try and fit a clearly zealous Home Guard into the anti-invasion plan at a time when even the most outlandish efforts—such as the siege catapult built by the Royal Mint to throw petrol bombs[21]—were being made part of home defence. By the summer, as we have seen, the War Office, under pressure from the LDV lobby, was also advocating a combat role for the Home Guard in the event of invasion.

Moreover, while the precise degree of aggressiveness in the anticipated fighting role did vary depending on the time and the source of
relevant instructions and orders (War Office, GHQ Home Forces, Command HQs and Area HQs, not to mention LDV organizers),[22] there
appears to have been a general consensus that whatever the LDV/Home
Guard might or might not be capable of in combat, it could function very
effectively *before* the invasion, in what the War Office had conceived of
as its original anti-Fifth Column and parachute-spotting security role.

By means of night patrols and observation posts, volunteers would be
able to spot any parachutes floating down to earth and sound the alarm.
Furthermore, through the manning of road blocks and the checking of
identity cards, members of the LDV would, as the War Office put it in
the June training instruction, be 'of the greatest value' in defeating the
Fifth Column and enemy spy threat.[23]

This was a role the volunteers were quite willing to play, caught up
like the rest of the population—and indeed most of those responsible for
home defence—in a collective sense of alarm fed by rumour and lurid
stories of captured spies and disguised paratroopers in the press. The
Sunday Express ran a typical story entitled 'Fifth Column plan to para-
lyse Britain', outlining a plot, now supposedly unmasked, for enemy
agents and sympathizers to seize power stations, sabotage railway trains,
and generally wreak havoc.[24]

The dangers of Nazi parachutists were also luridly portrayed in the
press. 'Each man is a trained engineer able to handle explosives,' the
Daily Mail breathlessly informed its readers. 'He can use all armaments,
from his standard sub-machine gun to a heavy tank—for he is supposed
to capture his chief weapons from his enemies.'[25] Rumour ran rife, and
people began to cast suspicious glances at their neighbours. 'Tolerance
is decreasing,' CBS correspondent Ed Murrow noted on 21 May, 'and
the temperature is rising.'[26]

Mystery writer Margery Allingham wrote of the mood after Dunkirk
and what it led to in terms of rumour and gossip.

It simply became generally known that any private suspicion whatever would be
treated with great sympathy by the police. If you thought anything or anyone
was a bit funny or a bit queer, you could go and talk about them to your heart's
content to your local bobby, who would put the magnificent machinery of the
C.I.D. in motion. Anything promising meant that M.I.5 would turn up, and

even though you heard no more about it you could rest assured that all had been gone in to. Well, what a chance! What an opportunity![27]

Nobody, it seemed, was above suspicion. Ed Murrow himself was to be mistaken for a Nazi spy in an Essex country pub and nearly arrested.[28] As a Ministry of Information observer wrote after watching an elderly clergyman in Hyde Park being accosted as a likely Fifth Columnist, 'innocent people may soon be molested'.[29]

Orders issued to LDVs going out on night patrol or manning road check-points reflected this sometimes almost paranoid fear of the enemy within. The volunteers of Painswick (Gloucestershire) were exhorted to 'keep an eye on the movement of suspicious persons and arrest them if necessary in the interests of public safety'.[30] In the city of Gloucester itself, the Home Guard battalion adjutant argued that volunteers should be educated to view with suspicion 'anyone, however plausible, who is inquisitive or appears to be hanging about for no particular reason'.[31] Another battalion in Gloucestershire were reminded that 'the wearing of a uniform constitutes NO proof of identity.'[32] Sentries at gas works in southern metropolitan London were warned that 'tricks or bluff may be employed by intruders for the purpose of obtaining access to the works', and that they should 'be on guard' against saboteurs at all times.[33]

General Ironside inadvertently added to an already tense situation in a rather inflammatory speech he gave to senior LDV organizers meeting in York in the first week of June. The C-in-C dwelt at some length on the Fifth Column threat and how important the LDV was in suppressing it. He occasionally added words of caution—'we do not want a spy complex' and 'we cannot assume the powers of the Home Office'—but overall Ironside's tone was decidedly belligerent. After going through the usual catalogue of stories about German paratroopers being guided in Holland by servant maids, the C-in-C urged his audience when seeing the enemy land to 'shoot them, shoot them, shoot them without any reference to taking any kind of care of their future'. Fifth Columnists were to get equally short shrift. 'If the intruder is a spy or an enemy,' he said at one point, 'you are entitled to shoot him'; adding almost as an afterthought that LDVs ought to be 'absolutely certain' before they acted. Ironside also heavily stressed the need to be suspicious. 'My experience is that the gentlemen who are the best behaved and the most sleek are those who are doing the mischief,' he said. 'We cannot be too sure of anybody.'[34]

In an atmosphere already laden with fears of a Fifth Column, this was bound to add fuel to the flames of suspicion and contribute to the LDVs' desire to take action. Ironside had been 'blunt' yet 'matter of fact', according to one observer, and the more level-headed paid most attention to what he had to say about serving as an example of stead-fastness to the population while quietly gathering information;[35] but at least some among the more headstrong in the audience came away under the (false) impression that the C-in-C had given them a virtual free hand. G. L. Wright, for example, drew the following conclusions at the meeting:

We (the L.D.V.) have *a right to arrest, search, etc,* suspected persons, and *then* take them to the police. This arrest and search is often a useful way to getting to inside information, re activities of Local Fifth Column. Remember that a person *making his or her way* in a rural area, is ipso facto suspect. If resistance is offered, slosh him. Warn him that if he tries to escape, you shoot, to kill. Remember that the greatest and best-behaved members of the public will often turn out to be the most effective Fifth Columnists.[36]

Primed to expect even the most innocent-looking pedestrian or motorist to be a Fifth Columnist or spy in disguise, volunteers manning check points and on patrol at night were in a frame of mind which one volunteer aptly described as 'suspicious alertness'.[37] Other law enforce-ment authorities, however, were becoming nervous. 'I am appalled', the Chief Constable of Southport, Major M. J. Egan, wrote to the Home Office after reading the notes of G. L. Wright, 'at what is likely to happen if the L.D.V.s begin to exercise their power of search and arrest as described.'[38]

In point of fact much of the activity undertaken by the LDV or Home Guard in an attempt to unmask Fifth Columnists, though sometimes irritating to those inconvenienced by security checks, was a relatively harmless display of zeal and self-importance. A pedestrian out for an evening stroll could be stopped and asked for his or her identity card, even if the volunteer had known the person concerned for years. 'One man', reported the *Daily Express* on 15 August after a night in which the Home Guard had been particularly active, 'said that he had been stopped 20 times on a journey of eight miles.' If an identity card could not be produced, then a person was liable, as one volunteer recorded of a scatterbrained friend who found himself in this predicament, to be 'taken to the police station by an LDV with a fixed bayonet'.[39] In one particular village, security precautions imposed by Brigadier Sir Percy Hobart (the zealous proponent of tank warfare then in temporary retirement and serving as an LDV section leader) were so rigorous that one army officer living there found that 'as time wore on the persistence of the sentries became such that it was well-nigh impossible to convince them that he had any right in Chipping Camden at all'.[40]

A ludicrous but true story was reported of a rector in Newchurch, Lancashire, being taken into custody by the local LDV for refusing to hand over the keys to an empty church school the commander wanted to investigate.[41] Cases of lovers in cars being interrupted by suspicious LDVs were common enough to become the subject of a Giles cartoon in *Reynolds News*.[42] 'Many a romance was shattered', as one volunteer put it, 'by the sudden demand for identity cards backed by a rifle pointing in the culprits' direction.'[43]

At the same time, however, the actions of volunteers on duty could occasionally be quite alarming, even fatal. In the best of circumstances, the Home Guard were likely to impede priority traffic; in a worst-case scenario, they might end up killing the wrong people.

Civilians could find that the instructions given by officious Home Guards concerning lights and identity papers were in fact wrong. Air raid wardens and other civil defence staff on their way to their posts could be stopped and required to produce their identity cards, causing considerable delay. During one of the first air raids on London, rescue parties and fire engines dispatched to a blaze in Chiswick could not get through because the LDV had set up a road block on a key arterial route.[44] Even the police were not immune. In various parts of the country policemen of all ranks found themselves from late June 1940 onward being continually stopped and challenged at gunpoint to produce their warrant cards, sometimes more than once by the same volunteer.[45]

Armed forces personnel were accosted, and while some—such as Field-Marshal Lord Gort, whose staff car was commandeered one night in August—were pleased at the eagerness of the LDV, many officers were furious at the high-handed ineptness displayed by some volunteers. 'Cases have been reported', the CO of the 7th Hertfordshire Home LDV battalion noted in June, 'where Army Officers have been stopped and asked for Identity Cards by L.D.V. who themselves could not establish their own identity.'[46]

There were also accidents and some fatalities caused through Home Guard actions. Motorists, not always able to see, hear, or comprehend efforts by volunteers to flag them down at night, risked serious injury or even death. Police were far from certain that the LDV actually had the legal right to stop and search, and light signals at night were sometimes unclear in meaning; but this did not prevent volunteers from letting fly if their instructions seemed to be being ignored.[47]

On the night of 2/3 June, LDVs shot and killed four motorists in separate locations.[48] Within days of these and subsequent accidents, the Ministry of Information home intelligence division was reporting that the propensity of some volunteers to shoot first and ask questions afterwards was a major topic of conversation in the north-east of England.[49] Military personnel travelling at night were equally at risk. 'I have lost two officers in the course of ten days,' the CO of the 2nd Anti-Aircraft Division wrote to GHQ Home Forces on 12 June, 'one shot dead in Eastern Command and one shot and dangerously wounded between Nottingham and these headquarters'; drily adding, 'We cannot afford these kind of losses and Officers are being distinctly discouraged from going about their work.'[50]

On 22 June the *Daily Herald* reported more trouble from northern England and Scotland, this time involving the wounding and killing of two motorcyclists and their passengers.[51] Four days later, in Gloucestershire, an ARP warden was shot and fatally wounded after failing to heed (or perhaps hear) an LDV challenge, followed by a motorist in Newport near the end of the month.[52] In Romford, a noisy exhaust prevented a car driver from hearing a challenge; four passengers were killed outright and a fifth seriously wounded.[53]

These do not, alas, appear to have been the only such incidents.[54] One of the worst cases of trigger-happiness occurred on 16 August. Attacking a group of Bf 110 fighter planes near Southampton, a section of 249 Squadron was bounced by Bf 109s. RAF Flight Lieutenant James Nicolson, his Hurricane on fire, continued to dogfight until forced to bail out after sustaining serious burns to his hands and face. He and a pilot officer were floating to the ground when they were suddenly shot at by LDVs under the impression they were German paratroopers. The pilot officer was killed when his parachute shroud lines were cut. Nicolson, already in tremendous pain from his burns, was wounded by rifle fire.[55] RAF aircraft as well as aircrew were occasionally taken to be the enemy and fired at. 'Mistakes have already been made,' a Home Guard county commander later noted severely in reference to indiscriminate shooting at aeroplanes, 'with deplorable results.'[56]

Equally problematic, from an official point of view, was the tendency of jumpy volunteers to raise the invasion alarm. Nervously expecting the enemy to drop from the sky at any moment, LDVs on patrol or manning observation posts at night time and again mistook strange sounds, lights, and shadows as evidence of a Fifth Column or a German parachute assault. Needless to say, there was usually a harmless explanation for such phenomena. Strange flickering lights assumed to be signals by Fifth Columnists to enemy aircraft could turn out to be marsh gas or even, in one case, a couple of glow worms. Furtive sounds and movements in the dark thought by nervous sentries to be stealthy Germans often revealed themselves on closer examination to be animals: horses, cows, sheep, and even hedgehogs. The white puffs of AA shell bursts, clouds, stray barrage balloons, and heaps of lime were mistaken for parachutes, and on one occasion the Home Secretary himself was reputedly called out of bed to deal with what turned out to be a false report of parachutists landing in Exeter.[57]

The dangers of prematurely crying 'wolf!' were made clear on the night of 7/8 September. GHQ Home Forces, aware that the tides were favourable for an invasion, sought to bring Eastern and Southern Command forces to a state of full alert. As troops were normally on eight hours' notice, the only means of preparing for immediate action, even if an enemy assault was likely rather than actually detected, was to issue the codeword for an invasion—'Cromwell'. Other commands were informed of this move, and word was passed down the chain of command for information purposes. Unfortunately, not all Home Guard commanders properly understood what was happening. In the town of Conway in Caernarvonshire, for example, the local Home Guard HQ had been rung up by the battalion commander, who would only say the word 'Cromwell'. After some confusion the meaning of the codeword was discovered, and the alarm sounded.[58]

Once one unit was behaving as if an invasion was in progress, it did not take long for others to become anxious. A report of events at the HQ of the 2nd Cheshire (GPO) Battalion Home Guard, based in Chester, where the Home Guard was called out at 9.35 p.m., gives a sense of how lack of information could leave the impression that the balloon had gone up.

10.20 p.m.   D. T. Control reported to Battalion Commander that the Inspector, P.O.E.D., Colwyn Bay, had informed them that the Conway Home Guard had been called out and was 'standing to.' He had no information as to the reason for this action.

10.25 p.m.   Attempt made to telephone Company Commander, No. 3 Company (Mr. Dowden) but no reply. The Postmaster, Conway, was spoken to and asked to make enquiries of local Home Guard commander or of Police.

10.40 p.m.   Postmaster, Conway, reported by telephone that he had made enquiries of the police who had informed him that an enemy aeroplane had passed over Conway and reports had been received that three parachutists had been seen to leave the plane near Tyngroes in the Conway Valley. The Conway Home Guard had been called out and had made a search. The police understood that the Home Guard were being recalled and dismissed.[59]

By this time, however, even assuming that this information on the stand-down was correct, many Home Guard units were convinced that a parachute assault was underway. Matters were made worse by the actions of the Vicar of St Ives in Cornwall, who on seeing the local fishing fleet returning from the west instead of the east (the usual route) mistook it for an enemy landing force and ordered the church bells to be rung—a signal that an invasion was in progress. Once one set of bells was heard, Home Guard commanders in nearby villages had bells rung to alert the population, and by late evening large sections of the country from Cornwall to the Western Isles were under the impression that the invasion had started.[60] Home Guards were called out practically everywhere, nervously expecting parachutists to appear. 'All one could hear', a columnist for the *Daily Herald* reported of the ensuing confusion, 'was the echoing and re-echoing of the Home Guard challenge "Who goes there?" with occasional rifle shots when the challenged party failed to stop.'[61]

It is worth stressing that not all such accidents were the fault of the Home Guard. Many Army units were primed to expect enemy parachute landings at any moment, and the order to fire at the unfortunate pilots of 249 Squadron had in fact been given by an over-excited Royal Artillery officer. The enemy, moreover, was actively promoting disorientation and rumour through the occasional dropping of 'empty' parachutes.[62] The confusion of the night of 7/8 September might have been avoided if GHQ Home Forces had possessed the means to bring troops to immediate readiness without using a loaded codeword, and it was from 3rd Corps HQ that one nervous Home Guard company commander had learned that 'landings by boat and parachute [are] confirmed'.[63]

On the other hand, by the autumn of 1940 there was growing evidence that while amateurism and over-zealousness could be fixed within the Army through discipline and training, greater command and control over the sometimes rather rogue behaviour of the Home Guard was much more difficult to achieve.

From early on, efforts had been made to caution volunteers against getting over-excited and acting beyond their authority. Orders were issued explaining that any group of parachutists numbering under six might well be the crew of a friendly aircraft, giving details of the uniforms and accents of the Poles, Czechs, and others fighting with the RAF, and pointing out that however dangerous Nazi paratroopers or aircrew could be, if they surrendered they were entitled to the protection of the Geneva Convention. 'The stories of German parties landing in Holland dressed in Allied uniforms or as civilians,' an order to the Northamptonshire Home Guard read, 'were often untrue and probably spread by the Germans themselves to create general distrust and panic.'[64] Orders were also sent out by GHQ Home Forces cautioning Home Guards to be sure that aircraft were those of the enemy rather than RAF machines before opening fire.[65]

Instructions were issued which stressed that 'the examination of a car, occupants of cars and their papers' was a matter for the police, and that volunteers should not impede the police, ARP, or Army in the course of their duties by setting up unauthorized road blocks and behaving as if their authority was greater than anyone else's.[66] 'What we want to avoid', the West Riding Home Guard county organizer explained in a circular to group organizers, 'is promiscuous shooting and the holding up of cars in a manner likely to cause accidents.'[67] Before opening fire, sentries should always flag down cars with lights that could be seen and challenge pedestrians in a loud enough voice to be heard (bearing in mind that there were deaf people on the streets). If, after two 'Halt, or I fire!' warnings, a pedestrian would not stop, then a sentry could shoot— 'aiming low to hit but not to kill'.[68] As for vehicles, if every effort was made and the driver still failed to pull over, then the sentry 'should fire at the tires and *not* at the occupant of the car'.[69]

Last but definitely not least, orders were sent out that under no circumstances were church bells to be rung by the Home Guard unless the commander had personally seen a minimum of twenty-five parachutes descending. Rumours, and bell-ringing in nearby towns and villages, were not to be acted upon.[70]

The problem was that such orders conflicted with more assertive instructions also emanating from higher authority, thus creating uncertainty. What was more, some Home Guard commanders were clearly unwilling to accept limitations on their security duties or accept orders with which they did not agree. This again was in part a function of the nature of the Home Guard itself. Having raised units and organized patrols without, as they saw it, much help from the War Office, many volunteers and organizers were reluctant to submit to orders from above when such orders seemed to impede their mission.

The situation in London illustrates this difficulty. In late June the situation in some zones had grown so serious that a branch of the Police Federation had sent a letter to Sir Philip Game, Commissioner of Metropolitan Police, complaining of the way the LDV (as it then still was) was becoming a positive menace to policemen going about their lawful duty.[71] Aware that the tendency of volunteers to shoot first and ask questions later meant that 'my life and limbs are also at stake', Sir Philip wrote on 1 July to the GOC London Area, Lieutenant-General Sir B. N. Sergison-Brooke, noting that while no constable had yet been killed, the LDV were 'becoming better shots daily' and that therefore it might be an idea to 'restrain their ardour'. The GOC passed on the request to Brigadier (retd.) James Whitehead, London Area organizer for the LDV. Home Guard commanders were in some cases rather touchy on the matter of the police—or anyone else, for that matter—not taking them seriously,[72] and Whitehead appears to have been affronted at the mere idea that volunteers were going too far. He wrote a letter to the commissioner defending their actions. The LDV, he stated, were stopping the police 'to ensure that disguises are not being made use of' by the Fifth Column. He would, if forced to do so, issue orders that this practice should cease; but, he warned, 'it must be remembered that a time may come when no one at all may be allowed to approach a post without being challenged, and that if he does not answer the challenge he does so . . . at his own risk.'[73]

Sir Philip, unperturbed, tried again. On 4 July he wrote two letters, one to Whitehead and one to Sergison-Brooke. The letter to Whitehead was appeasing in tone. 'I have not the least doubt', the commissioner explained, 'that the action of the L.D.V. is actuated by the highest motives'; all he was asking for was some attempt by the brigadier to limit 'undue exuberance' so as to restore 'a measure of common sense' to relations between the two forces. The letter to Sergison-Brooke was a request that the GOC do what he could to 'persuade him [Whitehead] to drop that pose of injured innocence!'. Over the following two days Game passed on the details of incidents where the police and others had been delayed or harassed, and politely enquired whether 'the L.D.V. might be told that until one German enemy is on our soil policemen might be accepted as such'. Brigadier Whitehead, conceding defeat, issued orders on 6 July to his subordinates that until further notice 'police are to be allowed to proceed without being stopped'.[74]

Similar problems of authority arose elsewhere.[75] In Glasgow, for example, enough instances of policemen and ARP wardens being held up by the Home Guard occurred for the Chief Constable, Sir Percy Sillitoe, to have notices published in the papers warning that if more restraint were not shown the police would be forced to take appropriate measures. This action infuriated the local LDV commander, who demanded that the notices be withdrawn and argued that it was the LDV rather than the police who bore the ultimate responsibility for securing Glasgow's safety. Sillitoe, rather less of a diplomat than his counterpart in London, at first took the uncompromising line that 'as long as Civil

Law continued to function within the city of Glasgow I would not accept "instructions" regarding my police duties and responsibilities from any military authority'. The Chief Constable, however, soon concluded that a more persuasive approach might be more effective, and, after the LDV commander had accepted his invitation to talk things over in person, the problem, as Sillitoe later recorded, 'was happily resolved between us'.[76]

Even persuasion, however, could not be effective in all cases. The eighty members of the Home Guard company in Newchurch, Lanca-shire, resigned *en masse* when their commander was asked to resign in the wake of the rather embarrassing affair of the parson taken into custody for refusing to hand over the keys to a school building.[77] 'I have intimated to the Company', the CO of a West Riding Home Guard unit wrote defiantly in December after protests from the Chief Constable, 'that neither the police nor anyone else, in my opinion, have the right to demand from an armed guard, duly mounted, either a Warrant or an Identity Card'.[78] Army commanders continued to fear that through checking passes the Home Guard would cause 'unnecessary delay on the roads' during an invasion.[79]

And no matter what instructions were issued by higher authority, the worrying fact remained that many volunteers felt free to question their commanders' orders. 'I am in the odd position', noted volunteer O. J. R. Howarth of the Downe Home Guard platoon, 'of saying exactly what I like to my officers, as a private soldier; they swallow it most generously.'[80] Even if a Home Guard zone organizer or battalion commander accepted an instruction from higher authority, there was no guarantee that it might not be queried or perhaps ignored by the junior commanders or the men themselves.

Frank Stirling, for example, Chief of Staff to Lawrence of Arabia in the First World War and now working with the GPO on telegraph and postal censorship, had done much to get an LDV guard mounted at the Central Telephone Exchange. He was, however, appalled when orders were issued that sentries should have a round only in the magazine, not the chamber. This was a prudent attempt to avoid accidental shootings, but the impetuous Stirling would have none of it. 'I took it upon myself', he explained in his memoirs, 'to countermand this order, which was utterly fatuous.'[81]

Similarly, though orders were issued that Home Guards were not to manufacture home-made weapons (due to a number of tragic accidents), everything from armoured cars to soup-tin grenades continued to be constructed in units where it was felt not enough weaponry was being produced by the War Office.[82]

Some of the more influential supporters of the Home Guard went even further, circumventing normal channels by communicating directly with an organization called the Committee for American Aid for the Defence of British Homes. This private US group had accumulated a quantity of donated revolvers and rifles and was looking for a way to get them into British hands. As the wheels of bureaucracy seemed to be moving too slowly, the committee was quite happy to accept private requests for shipment from the newspaper proprietor Edward Hulton, a great supporter of the Home Guard, and from another press baron, Lord Beaverbrook, who as Minister of Aircraft Production was quite happy to short-circuit normal channels in order to equip his MAP factory units.[83]

Moreover, once Beaverbrook had received the weapons he refused to give any of them up to the War Office. 'Nobody shall deprive me of the reward for well-doing,' he sharply informed Eden in early October when the latter requested that at least some of the donated equipment be turned over to him.[84] Beaverbrook also acquired a large amount of armour plate and produced several hundred special armoured cars— 'Beaverettes'—for the use of MAP factory Home Guard units. 'The whole conception', wrote Brooke, 'was fantastic. How could individual factories have held out and what part could they have played once the main battle for this country was lost?' Even within MAP there were those who thought this was going too far. Again, however, the Minister of Aircraft Production refused to hand over equipment which he had acquired for what the C-in-C Home Forces, desperately short of armour, acidly described as Beaverbrook's private army.[85]

And, despite efforts to limit and control the tendency, Home Guards continued to write to their MPs, GOCs, and the press whenever they felt discriminated against or unjustly put upon. Sir Ralph Glyn, MP, for example, wrote directly to an official in the Home Office to argue against preventing the Home Guard from searching cars and premises without a warrant. 'Clearly this is hopeless from our point of view,' Glyn concluded pointedly, 'and as we are anxious to get on with our work as quickly as possible I do hope you will be able to issue the necessary draft instructions in the immediate future.'[86] This particular effort came to nothing, but from the War Office perspective there was no doubting the fact that the Home Guard lobby remained active in and out of parliament and that the press continued to take a lively interest in the force.[87]

There was also the Prime Minister to consider. Ever since his initial intervention in the matter of the name of the force, Churchill had continued to keep an eye on developments and proved extremely reluctant to accept moves which he thought might damage public faith in the government's commitment to the Home Guard. In July he had intervened to prevent Pownall—who did not really want to be in charge of the Home Guard—from being transferred. 'It is only a few weeks since he was placed at the head of the Home Guard,' Churchill argued in a minute to Eden at the end of the month, 'and a great story made of the importance of this post.'[88] It was only with the greatest difficulty that Eden was able in August to persuade the Prime Minister that a temporary ceiling of about 1.5 million would have to be placed on Home Guard enrolment until the supply of arms and equipment caught up. 'I am anxious', Churchill explained, 'to avoid the disappointment and frustration which a stoppage of recruiting for the Home Guard is likely to cause to many people.' In the end a compromise was reached through the creation of a waiting list.[89]

What might be termed a tendency toward a culture of complaint within some sections of the Home Guard, combined with a habit of ignoring orders or acting impetuously, was a major concern of the War Office by the autumn of 1940. Remedial action, though, had to be considered in light of public and prime ministerial reactions, which may have caused a certain amount of hesitancy. As we shall see, it was news of the efforts of certain leftists to shape the Home Guard along radical egalitarian lines, to turn it into a people's militia of the Spanish Civil War variety, that finally spurred Whitehall to take decisive action toward controlling the force.

5 A People's Militia?
1940–1

> For the first time in British history the chance exists for Socialists to have a certain amount of influence in the armed forces of the country. The Home Guard is trembling in the balance . . .
>
> George Orwell, Primrose Hill platoon HG[1]

> The creation of private armies or of para-military armed formations has often proved fatal to the stability of the State and to the liberty of its citizens.
>
> Edward Grigg, War Office PUS[2]

While radical in terms of its tendency to question the motives and competence of higher authority (both within and outside the force) in relation to the perceived interests of its members, the Home Guard was not in structural and social terms a particularly left-wing organization. How could it be otherwise, given the way in which the county establishment was so prominent in its formation? Retired senior officers and members of the peerage abounded.[3]

Indeed, this was one of the reasons why the Communist Party, then taking the position that the war was an imperialist struggle inimical to working-class interests, was able to adopt a highly critical attitude towards the force. The *Daily Worker* went so far as to suggest that the Home Guard was 'a means of establishing an armed force directly under the control of the hunting-shooting-fishing oligarchy' to be used as 'an instrument of the class struggle'.[4]

Nor were the spokesmen of the Communist-dominated International Brigade veterans' organization at all supportive. A real people's militia in Britain, as an editorial in the *Volunteer for Liberty* explained, was impossible under present circumstances: 'the *only* basis on which such an army can be built is a People's Government—a government which the people have put in place to be *their* representatives, to do the jobs they want done, and to lead the way to a workers' state'. The Home Guard was a *de facto* instrument of imperialism, and those who joined it were 'helping the ruling class'.[5]

Lack of official encouragement, however, did not stop a small number of very active left-wingers outside the Communist Party from seeing in the Home Guard the basis for a future people's militia. Mostly intellectuals and publicists who had at some point in the past come into conflict with the Party line, such as George Orwell, Tom Wintringham, and John Langdon-Davies, they believed that what was needed to defeat Fascism was not just better weapons but a conviction that the war would bring about true democracy, a people's peace.

This view might have mattered as little as the beliefs of the small number of fellow-travellers of the Right involved in the Home Guard if it had not been very much in harmony with public sentiment in the summer of 1940. With the public increasingly critical of Chamberlain and the other 'Guilty Men' whose complacency, lack of moral fibre, and absence of creative thinking had supposedly allowed Britain to slide into its current parlous position, left-wing critiques of how the old guard were running the show and calls for a democratic, egalitarian people's war were increasingly common.[6] One of the popular series of BBC radio talks by the Yorkshire playwright (and LDV member) J. B. Priestley, in which he sought to articulate the mood of the 'ordinary folk' of England, gives a sense of the perceived nature of the struggle.

It so happens that this war, whether those at present in authority like it or not, has to be fought as a citizen's war. There is no way out of that because in order to defend and protect this island, not only against possible invasion but also against all the disasters of aerial bombardment, it has been found necessary to bring into existence a new network of voluntary associations such as the Home Guard, the Observer Corps, all the A.R.P. and fire-fighting services, and the like. . . . They are a new type, what might be called the organized militant citizen. And the whole circumstances of their war-time life favour a sharply democratic outlook.[7]

'Most of the public are criticizing our war effort,' a Ministry of Information home intelligence report dated 18 June noted, 'and particularly Chamberlain and [the] "old gang". People demand that [the] whole nation should be armed.'[8] With views such as these in circulation, it is not surprising that those who sought to link the Home Guard with the left-wing anti-Fascist struggle in Spain found a receptive audience.

George Orwell, for example, who had joined the Primrose Hill platoon of the 5th (London) LDV battalion in June, saw in the Home Guard a possible reincarnation of the best aspects of the anarchist POUM militia with which he had served in 1937. The Home Guard was, as his friend, publisher, and fellow volunteer Frederic Warburg wrote, seemingly ideal in relation to Orwell's rather unique mixture of personal, patriotic, and political preferences: 'it was unprofessional; it was volunteer; it was anti-fascist and anti-Nazi; it was rather inefficient (an important point this) and it was animated by a deep affection for the England he loved beyond all else.'[9]

Orwell, though only a section commander, had great hopes for the future of the Home Guard, which he saw as 'a democratic guerrilla force, like a more orderly version of the early Spanish government militias'. In his view, total war demanded total commitment, which in turn meant a political vision of the struggle with which ordinary people could identify, thus turning it into a people's war. 'It is our duty to pass that knowledge on to all who are potentially on our side,' Orwell wrote in the pages of *Tribune* in December 1940, 'which means the vast majority of the nation. In the case of the Home Guard—a million men, ninety-nine hundredths of them profoundly anti-Fascist in sentiment, but politically undirected—the opportunity is so obvious that it is amazing that it has not been grasped earlier.'[10]

In point of fact the opportunity *had* already been grasped by a fellow Spanish War veteran, Tom Wintringham. Formerly the commander of the British battalion in the International Brigade (but later estranged from the Party for personal reasons), Wintringham had been employed since the start of the war as military correspondent for *Picture Post*. Like Orwell and others, he viewed the war in ideological terms. 'The answer to totalitarian war', which Wintringham argued was the essence of Nazi success, 'is a people's war.'[11] Both Orwell and Wintringham were very much in favour of arming the people, and the enthusiasm for the Home Guard raised their hopes immensely. As Wintringham wrote some months later:

I could not help thinking how alike these two armies were: the Home Guard of Britain and the Militia of Republican Spain. Superficially alike in mixture of uniforms and half-uniforms, in shortage of weapons and ammunition, in hasty and incomplete organization and in lack of modern training, they seemed to me more fundamentally alike in their serious eagerness to learn, their resolve to meet and defeat all the difficulties in their way, their certainty that despite shortage of time and gear they could fight and fight effectively.[12]

He was disappointed, however, by the apparent indifference of the military authorities to the arming and training of the force, and highly suspicious of the way in which the 'Blimps' seemed to be running the show—something which he, again very much like Orwell, thought would impede the evolution of the Home Guard into a true guerrilla army.

On the other hand, with so much depending on initiative at the local level, there also existed the opportunity for those who knew what they wanted to make a mark while the Home Guard was still in the early stages of its development. Over dinner with Edward Hulton (owner of *Picture Post*) and his friend Tom Hopkinson one evening in early July 1940, Wintringham came up with a scheme to circumvent War Office delays and procrastination in the training of the Home Guard through the setting up of a private school. The Earl of Jersey was asked by Hulton to allow use of the grounds of his mansion at Osterley Park, just outside London. 'Could we dig weapon pits?' asked Wintringham, his imagination racing, 'Loose off mines? Throw hand grenades? Set fire to old lorries in the grounds?' Lord Jersey agreed to it all, as long as the house itself was not demolished in the process.[13]

Gathering together a small group of fellow Spanish Civil War veterans and experts in various aspects of guerrilla fighting, Wintringham was able to set up a weekend programme—heavily promoted in *Picture Post*—in what was termed 'ungentlemanly warfare' for interested Home Guards. On 10 July the first batch of eager pupils was attending classes in hand-to-hand combat, the ambushing of tanks, hit-and-run raids, and much else of a guerrilla nature. Osterley Park was an instant success, and news of it rapidly spread through word-of-mouth and the press. Demand for the lessons from the Osterley Park school, which Wintringham described regularly in *Picture Post*, eventually led to their being published as a book, *New Ways of War*. There is no evidence to suggest that Wintringham and his staff consciously sought to inculcate political values as well as tactical roles, but in drawing comparisons with the Spanish Civil War and promoting the methods practised by the militias—heavily grounded in personal initiative and passionate commitment to the anti-Fascist cause—both the school at Osterley Park and Wintringham's articles in *Picture Post* tended to invite empathy with the values that had inspired the Republican war effort.[14]

At about the time Osterley Park was starting to be talked about, another press- and Spanish Civil War-related initiative was coming to public notice. After a couple of false starts, the *Sunday Pictorial* had found a regular contributor for a column they were running called 'Home Guard Parade', devoted, as the title implied, to Home Guard issues. The man destined to write the column for many months and to go on a sponsored lecture tour among Home Guard units was John Langdon-Davies, a war correspondent who had covered both the Spanish Civil War and the Winter War in Finland and who was author of recent paperbacks on the Fifth Column and parachute menace.[15] Though not politically committed in the manner of Wintringham, Langdon-Davies made frequent references to the Spanish Civil War and guerrilla tactics (including those of the Irish Republican Army). 'The best Home Guard section', he noted on 6 October, 'is not necessarily the one with the best shots; it is the one which has grasped the adventure, the need for using the imagination, that has had to be called into existence to destroy Nazism.'[16]

This sort of thing was hardly likely to appeal to senior War Office officials and generals who viewed the radical left and unorthodox tactics with instinctive hostility and suspicion. Letters to the press supporting the idea of the Home Guard as a people's militia can only have added to the sense that left-wing elements were trying to subvert the loyalty of the volunteers. 'The only safeguard against the armed forces of Fascism and capitulation and treachery after the model of France, is that the people should be armed,' one fellow-traveller argued in a letter published in *Picture Post* on 13 July 1940. 'The rich, the privileged, will try to buy their security at the expense of the British people', but the armed citizenry, 'implacable', would resist and fight Fascism and its supporters 'to the bitter end'.[17]

There were, to be sure, signs that by no means all Home Guards agreed with this sort of thing. 'I am just about fed up with you and your publicity stunts,' one angry volunteer wrote in a letter to *Picture Post*. 'Where is this Buffalo Bill mentality supposed to get us? What do you think you are going to do with your little jampot bombs and Boy Scout poles?' To act like 'Marxist hooligans' was to overlook the unpleasant fact that it was the Nationalists rather than the Republicans who had actually won in Spain.[18] Indeed, within the ranks opinion on the issue of guerrilla tactics and people's war could be quite divided. The historian of the Ministry of Food Home Guard records that while some volunteers wanted it 'to be like the Red Army in 1917', others 'wanted the unit to be more like His Majesty's Brigade of Guards in the days of His Majesty King Edward VII'.[19]

Still, the left-wing influence was disquieting to those who had been enthusiastically prepared for troops to be sent earlier in 1940 to help the Finns against Soviet Russia. As early as 15 May the police had been instructed to weed out undesirable persons from the lists of applicants compiled at police stations, and both Fascists and Communists had been barred from joining the LDV in a secret War Office order dated 27 May. The police, however, sometimes had a rather different idea of who was or was not a security risk than the War Office; and in practice, as a staff officer later wrote, 'nearly all men on the police lists were accepted'.[20] Under these circumstances the Home Guard Inspectorate under General Pownall was far from sure that Wintringham and his colleagues were 'of an entirely suitable type', and asked MI5 to vet them as a potential security risk.[21]

MI5 was at this point overstretched by the demands of investigating Fifth Column reports, and generally believed that the direct security risk from the far left was considerably less than that from the far right.[22] They did, however, agree to investigate the staff of Osterley Park, and came up with a very mixed bag. Some, such as Stanley White, a chief instructor for the Boy Scouts, were clearly no threat. But there was a strong contingent of Spanish Civil War veterans, including several anarchist Spanish miners (who taught the use of explosives), Hugh Slater, one of Wintringham's subordinates from the International Brigade, and of course Wintringham himself, expelled from the Communist Party over an extra-marital affair rather than for ideological transgressions.[23] People such as these would not have endeared themselves to MI5, and only confirmed War Office suspicions. As for Orwell, he was regarded by his superiors as 'a dangerous red'.[24]

The War Office was also aware that the Spanish militia model being promoted at the school was attracting considerable press coverage and favourable comment, and that an attempt by Brigadier Whitehead to order London units not to attend courses at Osterley Park had only increased awareness and interest. In July, 1,000 men had attended weekend courses; at the end of August the monthly total had doubled, and seemed set to reach 3,000 in September.[25] Several months of dealing with the Home Guard had taught officers that a direct assault on left-wing influence would only result in a barrage of criticism in parliament and the press, and possibly a number of embarrassing resignations. The fact that newspapers like *Picture Post* and the *Sunday Graphic* were sponsoring men like Wintringham and Langdon-Davies and that they would be certain to complain loudly and in print at any infringement of their correspondents' liberties, was a definite deterrent to hasty action. Nor could the reaction of the Prime Minister be discounted. Who knew what he might do if he read that one of his favourite causes was being tampered with amid media protests? As General Pownall knew from bitter experience, the Home Guard could be coaxed and persuaded to act in a certain way, but it could not be treated like the Army where orders were simply orders.[26]

Yet it was clear that something would have to be done, not only about Osterley Park but also the general tendency of the Home Guard to get over-excited and behave as if the War Office ought to receive orders from it rather than the other way round. Gough's quip about a 'Frankenstein monster' mentality within Whitehall was an exaggeration, but there did exist a strong current of opinion that the Home Guard ought at the very least to be less of a loose cannon.

The solution arrived at involved the quiet removal of the less prominent Reds from the ranks of the Home Guard. As early as the first week of July, secret War Office letters were being circulated to company commanders stressing that if by chance a Communist (a label used rather loosely in view of the Party line on the LDV) was found to have been 'inadvertently' enrolled in a unit, he should be 'discharged under the heading "Services no longer required" without any amplification'. At the same time, however, 'the Company Commander should, in each case, confidentially inform the Police of the names and addresses of these men and the reason for their discharge'.[27]

As for those left-wingers whose public profile made direct confrontation seem inadvisable, a gradual, step-by-step series of moves towards co-opting or marginalization was pursued. In return for official sanction and material aid, Edward Hulton in September 1940 allowed the military authorities to get involved in the running of Osterley Park on condition that the existing staff be kept on. This compromise would, it was calculated, allow the Home Guard directorate to 'take over' the school. Media promotion of Osterley Park began to be actively discouraged—the BBC, for example, was prevented from running a story on the school—and the process of gaining greater control while keeping matters as much as possible out of the public eye continued as training at Osterley Park was wound down in favour of a smaller-scale school set up at Denbeis, near Dorking, under the command of a Regular Army officer with experience of the LDV, Lieutenant-Colonel H. A. Pollock.[28]

The Osterley Park staff, including Wintringham, were kept on in a consultant capacity, but—despite what Wintringham believed they had been promised—they were gradually divested of any real authority in relation to the running of the Home Guard. John Langdon-Davies, meanwhile, among other favoured writers, was being subtly wooed by the War Office.

'As a journalist,' Langdon-Davies stated at one point, 'I hate red-tape and instinctively mistrust Whitehall.'[29] The War Office initially felt much the same degree of mistrust toward Langdon-Davies;[30] a little flattery, however, in the form of a sympathetic ear to his criticisms of Home Guard arrangements within the Home Guard directorate and permission to quote from military training booklets in his column and books, led the journalist to change his opinion. Langdon-Davies, along with Wintringham, his associate Hugh Slater, and the novelist and newspaper editor John Brophy, joined a group of authors whose books were officially or unofficially approved by the War Office for Home Guard consumption.[32]

This is not to suggest that Langdon-Davies, Brophy, Slater, and the others became uncritical admirers of War Office policy toward the Home Guard, or ceased to be ardent left-wingers. All published ideas and schemes which were at times quite radical in their implications, and lobbied hard to try and get the War Office to accept them. The policy of getting rid of rank-and-file left-wingers on the grounds of 'services no longer required', moreover, did generate hostile comment.[33] But secrecy limited criticism, and like Wintringham at the Home Guard training school, now under War Office authority, those radicals not ejected from the ranks found themselves no longer entirely outside the system. Langdon-Davies eventually became involved in a semi-official Home Guard fieldcraft school supported by Southern Command, while Brophy was fed titbits of information by the Home Guard directorate and lulled by the way in which the War Office appeared constantly willing to listen to his ideas.[34] By the time Wintringham and Slater came to realize the extent to which they too were becoming co-opted or marginalized it was too late. In May of 1941, a frustrated Wintringham resigned from his post as adviser, correctly suspecting that his views were being quietly ignored. Slater, meanwhile, had been called up into the army.[35] 'Properly used,' as General Pownall had noted shortly after starting a press-cutting file in August 1940 to monitor what the papers were saying about the Home Guard, 'the Press can be a very useful adjunct.'[36]

Drawing the teeth of some of the more radical elements, however, was by no means a final solution to the overall problem of Home Guard independence. It was clearly time to look to the future, not least in the mind of the Prime Minister himself. On 3 September, at a meeting of the Cabinet defence committee, Churchill 'stressed the importance of giving the Home Guard a clearly defined status as part of the authorised and regular forces of the Crown', and suggested 'the introduction of ranks for the officers' as well as 'saluting'. In response the Army Council set up a special sub-committee, chaired by Edward Grigg, to examine current training and organization of the Home Guard and recommend whatever changes appeared necessary.[37]

Presenting their final report in October, the PUS and the two other principal members of the sub-committee, Lieutenant-General R. H. Haining (VCIGS) and R. J. Sinclair (D-G, Army Requirements), agreed that the Home Guard was above all an asset to national morale and ought to be supported as such. They also agreed that there were real problems with the current semi-independent and disparate nature of the force. 'The time has arrived when more direct control and administrative direction as distinct from guidance are required.'

This would mean, among other things, getting rid of the curious command set-up whereby Home Guard commanders did not hold commissions or Army-style ranks and could not discipline their men. The original motive behind creating a distinct rank structure had been to make sure that Home Guard commanders could never exercise control over regular officers and troops. However, it was clear that it had also helped prevent the evolution of a truly disciplined force, and had fostered the questioning of authority both within and outside the Home Guard to an uncomfortable degree. It had also given certain radical visionaries the idea that the Home Guard was entirely its own master, and that it could evolve into something entirely independent of War Office control and Army procedure. Moreover, the imposition of the Army rank structure would not only allow for greater discipline and control in the form of King's Regulations, but would provide an excuse for the War Office to weed out some of the more incompetent and difficult organizers and commanders through new officer selection boards.

Tighter control could also be achieved through an overhaul of the current administrative arrangements. At the War Office itself, a new, more powerful Home Guard directorate should be created. Lower down, at the zone and area level, administration ought to be more closely guided by county boundaries. Greater coherence could also be obtained by inserting regular personnel into the Home Guard in the form of a permanent staff instructor and an administrative officer for each battalion.

Arms and equipment, the sub-committee realized, were going to continue to be a problem given the needs of the Army and the size of the Home Guard. The replacing of the denim overalls with standard British Army battledress, however, would do much to keep up morale and make the men feel that they were being treated as real soldiers.

All this would, of course, require money, possibly as much as £2,750,000. But the Home Guard, both because it could potentially release regular soldiers for overseas service and due to its peculiar relationship to national morale, was not a body of men the War Office could afford to ignore. Indeed, 'everything possible should be done to maintain their keenness and increase their self-confidence'.[38]

The report was accepted by the Army Council without serious modification, and Edward Grigg set about preparing a parliamentary speech to announce the impending changes. As he admitted to Brendan Bracken, the new Minister of Information, the PUS was 'desperately anxious' for the War Office to regain the initiative in the House of Commons on Home Guard matters—'we always create the impression of having been kicked into things'.[39] Prudently, he sought the blessing of the Prime Minister, the biggest potential source of opposition to the War Office plans.

Churchill liked what he saw. 'I have read this most valuable and sagacious report with the greatest interest,' he noted in a minute to the War Office, 'and I find myself in almost complete agreement with its many conclusions of principle.' He was a little concerned at the effect commissioning would have on 'the equality of status . . . on which the Home Guard is founded', but did not press the point.[40] Moreover, the Prime Minister proved anxious to help Grigg make the best possible impression. 'This is not an occasion', Churchill advised as one parliamentarian to another on 4 November, 'for a general pronouncement, but just to tell the House in an agreeable way the story of the Home Guard, and the recent improvements which have been sanctioned.' Perhaps fearing that Grigg might suffer from stage fright, the Prime Minister wrote him a brief note of encouragement the following day. 'I want to let you know how good [the speech] is. I am sure it will go down well.'[41]

On 6 November, Grigg stood up in the Commons and announced what changes were being made in the Home Guard and why, passing over the concerns about lack of control and justifying the reform purely on the basis of military efficiency and morale. Hence, for example, the introduction of the Army rank structure was explained as being necessary in order that Home Guards could 'feel assured of full and unassailable military status', and great play was made of anticipated increases in the scale of weapons and equipment for the force. 'We hope by these new arrangements', the Under-Secretary of State for War concluded, 'to show that the value of their services is recognized by the State.'[42]

The speech itself, carefully tailored to provide some source of uplift to all, was so long that a joke went the rounds saying that it contained a personal word for every single Home Guard.[43] Generally speaking, however, the main points were greeted with favourable comment. Among the more traditional Home Guard commanders, the lack of Army ranks had long been a source of complaint. 'Everybody knows', Gough had written in a letter to *The Times* published in August 1940, 'that the exercise of leadership in battle and ordinary discipline cannot be enforced in any military unit without a properly constituted body of officers and N.C.O.'s whose authority is acknowledged by all concerned.'[44] Many agreed, had lobbied hard for army ranks, and were inclined to accept the regularization of the Home Guard happily.[45] Some units, in fact, had been using Army terminology and saluting informally from the beginning, finding that 'sergeant' and 'captain' (or a simple 'Sir!') rolled more easily off the tongue than, say, 'section commander' or 'platoon commander'.[46]

There were, to be sure, those who were not so keen on the changes. 'In my experience,' Lieutenant-General (retd.) Sir Douglas Brownrigg, now a Home Guard zone commander in London, wrote, 'it is true to say that those officers who set store by this [sense of their] rank are the ones least suited to hold it.'[47] There was considerable unease among those who wanted the Home Guard to remain a separate militia, a fear that army ranks would lead to retrograde regimentation. 'The Blimp mentality', Orwell noted in December 1940, 'has made a big come back.'[48] But even in left-wing circles there was a strong desire to see incompetent 'men of influence' weeded out to allow for greater efficiency and tactical training rather than mere boot-polishing and square-bashing. The Labour Party parliamentary defence committee, indeed, informed Grigg that they were all in favour of the Home Guard being 'effectively militarized'.[49] There was, however, one major scare over what commissioning might entail arising from a letter in *The Times*.

On 15 January 1941, a letter from Lieutenant-Colonel R. C. Bingham, CO of an [Army] Officer Cadet Training Unit, was published in *The Times*. In it Bingham lamented the fact that so many middle- and lower-class applicants were being granted commissions. Unlike the upper-class youths who had traditionally officered the Army, these men lacked the element of *noblesse oblige* necessary to look after troops properly and the moral character developed by good breeding necessary to lead them into battle. 'Man management', the colonel asserted, 'is not a subject that can be "taught"; it is an attitude of mind, and with the old school tie men this was instinctive and part of the philosophy of life.'[50] The resulting storm of protest led to the dismissal of Bingham and assurances from the new Secretary of State for War, David Margesson, that no class discrimination was being practised in the selection of officer-candidates.[51] It also raised questions about the upcoming selection of officers for the Home Guard.

On 4 February, Dan Frankel (Labour MP for Mile End) pointed out in parliament that a Home Guard zone commander had drawn the attention of those of his subordinates who might be involved in the selection process to Bingham's letter—which, the zone commander had said, was a good guide to choosing who within the Home Guard should be commissioned. Margesson tried to assure MPs that the matter was being investigated and that Bingham's opinions would not be followed, but suspicion remained. Seven days later Malcolm MacMillan (Labour MP for the Western Isles) demanded a guarantee from the War Minister that the zone commander in question would be sacked and that his replacement would 'ensure that Home Guard officers will be selected on merit alone'.

Margesson again tried to placate the critics, pointing out that an instruction to the selection panels had been recently issued which stressed that 'business, social or political prominence' would not be regarded as a qualification for commissioning. Unfortunately for the War Office, there were sufficient indications of apparent patronage to inspire further questions. Not surprisingly the selection of officers could in some instances lead to a feeling of having been unjustly treated,[52] and in true Home Guard fashion some of the offended parties were quick to voice their complaints in public. In February and March Frankel drew Margesson's attention to a case in one battalion where just before the selection panel was due to deliberate, a favoured civilian—technically not eligible for commissioning—had been hurriedly enrolled and then promoted to second-in-command 'over the heads of all the commanders who have been working for the Home Guard since Dunkirk'.[53]

Moreover, the War Office had from the start been anticipating that the commissioning process would involve the quiet weeding out of left-wing political undesirables as well as military incompetents,[54] which could lead to accusations of class bias. Alfred Edwards (Labour MP for Middlesbrough East), for example, pointed out that all but 19 of 319 senior Home Guard commissions granted in April 1941 were given to peers, baronets, knights, and retired generals.[55]

On the whole, however, the War Office had weathered a major shift in Home Guard policy rather well, bearing in mind the degree to which the Home Guard lobby might have made life difficult. There had been, however, one serious internal problem arising from the new order. The Prime Minister was not happy with the candidates for the new post of Director-General Home Guard.

Throughout the autumn of 1940, Churchill had continued to take an interest in the Home Guard and taken every opportunity to assure its members that, as he put it in the House of Commons on 5 November, he regarded the force as 'of the highest value and importance'.[56] He had liked the Grigg Report, but was not averse to making suggestions.[57] When he came across a short-list of the candidates, therefore, he was not willing to let what he saw as a bad choice become D-GHG.

The chief contender, General Sir Ivo Vesey, was aged 64 and currently on the retired list: hardly the man, from the Prime Minister's perspective, to provide the kind of dynamic, high-profile leadership the Home Guard would see as proof of the government's commitment to the force. 'Are there no younger men available for this strenuous administrative appointment?' Churchill asked in a note to General Sir John Dill (CIGS), on 19 October 1940. 'The bringing back of retired officers for these kinds of posts causes much criticism, both in and out of Service circles. Why not try to find a man still in his forties, and give him temporary rank.'[58]

From the perspective of the senior military staff at the War Office, it was an appointee's administrative experience which counted, not age. None of the three other short-listed candidates was under 55, and one of them, like Vesey, was on the retired list. Dill, divining that it was really the public relations aspect of the appointment that the Prime Minister was concerned about, tried to assure him that even if the D-GHG was a rather grey figure (in all respects), the Home Guard could focus on the activities of a largely powerless but high-profile Inspector-General, Lord

Gort. 'You might consider having the somewhat aged administrator,' Dill wrote back on 21 October, 'and getting Gort to devote much of his time to the Home Guard as Inspector-General to the Forces.'[59]

On the advice of the Permanent Under-Secretary, P. J. Grigg, Anthony Eden—shortly to become Foreign Secretary and be succeeded as War Minister by Margesson—also supported the appointment of Vesey. Writing to the Prime Minister on 22 October, he stressed that 'age and seniority count for a lot when it is a question of handling others tactfully, & smoothing over difficulties. This is what is wanted in a Director General of the Home Guard.'[60]

Churchill, however, not only refused to accept Vesey, but also refused to consider the three other candidates on the shortlist. His own choice was Lieutenant-General Sir Ralph Eastwood, who had take over from Pownall as Inspector-General Home Guard when the latter had finally obtained a transfer in early October. 'I formed a very favourable im-pression of him,' the Prime Minister noted in a letter to the CIGS on 6 November, 'particularly on account of his age, which is under 50.' To drop Eastwood after so short a time with the Home Guard directorate would, in his view, leave the government 'open to the most severe criticism'. Eastwood was young, competent, and was known to the Home Guard already. 'I am not prepared', Churchill warned, 'to agree to dismiss General Eastwood from the Home Guard Command [*sic*]. If you wish to set up this Directorate General, he must have it, as far as I am concerned.'[61]

By this point Edward Grigg was making his speech in the Commons and the Home Guard lobby had been alerted to the impending appoint-ment of a Director-General. To delay much further would be to risk questions in and out of the House about lack of official interest. Eastwood, moreover, was well thought of by Brooke and others. 'I therefore propose', Eden wrote in a letter to the Prime Minister on 16 November, 'to appoint Eastwood Director-General. I am strengthened in this decision because I know that this is your view.'[62]

The reasoning behind Eastwood's appointment was not forgotten. When two representatives of the oddly named Massachusetts Com-mittee of Public Safety arrived in England to assess the potential for setting up an organization similar to the Home Guard in early 1941, they were informed that the War Office had been enthusiastic enough to appoint 'one of the foremost young generals in the British Army' to the post of Director-General.[63] (The two Americans were impressed by how much effort was being devoted to the force and their report was favourably received.)[64]

By the spring of 1941 the War Office had reason to be optimistic about the state of the Home Guard. The force had, at least as far as left-wing extremism was concerned, been brought under a tighter rein. It would never function as the spearhead of a revolution. Steps had also been taken to make the Home Guard more efficient as a military organization through the commissioning process and more active involvement by regulars in administration and training. Even factory units, hitherto almost a law unto themselves, were brought into the military fold in May 1941 after careful negotiations with both the Trades Union Congress and the British Employers' Confederation.[65] With luck, there would be fewer accidents and false parachute sightings in future.

Yet problems remained. There was, to begin with, the matter of women in the Home Guard. In the spring and summer of 1940 women had been used in an unofficial auxiliary capacity in some units, while voluntary organizations had formed to teach women how to shoot. To strong-minded women such as Dr Edith Summerskill (Labour MP for West Fulham) and Marjorie Foster (winner of the King's Prize at Bisley) it seemed only right that ladies eager to do their bit should be allowed the same opportunities as men.[66]

Many of those men, however, were hostile to the idea. Apart from traditional concerns about fighting women interfering with what might be termed male combat motivation—defending family, hearth, and home—there seems to have been a disinclination to believe that the weaker vessel was really up to it. American correspondent Ed Murrow noted how an English friend of his had reacted to the idea in May 1940: 'a few million women with rifles was the most frightening prospect a man could face.'[67] The War Office was in addition concerned that allowing women into the Home Guard would deprive other important voluntary organizations, particularly the Women's Voluntary Service, of personnel, and in June 1940 it had been officially announced that 'women cannot be enrolled in the L.D.V.'.[68]

Dr Summerskill refused to accept this decision as final, and continued lobbying the War Office to allow women into the Home Guard. 'My first advances', she later related of efforts she made in December 1940, 'were treated with scant respect.'[69] But despite a series of rather rude rebuffs from P. J. Grigg, it was clear that the issue of admitting women into the Home Guard would be kept alive into 1941.[70]

There was also the thorny matter of the nature of the Home Guard in Northern Ireland. Concerned about the possibility of arms finding their way into the hands of the IRA, the government in Northern Ireland had decided in late May 1940 to raise the Ulster Defence Volunteers—equivalent in role to the LDV—as a branch of the Royal Ulster Constabulary.[71] As elsewhere in the United Kingdom the public response was very great. Within a week, the lists were full. The decision to link the UDV with the RUC, however, and thus with the dominant Protestant community, angered minority Catholics who felt that they were being discriminated against. Opposition MPs at Stormont such as John Beattie (Pottinger, Belfast) were not slow to react, and were able to cite cases of Catholics being turned away from the new force.[72]

By the autumn of 1940 the government of Lord Craigavon was coming under heavy pressure to place the Ulster Home Guard under military rather than police control as a way of solving the problem. Aware that the military in Northern Ireland were London's responsibility, and perhaps also conscious of the fact that while internal security was under the control of Stormont, responsibility for external defence—which was at least one of the functions of the Home Guard—was vested in Westminster, the Craigavon cabinet decided in late 1940 to pass the decision on to London.[73]

Churchill, meanwhile, had been made aware of the problem through the efforts of Maurice Healy, Hubert Gough, and other prominent Home Guard leaders in London who signed a petition directed at the government calling for an end to the sectarianism of the Ulster Home Guard. The Catholic Archbishop of Westminster, meanwhile, wrote a letter of support directly to the Prime Minister's office. Aware that any decision would have potential repercussions among Catholic communities everywhere, Churchill solicited the opinions of the Dominions Office as well as those of the Home Office and War Office.[74]

Ministers were divided about how to respond to the request. The Home Secretary, Herbert Morrison, was in favour of taking action on political grounds: 'there are loyal Catholics in Northern Ireland', he argued, 'who would join an Imperial defence force but are unwilling to join a force administered by a Government which they regard as a sectarian Government.'[75] David Margesson, however, was absolutely opposed to the idea of the War Office intervening in the affairs of Northern Ireland. 'You see,' he minuted to Morrison on 15 January 1941, 'I feel so strongly that, on the grounds of both military efficiency and of the absolute necessity of not involving the Army in the religious animosities of Ireland, we should not offer to take over this force.'[76] The Dominions Office, meanwhile, straddled the fence, explaining, as a Home Office official put it, 'that while they are not in a position to press strongly the importance of making such a change as has been advocated they would welcome any step which would diminish possibilities of friction in connection with this force'.[77]

Churchill himself would have preferred to let sleeping dogs lie, but the government of Northern Ireland had made this option problematic by asking that if London chose not to act, they be given permission to announce at Stormont that 'the Imperial authorities, having considered the offer made by the Government of Northern Ireland to transfer the Local Defence Volunteer Section of the Ulster Constabulary to the control of the Army Council, had requested the Government to maintain the force as a branch of the Ulster Special Constabulary'.[78] Either way London would be made the scapegoat.

In the end, after Sir John Anderson had been asked to assess the situation and had concluded that Catholics were unlikely to join a predominantly Protestant force no matter who controlled it, it was decided in March 1941 to let the Stormont cabinet know—with the minimum possible publicity—that the status quo should remain undisturbed. 'His Majesty's Government', John MacDermott, the Northern Ireland Minister of Security, announced at Stormont on 27 March, 'have come to the conclusion that it is in the interests of administrative efficiency and convenience that the force be maintained as a branch of the Constabulary Force under the control of the Government of Northern Ireland until such time as it may be necessary for the military authorities to assume control of the force for operational purposes.'[79] It remained to be seen if this would satisfy the critics.

There were also more general difficulties. Arms and equipment, for one thing, remained far below Home Guard expectations, while the

Home Guard lobby remained alert to any sign of indifference on the part of the authorities, such as the requirement that Home Guard officers travel third class while regular officers travelled first class on trains. And, despite the gradual imposition of discipline, there remained an alarming propensity for Home Guard officers to ignore the proper chain of command when making known their grievances. 'Instances were given', the minutes of a conference of Home Guard commanders in West Yorkshire held on 8 November 1940 recorded, 'where company and even platoon commanders had communicated direct to Area [HQ] and the T.A. Association without the knowledge of the Group Commander or even the battalion commander.'[80]

Last but not least was the question of what role the force was to play after Hitler had failed to invade in the summer or autumn of 1940. Did the country still need such a large force now that the threat of invasion appeared to have receded? And if it did, how should the Home Guard be developed: as a guerrilla force; a heavily-armed, perhaps even mobile, home defence reserve army; or something else entirely? These and other questions faced the War Office and government as the first anniversary of Eden's call for volunteers approached.

6 On Guard
1941–2

...a Home Guard weapon was one that was dangerous to the enemy, and, to a greater degree, to the operator.

Lt.-Col. J. Lee, HG Bn CO[1]

> Here lies a victim of them Huns;
> He had a pike and they had guns.
> But now he wonders, gone aloft
> Whether to blame the Huns or Croft.

'Bee', *Daily Mail*, Feb. 1942[2]

There is obviously a great deal of plain speaking in the Home Guard...

Lord Bridgeman, Feb. 1942[3]

Over the winter of 1940–1 it gradually became apparent that the initial public enthusiasm for the Home Guard was beginning to wear off. By the late summer of 1940 the Ministry of Information was detecting signs that after months of expecting an invasion any day, people were starting to think that perhaps the Germans were not coming after all, and while there were periodic mini-scares, by the first months of 1941 a mood of complacency prevailed.[4] 'There was little doubt', read a COS report in January 1941 paraphrasing the conclusions of Sir William Bartholomew (Chief of Civil Defence Operations Staff), 'that the public were taking the whole thing much more casually than they had last summer.'[5]

A corresponding slow decline in the strength of the Home Guard also became evident. In part this was due to the call-up of the younger volunteers into the regular armed forces and the forced retirement of the over-age and incompetent following the Grigg Reforms.[6] Another factor in declining numbers was a certain amount of disgruntlement at the slow arrival of weapons and equipment.[7] But a more general influence on resignations appears to have been a sense that the danger of invasion had significantly decreased. As four resigning Wellingborough volunteers put it in a letter to their CO on 9 December 1940, 'we feel that the crisis for which we joined the organization is now past'. If real danger manifested itself again they would volunteer again. 'We should like to add,' the four teachers concluded, 'that in case of further emergency we should be happy to undertake guard duties again, or similar duties, at a moment's notice.'[8]

Nor, it would seem, were those who remained keyed up to quite the same pitch of expectancy as they had been some months earlier. In May 1941 the Southern Regional Police noted that German airmen who bailed out were finding it difficult to get themselves taken into custody, since the Home Guard no longer seemed interested in arresting them. 'After all the trouble they take to come over and bail out,' the CO of a Buckinghamshire Home Guard battalion drily informed his company commanders, 'it is not right for anyone to totally disregard them.'[9]

The public were not, as it happened, that far off official thinking as to the chances of a German invasion over the winter of 1940–1. Winter weather precluded any large-scale enemy combined operations in the Channel, and by the spring of 1941, despite periodic enemy efforts at strategic deception designed to create the impression that operation Sealion would still be mounted, the Chiefs of Staff had cautiously concluded that an invasion was significantly less likely in the coming months than it had been in 1940. The airborne invasion of Crete in April 1941 led to a mini invasion scare, but in the following months alarm once more abated (although a curious concern in certain circles that the Germans might be digging a Channel tunnel lasted into 1942).[10]

The authorities, however, were far from happy with the prevailing public mood. Total war demanded total dedication, and complacency could easily lead to a diminishing will to win. As early as October 1940 the C-in-C Home Forces and the Chiefs of Staff were talking of the need to take counter-measures against complacency, and by March 1941 there was talk of reviving both public and Home Guard alertness through a new series of road-block ID checks.[11]

The Prime Minister was also concerned. Taking a great interest in Ultra and other intelligence sources, Churchill even at the height of invasion alarms had remained somewhat ambivalent concerning the reality of the Fifth Column threat and the inevitability of a cross-Channel assault.[12] Observing a Home Defence exercise early in 1941, the Prime Minister voiced his opinion that the umpires were inflating the likelihood of invasion. 'He even implied', an outraged Brooke later wrote, 'that this had been done in order to influence him into considering the threat greater than it was.'[13] Churchill was, however, quite determined that the general public should not cease to believe in such threats. One of his private secretaries, John Colville, noted in his diary after a dinner at Chequers in July 1940, at which various senior commanders were present, the PM's rationale:

He emphasized that the great invasion scare . . . is serving a most useful purpose: it is . . . keeping every man and woman tuned to a high pitch of readiness. He does not wish the scare to abate therefore, and although personally he doubts whether invasion is a serious menace he intends to give that impression, and to talk about long and dangerous vigils, etc. . . . [14]

This applied especially to the Home Guard, a central feature of Churchill's efforts to inspire a mood of belligerent optimism in the face of heavy odds and immediate danger. There was therefore a great desire on the part of both the Prime Minister and the War Office to restore faith within the Home Guard as to its central role in the nation's defence.

One obvious means of doing so was to take every opportunity to sing the praises of the force. And generals and politicians did not stint in their public admiration. On 9 February 1941, for instance, General Auchinleck, formerly GOC Southern Command and now C-in-C India, had made laudatory references to the Home Guard in a radio broadcast subsequently covered in the press. 'I have no praise too high', Auchinleck stated, 'for the way in which these men, a very large number of them old soldiers of all ranks and ages, have sacrificed their leisure and comfort to fit themselves to defend their country. It is magnificent, and no other word describes it.'[15] In March it was the turn of the C-in-C Home Forces, General Brooke. 'I attach the greatest importance', Brooke explained in a special Order of the Day, 'to the role of the Home Guard in its co-operation with Regular Forces in defense against invasion.'[16]

In May 1941, taking advantage of the first anniversary of the Home Guard, the War Office drew up a draft congratulatory message for George VI to sign, and took up a suggestion made originally by the King himself that volunteers from various London units be allowed to mount guard at Buckingham Palace on the 14th. Members of the Home Guard, the King's published message read, had made great progress, shown tremendous keenness, and were to be thanked 'for the service they freely give at considerable sacrifice of leisure and convenience'. His Majesty was confident that Home Guards in conjunction with the men of the field army 'will fit themselves to meet and overcome every emergency; and so make their contribution to the victory which will reward our united efforts'.[17]

The first anniversary was a public relations success, though somewhat overshadowed in the press by the sudden arrival of Hitler's deputy, Rudolf Hess (who on 10 May had parachuted into Scotland in an unauthorized and rather hare-brained attempt to personally negotiate peace between Germany and Britain).[18] Further efforts at morale boosting included widely publicized awards of George Medals for Home Guards who had displayed gallantry in emergencies, and the introduction of a series of proficiency badges in April 1941. Reactions to the badges were, however, somewhat mixed (perhaps the boy-scout analogy was too close for comfort),[19] and verbal assurances as to the worth of the Home Guard were obviously futile unless backed up by physical evidence in a short space of time.

The most obvious way to demonstrate a concrete commitment to the Home Guard would be to arm the force to the teeth, thus providing unambiguous evidence of the authorities' faith in the volunteers and belief in the threat of invasion. Arming the Home Guard, however, continued to pose serious problems.

The Army was expanding towards a projected strength of 55 divisions, and equipment losses at Dunkirk still had to be made good. What this meant in practical terms was that production of the standard infantry weapons—everything from rifles to mortars—was fully taken up by the needs of the regulars and nothing could be spared for the Home Guard. Symptomatic of this problem was the decision that as soon as rifles began to arrive in significant quantities from Canada and America the small number of .303 Lee-Enfields issued to Home Guards in May were withdrawn in the autumn of 1940 for distribution in the Army. Even Churchill, so often on the side of the volunteers, recognized that the regular forces had to have priority over the Home Guard.[20]

By the winter of 1940–1, most of the Home Guard were wearing battledress, complete with stiff leather gaiters, leather belt, gas cape, and helmet, and were armed not only with American P. 17 and Canadian Ross rifles but also with American Browning Automatic Rifles (BARs), old Lewis guns, various grenades, and even Thompson sub-machine guns of Chicago gangland fame. Quantity and quality, however, were a problem.

At the end of September 1940 the War Office forecast that even with the maximum use of private arms and shipments of First-World-War-vintage rifles and machine guns from across the Atlantic, the Home Guard would have somewhere under 847,000 rifles, 46,629 shotguns, and 48,750 automatics for a total of 1,682,303 volunteers—in other words, even under ideal conditions at least 740,000 Home Guards would have no personal weapon. Ammunition was also scarce. Given that most of the rifles issued to the Home Guard were .300 calibre rather than the standard British .303, ammunition had to be imported along with American arms, which allowed for a maximum of 50 rounds per rifle and 750 rounds for BARs and machine guns.[21]

What was more, many veterans were less than happy with what they got—especially if it involved handing in the beloved SMLE in exchange for a foreign weapon. The Canadian Ross and the US Remington and Springfield rifles, covered in the thick grease in which they had been stored for over twenty years, were longer and more unwieldy than the standard Lee-Enfield, and the Ross tended to jam when dirty (the reason it had been withdrawn from service in the First World War).[22]

The main problem, though, was sheer lack of weapons. Unit commanders complained, MPs asked awkward questions, and the press was constantly harping on the evident deficiencies.[23] Almost from the first the government had made implicit and often explicit statements to the effect that the Home Guard would be fully armed. In July 1940, for example, Lord Croft had stated in the House of Lords that 'very soon every man . . . will have some effective form of weapon with which to resist and if necessary to slay any Germans who seek to enslave him or his wife and family or to destroy the freedom of this fair land.'[24] Living up to such promises was going to be difficult.

There was, however, a potential solution—the development of special weapons that could be manufactured quickly, cheaply, and in quantity. This process had begun in the crisis atmosphere of the summer of 1940 when anything that could be provided quickly—'from the archaic to the apocalyptic'—seemed worth developing.[25] There were, for example, the Flame Trap and its cousin, the Flame Fougasse, static ambush weapons.[26] More common, and the first weapon universal to the Home Guard, was the official molotov cocktail, the No. 76 Self-Igniting Phosphorous (SIP) grenade.

First demonstrated in July 1940 and subsequently manufactured in vast quantities—over 6,000,000 by August 1941—the SIP grenade consisted of a half-pint glass bottle filled with phosphorous and other chemicals which ignited when the glass was broken. It was not, alas, a terribly effective weapon. Ordnance Board tests revealed that the glass would not break when thrown down on grass or even tarmac, and that it had to be dropped from a height of eight feet onto concrete before it would ignite. Once ignited, moreover, the grenade produced fumes which could choke the thrower if he was not careful.[27]

On the other hand it was very simple and cheap to mass-produce, and helped bridge the yawning gap in the supply of rifles. Optimistic instructions were produced suggesting that they could be a very useful anti-tank weapon. 'Six of these bottles breaking on a tank one after the other', one such instruction ran, 'should cause sufficient heat and smoke to develop all over the tank to bring the crew out.'[28] Any doubts about the weapon were firmly squelched by propaganda designed to highlight the grenade's effectiveness.[29]

Other grenades followed in 1941. There was the No. 73, commonly known as the Woolworth or Thermos bomb and designed to destroy tanks. It was, as a Home Guard later put it, 'just a lump of gelignite in a biscuit tin'.[30] Rather heavy, the Woolworth bomb could be thrown only short distances, and could easily injure the thrower if he was not behind cover.[31] It did, however, make a satisfyingly loud bang when exploded.[32]

There was also the No. 74 grenade, better known as the Sticky bomb. This had been developed as a stop-gap anti-tank weapon—'I don't mind where they come from,' Eden had minuted in June 1940, 'as long as we get them'[33]—but after tests was rejected for use by the Army by the Director of Artillery. Churchill, however, insisted on further tests, and after viewing a demonstration on 28 July personally ordered that the weapon go into mass production.[34] Chiefly composed of a glass flask filled with nitro-glycerine and covered with a sock coated in adhesive, the Sticky bomb seemed alarmingly prone to breakage and leakage, and would not stick to wet or muddy surfaces. 'The whole article', as an Ordnance Board official put it, 'is most objectionable.'[35] The Prime Minister, however, remained adamantly in favour of the grenade. When Ordnance Board opposition seemed to be causing delays, he sent a sharp note to his scientific adviser, Professor Lindemann: 'Sticky Bomb. Make one million. WSC.'[36] So despite its flaws the Sticky bomb went into service with the Home Guard, most of whom seem to have viewed it with a certain affection. 'It was rather popular with the men,' the historian of the 45th Warwickshire Battalion relates, 'except that when throwing it, it was wise not to brush it against your clothes, for there it was liable to stick firmly, and blow up the thrower instead of the enemy objective.'[37]

Grenades of this sort—as well as the more commonly used Mills bomb and Hawkins anti-tank mine—were helpful, but what was really needed was some sort of close-support weapon that could be fired and required a crew. That would absorb excess manpower, give the men concerned a sense of involvement, and add to the sense that the Home Guard was a front-line force.

Heavy US Browning and old Vickers machine guns, to be sure, could have partially fulfilled this function. As a member of an Edinburgh company explained:

The Vickers was undoubtedly the aristocrat of our weapons at this time [early 1941], and was sedulously groomed by the men, who delighted in dismantling it and reassembling it. A convoy of no less than three cars was allotted to carry it and its warlike paraphernalia and attendant acolytes about the country.[38]

Unfortunately such weapons—especially the Vickers, which was also used by the Army—were in very short supply, and thus could not absorb many men.

This was where the grandly named Northover Projector came in. Like other Home Guard weapons, its origins lay in the panic days of 1940. Designed by a Home Guard officer, Major H. Northover, on his own initiative, it was a simple line-of-sight weapon, easily manufactured and very cheap (just under £10 each). Consisting of a hollow metal tube mounted on a simple cast-iron tripod, the Northover Projector fired SIP grenades with the aid of a toy pistol cap and a black powder charge. Writing directly to the Prime Minister, Northover arranged a demonstration of his weapon which led to a personal endorsement by Churchill and a decision to mass-produce the Projector in October 1940. 'You see,' Brigadier Whitehead confided to Ralph Glyn, 'each of these weapons requires more than one man and if a Northover team consists of three men, they all feel it belongs to them and forget, for the moment at any rate, that they have not got a rifle.'[39] Orders were placed for enough Northover Projectors to equip the Home Guard on a scale of one per platoon, and by August 1941 over 8,000 were in service.[40]

Simplicity and low cost, however, were matched by design defects. The Northover was rather cumbersome, often would not fire in wet weather (the charge became too damp), had a feeble discharge pressure, and was not accurate beyond 150 yards. The cast-iron tripod also tended to crack if dropped, and quality control of both the weapon itself and its SIP ammunition was minimal. Bottles could sometimes explode in the barrel if the black powder charge was too great, fall dangerously short, or fail to explode at all after being fired. Worst of all, the Northover gave off a dense cloud of white smoke when fired which obscured the target, gave away the advantages of concealment, and took about a minute to dissipate.[41]

Home Guards were initially rather taken aback by the Heath Robinson quality of what one volunteer characterized as 'a piece of drainpipe on three legs'.[42] The Northover did indeed look uncomfortably like the comic illustrator's First World War contraptions and the current work he was doing on Home Guard techniques.[43] Some officers never accepted it as useful while others had total confidence; but for the most part, with the War Office propaganda machine put into high gear ('an amazing weapon—effective—accurate—simple in construction—easy to operate, requiring no expert technique—no maintenance problem—produced at low cost'),[44] its flaws were overlooked or worked around, three or more men assigned as crew, and the Northover viewed, in the words of one Home Guard, as 'something to be accepted gratefully until something better arrived'.[45]

That something, at least in theory, was the Blacker Bombard, which began to appear in small numbers towards the end of 1941. The invention of a TA artillery officer, Lieutenant-Colonel L. V. S. Blacker, the original design for the weapon had been rejected by the War Office in favour of the standard 2″ mortar in 1939. In the summer of 1940, however, Blacker had become involved in the same section of the Munitions Directorate (MD1) which had promoted the Sticky bomb, and convinced his superiors later in the year that a modified version of his original design could serve as a combined anti-tank and bombardment weapon which—or so he claimed—would have the anti-tank capabilities of the 2-pounder gun and almost the same range as the 3″ mortar. The Director of Artillery and others were not particularly enthusiastic, but after a demonstration on 18 August which Churchill attended the Bombard's future was assured. 'As Prime Minister,' he informed the director of MD1, 'I instruct you to proceed with all speed with the development of this excellent weapon.'[46]

With the Prime Minister having adopted the Blacker Bombard as 'one of his pets' (as Brooke rather disdainfully put it)[47] Margesson was converted—'the 2 pdr. is much better, but we cannot get enough quickly to arm the Home Guard'[48]—and production went ahead on a projected scale of one per company. The Blacker Bombard, bearing a striking resemblance to a medieval siege gun in more than name, worked on the principle of a heavily sprung steel rod (the so-called spigot) inside a short barrel-like 29 mm tube being released to strike a small charge on the end of a projectile, the projectile thus being propelled towards the target.[49]

The Bombard, or Spigot Mortar (a less archaic title soon adopted for the weapon) was certainly more imposing than the Northover. It too, however, had problems. Despite the claims of its inventor, it did not come anywhere close to the 3″ mortar in effective range, its accuracy was questionable—General de Gaulle had almost been killed at its first demonstration[50]—and its rate of fire was agonizingly slow. Weighing 360 lb and possessing a recoil of twenty tons per square inch, it had to be dismantled in order to be moved and was difficult to sight after the first bomb had been fired. The anti-tank ammunition, moreover, when finally available, proved to have such an insensitive impact fuse that it would pass right through an unarmoured vehicle such as a car or lorry or hit the ground without exploding. When bombs did explode, the remains of the tail fins had a nasty habit of hurtling back towards the crew.[51]

Yet once again the Home Guard appear to have looked on the bright side. Unlike the Northover, the Spigot Mortar did pack a significant punch in the form of a 14 lb anti-personnel bomb and a 20 lb anti-tank bomb, and the War Office did its best to present it in a favourable light. 'Not everyone understands what we want the Bombard for,' as Margesson put it in a letter to Beaverbrook. 'It is not an anti-tank *gun* but it is an anti-tank *weapon* . . . for use in an ambush.'[52] As with other Home Guard weapons tactics were designed around the Spigot's short-comings: if well-concealed and pre-sited (perhaps on a concrete base), a Spigot Mortar could conceivably score a direct hit on the first shot— always bearing in mind that its five-man crew were unlikely to get a second chance.[53] Once again the introduction of a new piece of sub-artillery requiring the attention of a number of otherwise unarmed volunteers amid much favourable propaganda was, in general, a public relations success. 'It was a heartening acquisition,' as the Ministry of Food battalion historian wrote, 'and showed the Home Guard that they were at last being taken very seriously indeed.'[54]

The various bombs and other weapons distributed to the Home Guard in 1941–2 did not by any means end calls for more arms, especially in light of the fact that Army commanders were calling on the Home Guard to perform more functions in lieu of regulars being posted overseas. A conference of Home Guard commanders in the South Midland area on 30 June 1941, for example, gave rise to much criticism.

Everyone present emphasized the bad effect shortage of arms was having not only on the efficiency but on the morale of the Home Guard. Zone Commanders present pointed out that men were being called upon to perform duties under Operational Instructions from the Area which could only be efficiently carried out provided there were sufficient arms and ammunition.[55]

The issuing of new weapons, however, did have at least a short-term positive effect on morale, and without them criticism would doubtless have been much greater.

Perceptive observers recognized that the true value of grenades and sub-artillery lay more in boosting flagging morale than in improving fighting ability. 'In these circumstances,' the CO of the 5th Battalion Devon Home Guard wrote of the decreasing prospect of invasion in 1941–2, 'the great influx of new weapons into the Bn was fortunate. It gave us something to think about, something to chew with our mental teeth.' As another battalion commander put it, 'everything was new to the men and they were vastly interested'.[56]

There was, however, one weapon issued by the War Office which was an unmitigated public relations disaster. This was the infamous pike, issued to disbelieving and outraged volunteers at the beginning of 1942.

As with several other weapons eventually issued to the Home Guard, the advent of the pike was due in large part to the intervention of the Prime Minister. At the beginning of December 1941 in the course of a speech on Home Guard affairs, Churchill had stated that even where rifles were not available efforts were being made to provide simpler hand-held weapons such as 'a pike or a mace' as an interim measure until all volunteers were armed. 'After all,' the Prime Minister added artlessly, 'a man thus armed may easily acquire a rifle for himself.'[57] At the time this reference to pikes and maces seems to have been overlooked or dismissed as a piece of Churchillian rhetoric, conveying more spirit than substance. But in point of fact the Prime Minister had been quite in earnest.

At the end of June 1941, Churchill had written to the War Office ordering that 'every man must have a weapon of some kind, be it only a mace or pike'.[58] Taking the Prime Minister at his word, the War Office began to issue truncheons to some Home Guard units, and in July placed orders for the production of 250,000 long metal tubes with surplus sword bayonet blades spot-welded in one end—pikes, as ordered by the PM.

In light of how negatively the pike was to be received, it is worth asking why production went ahead. It was true that Churchill himself had pressed for pikes to be manufactured and issued, but P. J. Grigg, among others, was not averse to occasionally ignoring orders from 10 Downing Street which he considered foolish if he thought he could get away with it.[59] If not overawed by Churchill's 'Action this Day' tone, the explanation may be that the War Office itself was genuinely misled into thinking that pikes would be welcomed by the extent to which foot drill, smartness, and bayonet fighting were encouraged in some Home Guard units.

It was a constant refrain of the left-wing lobby and others within the Home Guard that the 'Colonel Blimps' who commanded many Home Guard units emphasized square-bashing, boot and button polishing, and the value of cold steel over camouflage, modern battle tactics, and squad fighting.[60] It is not difficult to find examples of such behaviour. In the 2nd (Chester City) Cheshire Battalion, for instance, the second in command ordered that 'Boots, belts, and anklets should be polished . . . Buttons and badges should be bright' in order to instil pride—a policy followed in, among other units, the Loughborough College Home Guard (where smartness was evidently considered one of the primary virtues).[61] A gleaming bayonet was also important. An article in the February 1941 issue of a west country unit magazine extolled 'The Spirit of the Bayonet', and as late as August 1943 members of the 3rd Argyll Battalion were being told that 'The bayonet isn't obsolete' and that bayonet drill also 'has the advantage of warming men up on cold evenings and takes the place of P.T.'.[62]

Under these circumstances, it might have appeared in the War Office that the more traditional among the Home Guard would welcome an extra issue of cold steel. A bayonet, however, was one thing in the minds of enthusiasts; a pike was quite another, as the authorities were soon to discover.

Many of the pikes, like the Spigot Mortar, were assembled in factories under the auspices of the Ministry of Aircraft Production. For all his faults—and there were many—Lord Beaverbrook could see the kind of negative reaction pikes would generate. Metal tubing, in his view, could be put to much better use and was in any case in short supply. 'What about bows and arrows?' he asked sceptically in a letter to Margesson on 4 August. 'In this event we must lay in a supply of string. String is very short, too.' The Minister of Aircraft Production found the whole thing farcical. 'There is also a plentiful supply of flint at Cherkley [Beaverbrook's home], which we could turn into flintlocks,' he added. 'Would these be of any use?'[63]

Margesson, however, knew from experience that when Churchill intervened on behalf of the Home Guard, it was wise not to obstruct too often. 'First of all,' he pointed out in a letter of reply, 'the Prime Minister ordered them, and if you think they represent an interruption of something else which is more important, I think you must have a word with him.' The War Office was also concerned at the slow pace of production of other weapons for the Home Guard, and worried that criticism would only increase if something were not done immediately. 'We are short a million personal weapons,' the War Minister lamented.

He would have preferred firearms if they were available, but pikes were still a step up from 'bare fists or stones'.[64] It soon became apparent, however, that members of the Home Guard had a rather different perspective.

The truncheons were not particularly popular,[65] but the pikes generated a tidal wave of anger and disgust. Something which might just have been acceptable at the height of the invasion panic in 1940 was by early 1942 clearly an affront to Home Guard dignity and self-esteem. How could the authorities possibly issue such an anachronistic piece of equipment unless they had no intention of treating the Home Guard as a real fighting force?

Almost without exception, incredulous COs and quartermasters unwrapped bundles of pikes and hurriedly put them into storage, aware of how the men would react if they were handed out. Their mere existence, however, cast doubt on the competence of the Home Guard Directorate and gave rise to suspicions that once again volunteers were being slighted.[66]

As always Home Guard complaints were not slow to find their way into the press. The opportunity for satire was irresistible, and cartoons of Home Guards armed with bows, swords, and other medieval paraphernalia appeared everywhere. Columnists and editorial writers had a field day castigating the authorities for such a retrograde move. A *Daily Mail* editorial was particularly sarcastic.

You never know. The pole-axe may return. Crossbowmen of the thirteenth century might be useful behind the hedges. Archers with poisoned arrows might take tips from Harold at Hastings. The War Office may be found studying reproductions of Bayeux tapestry and using medieval manuscripts as military manuals. Did not head-piece armour return in the last war?[67]

Other Fleet Street columnists did not find the matter so humorous.

Pikes would be worse than useless because of the demoralizing effect on the men called upon to use them. These men would be well aware that the invader was well armed to the teeth with every weapon and every scientific devilment known to warfare.[68]

In parliament, another traditional venue for the airing of Home Guard frustration, the pike issue was quickly taken up. 'I think the provision of pikes for the Home Guard,' Captain Godfrey Nicholson (Tory MP for Farnham) remarked angrily, 'if it was not meant as a joke, was an insult.'[69]

Even in the House of Lords, where debate was generally more courteous than in the Commons, the mood was one of anger. 'I think that the Home Guards throughout the country are waiting rather anxiously to ascertain whether they are going to be supplied with any other medieval knick-knacks of a similar sort,' Lord Mansfield (a Home Guard himself) stated, 'because, frankly, the Home Guard honestly regard these pikes as little less than an insult.' Lord Cork asserted that as a result of the appearance of pikes he had received letters from all over the country doubting whether the government was 'really serious in dealing with the danger of invasion and whether they really wanted the Home Guard'.[70]

It was Churchill who was really responsible, but it was Lord Croft as Under-Secretary of State for War, displaying the valorous but politically dubious adherence to principle that was the hallmark of his parliamentary career, who chose to make himself a target by speaking in defence of the weapon. Replying to complaints about lack of rifles for the Home Guard, on 4 February 1942 Croft stated his opinion in the Lords that other weapons—including pikes—could be more effective at close quarters. 'If I were a bomber in . . . a [hand-to-hand fighting] formation . . . ,' he claimed, 'I should like to have a pike in order to follow up my bombing attack, especially at night. It is a most effective and silent weapon.'[71]

From then on the pike issue was always attributed to Croft, and much to his annoyance cartoons appeared of him in full armour and the weapons themselves became known as 'Croft's pikes'.[72] To go as far as to withdraw the weapon would be to admit that the whole thing had been a colossal mistake—and therefore not something the authorities could contemplate. On the other hand, as a public relations officer at GHQ Home Forces advised the chief of staff, 'the less there is said on the subject the better'.[73]

The pike fiasco was especially bothersome to the authorities because it undermined the positive effect of the Northovers and Spigots and gave ammunition to those Home Guards who were still dissatisfied with how they were being treated by the authorities. For, quite apart from weapons, there were several issues which continued to cause friction.

Paradoxically, one source of difficulty arose from GHQ Home Forces and lesser HQs coming to rely too much on the Home Guard. Even among the more optimistic Army commanders, claims as to the value of the Home Guard in battle in the summer and autumn of 1940 had a somewhat desperate air to them, a sense that ill-armed, untrained volunteers were better than nothing at all. By the middle of 1941, however, with the Home Guard receiving more equipment, being organized in a more orthodox manner, and (theoretically, at least) now better trained through the use of training manuals and attendance at Denbeis and similar schools, GOCs began to integrate the Home Guard into their operational plans. The C-in-C Home Forces, General Brooke, took the lead in this, his continuing anxiety over the threat of invasion apparently leading him not only to ask for Home Forces to be enlarged but also to place more faith in the Home Guard.[74]

Unfortunately, not all staff officers understood the limitations placed on the uses of the Home Guard by its local organization and part-time nature. 'Considerable resentment was felt by many senior H.G. Commanders', an officer with Scottish Command HQ later wrote, 'at thoughtless demands or instructions received from Command and District Headquarters.'[75] Linked to this problem was the increasing amount of paperwork unit HQs were being expected to process. From the Home Guard perspective higher authorities seemed blissfully unaware that Home Guard officers had day jobs, and that what worked in the Regular Army and civil service would not necessarily be appropriate in the Home Guard. The number and variety of regulation forms, requests, and instructions crossing the desks of harassed Home Guard unit HQ staffs seemed to be creating more confusion than order. 'There seemed to be a paragraph and sub-paragraph to cover every tiniest event which could possibly happen,' John Brophy related, 'not only to every man, but to every buckle and bootlace.'[76] Among the more baffling missives from higher authority was a detailed set of instructions for the interring of Muslim casualties issued in April 1941. 'The most pressing need . . . felt by Company Commanders at the time', a Buckinghamshire battalion commander later wrote, 'was for more rifles, not burial instructions.'[77]

The role of the Home Guard also continued to cause problems. Despite the opening of the Eastern Front in June 1941, GHQ Home Forces remained, in the words of the GOC Western Command, 'obsessed with the fear of an imminent invasion'.[78] Brooke, eager to make the Home Guard a more integral part of home defence as troops were transferred to other theatres, introduced an ambitious new scheme for the Home Guard. Instead of just observing and harassing the enemy, and then retiring before superior odds, the Home Guard would create 'nodal points', defensive positions built around villages and important road junctions. Faced with superior force, the Home Guard would retreat to these nodal points and fight it out until overwhelmed. The idea was that while the invader would initially overwhelm these defensive positions, they would, as one after another was dealt with or circumnavigated, delay and obstruct any enemy advance and allow time for Home Forces to organize a field army counter-attack.

From the perspective of GHQ Home Forces, this was a role for which the Home Guard now seemed admirably suited. The force was now better equipped to fight than it had been in the summer of 1940, and a certain amount of unit-level tactical training and local exercising was taking place. But beyond the local level its limitations were glaringly apparent. Its lack of transport, the absence of a logistical tail, the lack of command and control beyond the battalion level, the 'one off' nature of its sub-artillery, all pointed to a short static fight rather than a prolonged, mobile engagement.

There was also Home Guard parochialism to consider. 'For the men of Devon,' Lieutenant-General Sir Frederick Morgan (GOC South-Western Area) wrote, 'those of Cornwall were nothing but a lot of damned foreigners who, as like as not, would welcome the Germans: while the Cornishmen reckoned those of Devon to be a soft lot who could be relied upon in no way to resist the enemy.'[79] Elsewhere in England the situation appeared no better. 'It would be wrong to say that there was any animosity between the men of Suffolk and Cambridgeshire,' the historian of the Cambridgeshire Home Guard reflected, 'but they were cousins rather than brothers, and sometimes distant cousins at that.'[80] In Scotland, according to Compton Mackenzie (then commanding the Barra Company of the 2nd Inverness-shire Home Guard battalion), friction between the Home Guard of the northern and southern parts of the Highlands was such that the 'Cameron and Seaforth Highlanders were at war with the Black Watch and the

Argyll and Sutherland Highlanders'.[81] Co-operation among mobile units crossing county boundaries might therefore be problematic.

In the wake of the German airborne invasion of Crete, however, during which it had been learned that enemy parachutists were at their most vulnerable within the first few minutes of landing, the C-in-C Home Forces was willing to allow for a certain degree of local mobility within the framework of nodal-point defence. What Brooke wanted, as he explained in an order issued at the end of June 1941, were 'small fighting patrols' of younger men, who, with the aid of bicycles or cars, could be dispatched to the scene of a parachute landing and either nip the threat in the bud or inflict severe losses before retreating to the static nodal-point defences.[82]

As usual, however, there were those enthusiasts who had their own ideas as to the proper role of the Home Guard in the event of an invasion. Some, for instance, had already formed such patrols prior to official sanctioning, and were now looking for a more aggressive and active function. 'There is one school of thought', Major-General Lord Bridgeman (the Deputy-Director Home Guard) pensively put it, 'which is for ever anxious to "make the Home Guard mobile".'[83] As John Brophy explained in the *Sunday Graphic* in May 1941:

Rightly or wrongly, many [volunteers] feel that the Home Guard is not being asked or trained to do all it might do.

They feel that an undue emphasis is being placed on the duty to observe and report: the emphasis was right in 1940 but wrong to-day.

What they have in mind is that the Home Guard now is ready to tackle, in this or any other order, airborne troops, tanks and dive-bombers. That is how they see the job confronting us.

To do that job effectively all we need is the right weapons—which cannot be delivered too fast—and more emphasis placed on our local striking power than on limitations we have outgrown.[84]

The same month, Lieutenant-Colonel Sir Thomas Moore (Tory MP for Ayr Burghs and a leading Home Guard advocate) was asking the War Office to allow the Home Guard to use cars laid-up because of the petrol shortage for transport purposes. Hore-Belisha, the former War Minister, went even further. 'The Home Guard,' he argued during the debate on the war situation on 6 May, 'like the Army as a whole, should become mobile and armoured.'[85] Perhaps dissatisfied with the rather limited striking role advocated by GHQ Home Forces, John Brophy seconded this idea. 'We have progressed from static defence to local mobility,' he argued in the *Sunday Graphic*. 'Let us hurry on a stage further to Armoured Mobility.'[86] Not all Home Guard commanders agreed with such grandiose ideas, but there were some who certainly did, including those who requested that Northover Projectors and Spigot Mortars be equipped with wheels to facilitate motor transport.[87]

What was more, lack of adequate liaison between GHQ Home Forces and the Home Guard Directorate meant that when a special Home Guard instruction was issued in the summer of 1941 explaining the new policy of mobile patrols it contained none of the qualifying clauses included in the original GHQ order. As a result, official blessing appeared to have been given to a much more mobile and aggressive role than in fact the C-in-C contemplated.[88] Brooke, indeed, was worried that if units became truly mobile they would charge off on a 'wild goose chase' in search of the enemy rather than defending their locality.[89]

And while Bridgeman may have been rather more willing than Brooke to see the Home Guard become more mobile, there was little support for the idea of giving the Home Guards armoured vehicles—as Churchill discovered in October 1941 when, responding to Home Guard enthusiasm, he pressed the idea of special Home Guard 'mobile formations' on Margesson after once more brandishing the threat of invasion. 'Once the Russians have been reduced to a second-rate military power,' he rather implausibly argued in light of official studies which suggested that a successful landing was at that point in the war highly unlikely, 'the Germans could quickly mount an invasion of this country.'[90] The War Minister, however, after consulting his staff, pointed out the obvious difficulties in such a plan. The Home Guard was organized and trained only up to battalion level and could not therefore easily form brigade-strength units; it was part-time, limiting the amount of specialized training it could undertake; and above all it could not be fully equipped in an armoured role.[91]

The Prime Minister, however, was not to be put off so easily. Writing to Margesson on 23 November, he proposed a smaller-scale armoured role. Special battalions, with minimal extra training, could be formed from 'the great mass of hefty manhood now in reserved occupations' who had joined the Home Guard, and equipped with 'rifles, machine guns and bren carriers'.[92]

Margesson remained firm. Part-time service allowed the Home Guard to learn adequately the single set of skills necessary for static defence. Mechanized warfare, though, was quite another story. 'Training for a mobile role involves collective training for a variety of operations of war,' he explained in a letter dated 22 January 1942, 'any one of which a mobile unit might be required to undertake at short notice. It also requires the training of a number of specialists. Such training, I am advised, cannot be carried out on a part-time basis.' The Ministry of Labour, furthermore, would be very unhappy if men in reserved occupations lost work time due to extra Home Guard training, and valuable equipment would still have to be diverted from the regular forces.[93] It was a watertight case.

Calls for the Home Guard to become armoured and mobile were a problem. Of equal concern to the military authorities, however, was the revived interest in guerrilla warfare. As noted, the left-wing influence evident in the early days of the LDV had been effectively marginalized by the first months of 1941. But the German invasion of the Soviet Union beginning in June 1941, and the consequent eulogizing of the heroic resistance of Britain's new Russian allies, had focused attention not only on the Red Army itself but on the patriotic activities of partisans behind the lines on the Eastern Front. If ordinary people in Russia could contribute so much to defeating the enemy, then surely the ordinary British citizen should be trained and equipped to do the same in the event of an invasion? Talk arose, as in the spring of 1940, of a People in Arms—sometimes meaning just the Home Guard, at other times the entire civilian population—turning to guerrilla tactics and nimbly harassing the enemy behind the lines to the point of paralysis.[94]

Left-wing enthusiasts took new heart from events in Russia. Tom Wintringham, for instance, though he had resigned from the Home Guard school in June with a feeling of defeat, was soon renewing his calls for a people's militia. 'To put the matter in Marxist terms,' he wrote enthusiastically in *Tribune*, 'I consider that guerrilla warfare and mechanized warfare are dialectical opposites which can and will interpenetrate.'⁹⁵ Another correspondent wrote that the training given at Osterley Park, 'mainly by socialists', had been more than vindicated 'by the recent events on the Eastern Front'.⁹⁶

A book written by Hugh Slater, another former Osterley Park instructor, entitled *Home Guard for Victory!*, had gone through six printings by October. It was mostly technical in nature, but had definite political overtones. 'The reforms it suggests', Orwell had noted enthusiastically in the *New Statesman*, 'all have the implied aim of making the Home Guard more definitely into a People's Army and breaking the grip of the retired colonel with his pre-machine-gun mentality.'⁹⁷ Even Liddell Hart eventually got in on the act with a series of articles for the *Manchester Evening News* decrying attempts by the War Office to dampen the voluntary tradition—'the very essence of England'—by being rigid and not allowing the Home Guard to develop guerrilla tactics.⁹⁸

By no means all unit commanders agreed with all this talk of guerrilla warfare. 'Our intention', the historian of the Rutland Home Guard wrote, 'was to train good irregular soldiers and not dubious guerrilla bands.'⁹⁹ Others, however, were quite enthusiastic, especially those who had not liked the gradual militarization of the force. An Edinburgh company commander, for example, 'worked strenuously' in 1941 'to turn his unit into a body of first-class guerrillas or "banditti" rather than second-class regular soldiers'.¹⁰⁰ Maurice Petherick, MP, noted scathingly in a letter to the War Minister in March 1942 that in the South-Midland Area 'the H.G. had got it into their heads that, if attacked by a superior force of Germans, they should hide and perhaps indulge in a bit of genteel harassing'.¹⁰¹

It was difficult for the War Office to argue against a guerrilla role, especially as Lord Bridgeman, who became Director-General Home Guard when Eastwood moved on to become GOC Northern Command in the summer of 1941, had spoken publicly in terms which suggested he favoured the idea. In August 1941, for example, in discussing the training of the Home Guard with the press, Bridgeman made the following comments:

The Russians have laid stress on the importance of sabotage and similar activities behind the enemy lines. This is a task for which, if invasion comes, the Home Guard will be particularly suitable. They will be able to undertake all those harassing enterprises which interfere with the enemy's communications and keep him looking over his shoulder. The Russian campaign is extending our knowledge of what can be done.[102]

In a speech before senior Home Guard commanders at the Royal United Services Institution at the end of January 1942, the Director-General argued the merits of 'ungentlemanly warfare'.

Don't let us forget that this is a cad's war. There are no rules, except to kill any German who lands in this country by any available means; and the more lowbrow the battle is, the greater the likelihood of achieving the essential ingredient of victory, namely surprise, by which the Home Guard, if it uses it rightly, can discount whatever advantages of training and equipment the enemy may possess.[103]

Bridgeman, indeed, was so certain that guerrilla warfare was a practical proposition for the Home Guard that he pressed GHQ Home Forces to issue official instructions on the subject.[104]

There were, however, problems in promoting guerrilla warfare. For one thing, a clandestine guerrilla organization already existed. Created in the summer of 1940, its members dressed like Home Guards to avoid curiosity among local people when in training or preparing arms caches but were in fact totally separate from the force.[105] To allow the real Home Guard, in which just about every aspect of equipment and training tended to be discussed in public, to take on this role might easily compromise the so-called 'Auxiliary Units'.

GHQ Home Forces, responsible for both organizations, in any case saw problems with any change in role, be it towards fluid guerrilla tactics or in the direction of semi-armoured mobile thrusts. The rather orthodox and humourless Lieutenant-General Sir Bernard Paget, Chief of Staff (and the man who succeeded Brooke at the end of 1941 when the latter became CIGS), was not the sort of man to share Bridgeman's enthusiasm for promoting guerrilla warfare, and may indeed have been irritated by the fact that the Director-General Home Guard was speaking out on operational questions the responsibility for which resided in GHQ Home Forces, not his (administrative) directorate.[106]

A memorandum drawn up by Major G. E. O. Walker of the GHQ general staff listed the main practical objections to the Home Guard assuming a guerrilla function. Calling themselves guerrillas might add to their self-esteem, but the plain fact of the matter was that volunteers had not been trained for the job. Moreover, if Home Guards were left to roam about the countryside pretending they were partisans they would be 'liable to confuse our own troops'. The Home Guard were supposed to be relatively static and entirely local in their operational role, ready to fight to the death in nodal points. To allow the impression that they would turn to guerrilla fighting would negate the possibility of seriously tying down the enemy. 'Owing to the unavoidable lack of discipline and training in the Home Guard,' the memorandum concluded, 'it will be difficult enough anyway to get them to stick to their posts without giving them a loophole which satisfies their personal desires and can be made to satisfy their conscience.'[107] Paget whole-heartedly agreed.[108]

In March 1942 orders were issued that under no circumstances were the Home Guard to arm the civilian population and form partisan bands. Calls in parliament and the press to 'Arm the People' there might be, but from the military perspective sanctioning *francs-tireurs* would only lead to confusion and unnecessary civilian casualties.[109] Then in the spring of 1942 Paget issued a general instruction laying down the law concerning the role of the Home Guard.

There has been a good deal of pressure lately, encouraged by the Press, for Home Guard[s] to become guerrillas. This is unsound; they are not trained or equipped for this sort of fighting and they would be a menace to the Field Army. It must not be allowed except in sparsely populated areas where there are no Nodal Points, and the country is particularly suitable for it. Instructions issued must NOT detract from the overriding principle that there will be no withdrawal from Nodal Points while there are any men left to defend it [*sic*].[110]

Time would tell how effective or otherwise such instructions really were in dampening Home Guard enthusiasm for alternative roles.

As it happened, towards the end of 1941 a new role began to evolve for the Home Guard that had nothing to do with static or mobile defence, nodal points or guerrilla hideouts. The force was about to enter the front line of Anti-Aircraft Command.

In its increasingly avid search for men for the field forces, the War Office had in September 1941 decided that 50,000 men should be drafted from Anti-Aircraft Command now that the threat of air bombardment appeared to have diminished. Not surprisingly, the GOC AA

Command, General Sir Frederick Pile, was not anxious to see the number of manned guns and searchlights diminish. At a meeting with the Prime Minister on 7 October, he pushed Churchill to accept the idea of replacing the drafted men with women in the ATS and men of the Home Guard.[111]

The Chiefs of Staff agreed in November that with a nucleus of regular personnel to help train them, Home Guards as well as ATS could serve as effective substitutes for the gunners called away to other duties.[112] Certain units had been manning beach defences and guns for some months, and by May 1942, over 11,000 Home Guard volunteers were being trained as anti-aircraft gunners.[113]

Meanwhile, the War Office had been grappling with the implications of a proposed new National Service Bill. Designed in part to extend the age range of call-up for military service, the bill would also require anyone from age 18 to 60 to undertake some form of national service, with the government empowered to direct people into needed jobs. This would increase the size and effectiveness of the civil defence services and the ATS. What, though, of military service outside the regular armed forces? Should Home Guard attendance, as would be the case in the other part-time volunteer organizations, be made compulsory for current members? Should people in reserved occupations be directed into the Home Guard?

There were good arguments to be made for and against the idea. On the one hand, the Home Guard had always been a voluntary organization, and to conscript men into it—or even to prevent those already enrolled from resigning on two weeks' notice (the so-called Housemaid's Clause)—might substantially change the character of the Home Guard and lower morale.[114] On the other hand, attrition due to the call-up age and declining interest meant that in the last six months of 1941 the Home Guard lost a net total of 150,000 men.[115] In the East and South-East of England, indeed, units were sometimes considerably below strength and unable effectively to carry out the tasks they had been assigned in the event of invasion. Compulsory enrolment in other part-time services would in addition curtail Home Guard recruiting. There was also the public relations angle to consider. To leave the Home Guard out of the new bill when every other service was involved might create the impression that the force was regarded as less important.[116]

Opinion on the subject within the Home Guard itself was divided. In the north, where there were generally enough volunteers, there was not much liking for the idea. In the south, on the other hand, doing away with the housemaid's clause had been advocated for some time.[117]

The matter was tricky enough to be taken up in the War Cabinet on 28 November 1941. It was decided that while a scheme for compulsory enrolment in selected areas in the South-East was theoretically sound, no decision should be taken until there had been 'an opportunity to test feeling in Parliament by a debate'.[118]

On 2 December, the Prime Minister rose in the House to speak on the provisions of the new National Service Bill, taking care to emphasize the importance of keeping up the strength of the Home Guard.

It has become a most powerful, trained, uniform body, which plays a vital part in our national defence. We must make sure that this great bulwark of our safety does not deteriorate during the inevitably prolonged and indefinite waiting period through which we have to pass or may have to pass. Power must now be taken by statute to direct men into the Home Guard in areas where it is necessary and to require them to attend the drills and musters indispensable to the maintenance of efficiency.

Regulations to this effect, Churchill added, would be discussed in parliament before being implemented.[119]

Notice having been given, the War Office issued a White Paper on the future organization of the Home Guard on 17 December, and the following day Margesson explained why the decision to include the force in the National Service Bill had been taken. First of all, there was the simple fact that all other part-time services would be subject to the bill once enacted. 'It would obviously be unjust', the War Minister argued, 'to exclude one part-time service, namely, the Home Guard, from this general obligation. I am certain the Home Guard would never wish to claim such a privilege.' The force, furthermore, was as the Prime Minister had stated vital to the defence of the country, and was at present under-manned in some areas. Compulsory enrolment would only be applied in areas where units were below strength, but for the sake of fairness those already in the force would also be required to stay on after being given some time to decide whether or not to resign before the new regulations came into effect. Those who failed to attend up to a maxi-

mum of forty-eight hours training per month would be liable to prosecution in a civil court. 'I hope and believe', Margesson concluded in
reference to the proposed regulations, 'that they will commend themselves to the House, to members of the Home Guard itself, and to the
country as a whole.'[120]

The War Office, it appeared, had calculated correctly. The response
in parliament and the press to Margesson's proposals was generally
favourable, *The Times* taking the lead in suggesting that this was a sign
the government was serious about improving the standard of training
and effectiveness of the Home Guard.[121] Within the Home Guard itself
there was a certain amount of anxiety at the idea of taking on reluctant
conscripts and some nostalgia for a vanishing amateur *esprit de corps*;
but there was also a general sense that the authorities were genuinely
concerned about the prospect of invasion and really did see the force as
playing a key role in the defence of the United Kingdom.[122]

Two years after its birth, the Home Guard was better armed and
equipped than ever before. It was seen by GHQ Home Forces as an
integral part of active Home Defence in the form of the nodal point
scheme, and the decision to include the force in the National Service Bill
appeared to confirm that the utility and importance of the Home Guard
was now fully appreciated by the War Office and the government. In
Northern Ireland, meanwhile, overt criticism of the association of the
Ulster Home Guard with the RUC had significantly declined by the end
of 1941.[123] A progress report drawn up in the War Office in April 1942
was cautiously optimistic. 'If no unforeseen development, political or
operational, occurs,' the report concluded, 'it may be confidently
thought that the development period of the Home Guard is well nigh
over and that the Home Guard and its commanders can now settle
down.'[124] Whether this would in fact be the case remained to be seen.

7 Waiting for Hitler
1942–3

I do wish the average Englishman would grow up. An adult outlook on military training is so much less painful—for the instructor.

Captain S. Fine, Regular Adjutant to HG Coy, 1942[1]

Awake for Hitler in the sky at night
Has hurled his planes to fill the land with fright.
He does not know the Guard is on its toes
But England knows and knowing sleeps all right.

F.B., HG, 'After Fitzgerald'[2]

'I don't want to hear any more about your bloody women.'

P. J. Grigg to E. Summerskill, Commons Lobby, 1942[3]

As spring gave way to summer in 1942, the most central question facing those responsible for the Home Guard was its role. For despite the various orders issued by GHQ Home Forces to try and dampen enthusiasm for guerrilla warfare and mobility, the confusion over how the force was to operate in the event of an invasion increased rather than diminished.

This was not, however, simply a matter of headstrong Home Guard commanders ignoring instructions or interpreting orders to suit their personal predilections. Much of the fault lay within the Home Forces command structure itself. For what GOCs and their juniors thought appropriate for the Home Guard did not necessarily match the thoughts of the C-in-C, and they too could engage in a certain amount of creative interpretation.

In Scottish Command, for example, where General Thorne did not at all like the idea of mobile Home Guards (guerrilla or otherwise), Paget's cautious advocacy of small mobile patrols—where appropriate—was deleted from orders that Command HQ issued to lower formations. In a directive dated 7 July 1942, Thorne sought to clear up evident confusion over the mixed mobile and static role by coming down heavily on the side of village defence. 'Under no circumstances', the directive cautioned, 'must there be any withdrawal in defence without definite orders to this effect from superior Command. In default of such orders, resistance must be continued to the last man and the last round.'[4]

A similar stance was taken in Southern Command by Lieutenant-General H. C. Lloyd. 'The word "Guerrilla" will not be used in future,' Lloyd instructed in a memorandum to his corps commanders in early June 1942, 'as it is often misunderstood and if guerrilla activity is generally regarded as a possible secondary role for Home Guard there is great risk that the obligation to fight to the last in defended localities will not be met.'[5]

In other parts of the British Isles, however, the reaction to Home Forces' position was quite different. In Western Command, for example, General Sir James Marshall-Cornwall, the GOC, had taken exception to what he saw as an attempt by GHQ to tie down the Home Guard. Home Forces was sending mixed signals, some of which seemed to indicate that offensive action on the part of the Home Guard was not to be encouraged. He, on the other hand, had been working on the assumption that the Home Guard *should* adopt an offensive mentality. As Marshall-Cornwall put it in a letter to the CGS at Home Forces, Lieutenant-General J. G. Swayne:

I feel very strongly on the subject. If we are only going to allow offensive patrols 'in certain districts', and if the formation of mobile units is a matter in which authority is centralized solely in G.H.Q., and then only in special circumstances, we seem to be striking at the whole principle of local mobility, local counterattack, and tank-hunting activities which are essential if we are to defeat a ruthless and vigorous invader, and we shall be making our Home Guards pillbox-bound and impotent for war.[6]

In Eastern Command, mobility was considered sufficiently important for a special request to be made for Spigot Mortars to be fitted with wheels.[7] In South-Eastern Command, meanwhile, an even more headstrong GOC, Lieutenant-General Bernard Montgomery, was making comments which could have been tailor-made for those dreaming of mobile assault parties and guerrilla raids. Montgomery believed fervently in treating the Home Guard as front-line troops, and missed no opportunity to make this clear. 'First of all,' as Monty typically put it at one of his famous cinema lectures to both regular and Home Guard officers, 'an offensive mentality must be encouraged in every way. . . . Troops must be trained to fight and adapt themselves to any form of fighting.'[8]

Little wonder, therefore, that many Home Guard units in the summer and autumn of 1942 continued to assume that guerrilla fighting was one of their duties. An Auxiliary Unit officer noted as late as October that many Home Guard commanders, especially in the Eastern Counties, 'have laid down a policy of guerrilla warfare for their people and say quite openly that they are going to "take to the woods"!'. As someone whose job really was guerrilla warfare, this officer was not impressed. 'I cannot see that they will be of the slightest use in this role,' he argued in a letter to GHQ Home Forces, 'and [they] will *not* function at all in the face of some Boche attack pressed home. In my humble opinion they will run like stink without firing a shot.'[9]

The majority of units, however, appear to have been more confused and frustrated than anything else by the variations on the guerrilla–mobile–static theme handed down to them by everyone from the C-in-C Home Forces to the local Area Commander.[10] The sometimes rather drastic swings in official instructions on training even inspired a well-known poem, *Home Guard Training*, by J. A. A. Griffen, the officer in charge of the Home Guard in the Essex sub-district.

> The Brigadier we had last spring,
> Said 'static roles are not the thing;
> As mobile as the midnight flea
> Is what the Home Guard ought to be.'
>
> He went; another came instead
> Who deemed mobility quite dead,
> And thought the Home Guard, on the whole,
> Far safer in a static role.
>
> . . .
>
> No doubt some high strategic plan
> Beyond the ken of common man

1. LDV recruits learning rifle drill movements, Buckhurst Hill, 1 July 1940.

2. *Punch* cartoon, June 1940.

" I've laid your uniform out, my Lord."

3. *top* Anthony Eden greets Home Guard officers at a road block in Woodford, Essex, 1940.

4. *above* Winston Churchill acknowledging the salute of the 1st American Squadron Home Guard, January 1941. Clementine Churchill to his right, Brigadier Sir Basil Sergison-Brooke to his left.

5. The art of concealment. Members of the Dover Home Guard demonstrate the latest camouflage techniques.

6. Home Guards learn how to use the aircraft Lewis Gun, Wealton Training School, Western Command.

7. Home Guards learn how to use the Browning Automatic Rifle in Western Command, September 1940.

8. A member of the 1st London (Westminster) Home Guard relieves a Grenadier Guardsman, Buckingham Palace, 14 May 1941.

9. Preparing to meet the Fifth Column in Scotland. An enemy agent masquerading as an innocent nursemaid shoots a Home Guard sentry, and is himself then shot by covering marksmen of the Tain Home Guard, Ross, August 1941.

10. *top* Courage against steel. A demonstration of how Home Guards can defeat an enemy 'tank' with beer-bottle Molotov Cocktails at a road block, 1940.

11. *above* A section of the 5th Battalion (Doncaster) South Yorkshire Home Guard capture a 'Nazi' parachutist during an exercise, 1941.

" O.K., Buddies. Reach for the ceiling. This is a stick-up."

" I want you men to imagine the enemy are approaching in large numbers,
supported by tanks, flamethrowers, paratroops, etc., etc. . . ."

12. Road block and Home Guard exercise, as viewed by Giles.

13. A Northover Projector and its Cardiff Home Guard crew in firing position, watched by a group of interested schoolboys, October 1941.

14. A Blacker Bombard, later renamed Spigot Mortar, being demonstrated by members of a Home Guard Travelling Wing, Saxmundham, Suffolk, July 1941.

15. *top* Professor Lindemann, Churchill, Captain David Margesson, Sir Archibald Sinclair, and Lord Beaverbrook observe with varying degrees of enthusiasm a demonstration of the Smith Gun, June 1941.

16. *above* Liverpool Home Guards man a rocket projector of an Ack Ack 'Z' Battery, Western Command, January 1942.

17. The return of the cavalry. A mounted Home Guard patrol in Wales, August 1942.

18. The Home Guard navy. Members of the Trent River Patrol, February 1943.

19. A Home Guard sergeant inspecting the identity papers of a local bobby during an exercise in 1942. Relations between the Home Guard and police were not always so cordial in 1940–1.

20. In a 1943 exercise in which the Fifth Column figured prominently, a car is stopped for an identity check by members of the Worthing Home Guard. At night in the summer of 1940 things did not always go as smoothly.

21. A Home Guard bayonet charge.

22. Throat slitting by numbers. Commandos demonstrate on Dundee Home Guards the correct technique for overpowering sentries, July 1943.

23. *above left* Lieutenant-General Sir Henry Pownall, Inspector-General Home Guard, 1940.

24. *above right* Not fade away? General (retd.) Sir Hubert Gough, Zone Commander, London, 1941.

25. *right* His Majesty King George VI inspects men of the London Home Guard, 10 August 1940.

26. General Sir Alan
Brooke, C-in-C Home
Forces, 1940–1.

27. General Sir Bernard
Paget, C-in-C Home
Forces, 1941–4.

28. Lieutenant-General
S. R. Eastwood, Director-
General Home Guard,
1940–1.

29. Major-General Lord
Bridgeman, Director-
General Home Guard,
1941–4.

30. *top* The most popular of Home Guard activities.

31. *above* Home Guard stand-down parade, London, December 1944.

Dictates these changes in our job
From 'mob' to 'stat' and 'stat' to 'mob'.

Still it would help us all to know
More positively where to go,
In case, when Boches do appear
We cannot find a Brigadier.[11]

The existence of a few 'special case' Home Guard units which through the circumstances of their birth had come into possession of sufficient transport to allow them to be mobile beyond their locality and were being used differently by GOCs—the Cambridge University OTC, the Royal Arsenal Home Guard, and the 1st Warwickshire battalion, for instance, had each collected several dozen obsolete armoured cars and even (in Cambridge) a light tank to form mechanized squadrons—only added to the confusion over role.[12]

In response to all this, GHQ Home Forces continued to reiterate that while limited mobility was to be encouraged, it should never be at the expense of adequately defending the nodal point (or 'Keep', the term more often used in 1942–3). It was carefully explained to Marshall-Cornwall, for instance, that in fact the C-in-C was by no means against *all* mobile activity on the part of the Home Guard—Paget just wanted to make sure that fortified positions were not left undermanned and that Home Guards were not 'turning into mobile counter attack units to be used as striking forces outside their own district'.[13]

A lecture given by a General Staff officer at a Home Guard company commanders course in August 1942 highlights the role Home Forces was trying to impress upon the force. Offensive patrols were possible, but only 'provided they are not carried out at the expense of the defence of the locality' and the vital task of observation. Reconnaissance, in fact, remained the prime task of the Home Guard, even though many members wanted to be more aggressive. 'I have found in all schemes', the major admitted, 'that the normal Home Guard wants to fight and that it is very difficult to explain to him that his task is to become expert in field-craft.' Reconnaissance, however, did not mean the Home Guard were to see themselves as Partisans.

Guerrilla tactics are all right in Russia, but personally I feel that providing you carry out your role of keeping the towns and communications open then a great step will be taken in the defeat of the enemy. Guerrillas, to my mind, in this country are a waste of good man power. Also there is the temptation that Home Guard men may leave their posts to join in with any mobile parties of that nature.[14]

In November 1942 a new general instruction was issued to Commands which sought to make clear once and for all the limits on mobile and guerrilla tactics. 'It must be clearly understood by all Home Guard that their role is to fight to the last in a defended locality unless they are specifically allotted the role of fighting patrol,' the instruction read. 'The use of the term "guerrilla" will be strongly discouraged, as if guerrilla activity is generally regarded as a possible role for Home Guard there is grave risk that the obligation to fight to the last in defended localities will not be met.'[15]

By 1943 the message appears to have got through in some, but by no means all, localities.[16] As for the brief revival in the fortunes of the People's Militia lobby, the tactics used in the past were evidently enough to prevent any further developments. As early as August 1942 a Home Guard correspondent, reflecting on the attitudes of his middle-class compatriots, wistfully admitted in *Tribune* that 'I have come across no signs of dissatisfaction among these people with the social order'.[17] 'The Home Guard still exists in as great numbers as before,' a discouraged Orwell was to write in a letter to *Partisan Review* exactly twenty-four months later, 'but . . . seems now to have no political colour of one kind or another.'[18]

The primary *raison d'être* of the Home Guard, meanwhile, seemed to be passing away. The Germans were still fully engaged in the East, and as the months passed the prospects for a cross-Channel assault continued to diminish. As early as November 1941 the Joint Intelligence Committee had indicated that an invasion attempt in 1942 was unlikely, and the Chiefs of Staff thought if one was mounted at this stage it would certainly fail. By late autumn 1942 the JIC was forecasting that even if Russian resistance collapsed and the Allied invasion of French North Africa failed, German air and seaborne forces would not be adequate to mount a credible assault.[19] As the GOC 1st Corps District recalled, 'it was hard to work up much enthusiasm in the preparations to meet so unlikely an event as a German seaborne invasion'.[20]

Under these conditions, the presence of an anti-invasion force numbering 1,565,000 men in the summer of 1942 might have seemed something of an anachronism.[21] There were, however, good reasons for maintaining—indeed, even augmenting—the strength and self-regard of the Home Guard in 1942–3.

GHQ Home Forces, for one thing, was less certain than the Chiefs of Staff and others that the threat for which it had been planning and training for over two years was becoming a thing of the past. Marshall-Cornwall in Western Command found GHQ staff 'obsessed' with the need to continue to prepare against enemy attack.[22] General Paget thought that airborne or seaborne raids were still a very immediate threat and even believed that a full-scale invasion might still be mounted in the spring of 1943 as a 'desperate final gamble' if the Russians were suddenly defeated.[23] With regular troops being transferred to more active theatres, the Home Guard remained a crucial part of home defence in the minds of Home Forces planners, as well as Lord Croft (Under-Secretary of State for War).[24]

The extent to which the Home Guard had come to be seen as an integral part of, rather than supplementary to, the regular field force was most evident in South-East Command, where Montgomery was striving with typical energy and single-mindedness to train the Home Guard up to the standard of his regular units.[25] Even in Scotland, where the danger of enemy raids was slight, General Thorne found that the Home Guard was extremely useful in asserting a military presence in a Command where regular units were undermanned and (in many areas) few and far between.[26]

General Pile, at AA Command, was even more interested in maintaining the Home Guard—although with a rather different end in view. Having already been forced to dispense with 50,000 men in late 1941, Pile was informed in July of 1942 that he would lose another 16,000. Under these circumstances, the Home Guard represented a vast pool of potential gun and searchlight battery crews. Indeed, by the summer of 1942 the need was great enough for special Home Guard factory unit light AA gun batteries to be formed and for the Ministry of Labour to begin placing compulsory-enrolment Home Guards directly into Home Guard Heavy Ack Ack units.[27]

A further reason for maintaining the Home Guard was its potential usefulness in civil defence. Ever since the Blitz of 1940, Home Guards on duty had been encouraged to pitch in to help clear rubble, direct traffic, and in general make themselves useful in crisis conditions. The results had sometimes been rather mixed—liaison between the civil defence services and Home Guard unit commanders was not always good, and Home Guards could be officious—but the potential useful-ness of part-time Home Guards in freeing up civil defence workers for military service was evident.[28]

In early 1942 the C-in-C Home Forces had sent out instructions asking Home Guard units to train to assist civil defence personnel in ways which did not interfere with their military duties. By the autumn, re-emphasizing this role to home commands, GHQ was making it clear that as the likelihood of invasion decreased the use of Home Guard personnel in civil defence duties should increase. 'It is not desirable', an instruction dated 19 October indicated, 'to lay down any rigid division of time between Home Guard and Civil Defence duties.'[29]

The Home Guard, in short, was by no means an anachronism. Indeed, the potential usefulness of the force in the variety of roles outlined above led the War Office in May 1942 to extend compulsory enrolment to the whole country and in June to raise the Home Guard ceiling from 1,800,000 men to a maximum of 2,500,000.[30] At the same time, how-ever, despite the introduction of compulsory enrolment, the Home Guard continued to assert its self-made identity in parliament and the press. Maintaining the morale of the Home Guard was therefore also very much a priority. As in previous months, public praise for the force combined with the introduction of new weapons were key elements in this endeavour.

The second anniversary of the Home Guard, like the first, saw a host of measures designed to bolster the self-esteem of the force. On 10 May, the War Office announced that the following Sunday would be cel-ebrated as 'Home Guard Sunday', complete with public demonstrations of training and weapons and local church parades. On 12 May, General Paget issued a special order of the day to be distributed to the press and all Home Guard units. Paget wanted to express his 'high appreciation' of the progress made by the force, and to applaud the 'spirit of service and self-sacrifice' volunteers had shown, a spirit which was now being rewarded with a steady flow of new arms and equipment. 'Yours is a great responsibility,' the C-in-C asserted, 'having in mind the vital part you have to take in the security of the United Kingdom.'[31]

The Prime Minister, aware through debates in parliament and the press that confidence in his military leadership was slipping in the wake of disasters overseas, had his own reasons to demonstrate his commitment to the Home Guard. According to a Mass-Observation poll, while 32 per cent of the public still supported him unreservedly in the spring of 1942, a disquieting 21 per cent expressed unambiguous disapproval.[32] Churchill therefore sought indirectly to bang his own drum in a speech to the Palace of Westminster Home Guard (subsequently reported in the press) which dwelt on the importance and achievements of an organization Churchill had helped foster. 'This body,' the Prime Minister declared to the assembled MPs, 'engaged in work of national importance during all hours of the day ... is nevertheless an invaluable addition to our armed forces and an essential part of the effective defence of the island.' And while once it could be said that the Home Guard was under-equipped and insufficiently trained to meet an invader, this was certainly no longer true.

Now, whenever he comes—if ever he comes—he will find, wherever he should place his foot, that he will immediately be attacked by resolute, determined men who have a perfectly clear intention and resolve—namely, to put him to death or compel his immediate surrender.[33]

The Crown too became involved in the anniversary celebrations. Brooke had been opposed to the idea of asking the King to assume figurehead leadership of the Home Guard, but Paget was quite enthusiastic when approached by Lord Bridgeman.[34] P. J. Grigg floated the idea in a letter to the King's private secretary, and received the welcome news that George VI would be 'very pleased' to forge a closer link with the force.[35] On 13 May a special Royal Message, drafted in the War Office (though slightly modified by the King), was circulated to Home Guard units and issued to the press. 'In order to mark my appreciation of the services given by the Home Guard with such devotion and perseverance,' the King announced, 'I have to-day assumed the appointment of Colonel-in-Chief of the force, and I send my best wishes to all its members.'[36]

New weapons were also issued in the spring and summer of 1942 in an effort to keep up morale, beginning with the one piece of equipment that proved satisfactory enough to be issued to the regular forces as well. Rumours had been circulating within the Home Guard for some time that a new personal weapon was being manufactured in large quantities. When it finally appeared in the spring of 1942 this turned out to be the famous Sten gun, a replacement for the Thompson sub-machine gun. Designed at great speed, the chief characteristics of the Sten in comparison to the Thompson were its simple mechanism, lightness, and low cost (reputedly a mere thirty-five shillings a piece).[37] The all-metal Sten gun was at first treated with great suspicion, and dubbed among other things 'the Woolworth Gun' and 'Gas Lighter'; but once it had been fitted with a trigger guard it soon proved itself to be an easy and popular weapon to handle, and as well as being issued to the Home Guard at a gun-to-man ratio of one to six in July (increased in September to one to four) the Sten was soon being used by regular troops to great effect on battlefronts around the globe.[38]

Rather more problematic was the No. 68 EY rifle grenade, designed to be fired as an anti-tank projectile from a discharger cup fitted to the barrel of a rifle. Through a mixture of poor training in its use and lack of quality control, the EY rifle-grenade system was inaccurate and developed a bad reputation among some units for premature explosions.[39] And when it did not explode prematurely, it might do little damage or not explode at all. Despite official claims that the No. 68 grenade fired from an EY rifle 'will penetrate anywhere on all German tanks except the largest vital parts on the largest tanks',[40] a member of the 22nd London (Royal Arsenal) Home Guard Battalion related that when attempts were made to use an old Matilda tank as a target, the grenade 'bounced off the curves and corners of the tank without exploding with a disheartening regularity, and the few that did hit fair did little more than scorch the paint'.[41]

A rather more successful new weapon was the third and final piece of sub-artillery issued to the Home Guard: the Smith gun. Like its predecessors, this weapon was unorthodox in origin, and its appearance was very odd indeed. It consisted of a short 3″ inch smooth-bore barrel mounted on something which looked like a two-wheeled baby carriage, which to be fired had to be tipped over so that one of the wheels could serve as a baseplate. The invention of a Major (retd.) William H. Smith, the managing director of a civil engineering firm which manufactured toys, the gun had first been conceived in the crisis of 1940 as a cheap, easily produced anti-tank weapon. The Ordnance Board was dubious, but Churchill saw it demonstrated, and orders had been placed in 1941. Production teething troubles, however, delayed the appearance of the first of 4,000 Smith guns for the Home Guard until the summer of 1942.[42]

Opinion of the Smith gun was not entirely favourable. It had a very low muzzle velocity, was inaccurate, and had an effective range of only 100–300 yards. To sceptics such as Captain H. G. Smith of the 7th Essex Battalion, it was 'a brute of a weapon, very heavy and awkward to handle', and due to faulty fuses on the shells it initially developed what was described in a technical manual as 'a reputation for lack of safety':[43] to be more precise, as a Cornwall battalion commander bluntly stated, it had 'a terrifying reputation for killing its crew'.[44]

The authorities, however, while seeking to repair some of the weapon's more glaring defects, portrayed the Smith gun as a useful addition to the Home Guard armoury. In the late autumn of 1942, for example, a special instruction on the employment of the weapon was informing readers that 'the Smith Gun is a simple, powerful and accurate weapon which, if properly handled, will add greatly to the fire power of the Home Guard'.[45] As in the past, initial scepticism seems in many cases to have been replaced by a desire to make the best use of a new weapon and a growing sense of affection. When a letter appeared in *The Times* towards the end of the war which seemed to be suggesting that the Smith gun was a junk weapon, letters poured in from angry Home Guards who maintained that the weapon had been highly satisfactory, and indeed one of the best pieces of equipment ever issued to the force.[46]

By the end of 1942 a quite high percentage of the Home Guard were equipped with a wide array of weapons. By the start of 1943, 18,919 Northovers, 18,691 Spigots, and 3,049 Smith guns were in Home Guard service, in addition to almost 900,000 rifles, 30,145 shotguns, 23,630 BARs, 248,234 Sten guns, 12,895 Thompson sub-machine guns, and over 20,000 Lewis, Browning, and Vickers light and heavy machine guns (not to mention the several hundred 3″ anti-aircraft guns and

'Z' rocket batteries being manned by the new Home Guard battery crews).[47]

The operational scope of the force was also expanding. By May 1943, 111,917 volunteers and conscripts were enrolled in Home Guard AA units.[48] In addition, GHQ Home Forces had sanctioned the formation of auxiliary Home Guard bomb disposal units up to a maximum strength of 50,000 men, and special Home Guard motor transport companies to help the regular forces in the event of an emergency.[49] Within regular Home Guard units, meanwhile, specialization had reached the point where in addition to mobile and static platoons, there were often medical teams, intelligence sections, catering parties, chemical warfare subsections, signalling parties, and even pigeon handlers.[50]

The amount of training the Home Guard was receiving was also at a new peak in 1942–3, with greater co-operation from the regular forces (especially those which had been under Montgomery's control), three permanent Home Guard training schools, numerous special courses, and over two dozen mobile training 'wings' going round the country all making a contribution to a higher degree of tactical sophistication.[51]

At the same time, however, problems remained. For one thing, despite more training, the force retained a tendency to act independently, as Home Guard exercises demonstrated. War games are difficult to conduct at the best of times, and some of those involved will inevitably dispute that they have been 'killed'. Even so, the Home Guard could on occasion demonstrate an unusually blatant disregard for the rules and enthusiastically indulge in questionable improvisations and Fifth Column tactics.[52] 'The Cornish miners,' General Morgan later wrote of Home Guard exercises in South-Western Area, Western Command, 'finding the official fireworks for the simulation of shell and bomb too short of realism for their liking, were in the playful habit of tossing the odd dynamite cartridge at each other.'[53] The propensity of the Home Guard to adopt disguises and suspect everyone of being a Fifth Columnist reached such proportions that in the instructions for an exercise in the West Riding of Yorkshire in November 1941 it was laid down that 'Umpires will be assumed to be in possession of Identity Cards and necessary passwords and [will be] free to move in all circumstances'.[54] For an exercise held in July 1942 by the 19th Kent (Farningham) Battalion Home Guard it was specified in the preliminary orders that 'No fifth column activities will be employed prior to or during the exercise'. Despite this remonstrance, in a mock battle with a regular unit the following month a platoon of the Farningham Home Guard decided to forgo the normal umpiring process and make the battle more exciting by firing small green apples from their Northover Projectors—an innovation which they found 'quite effective' in driving off the enemy.[55]

The vocal questioning of authority so characteristic of the Home Guard could lead to exercises which degenerated in a manner best described by an Edinburgh company commander.

The vexed question of who shot who arises early in the proceedings; and is further complicated by the tendency of riflemen on these occasions to credit themselves with a standard of marksmanship which bears little or no relation to their performance on the range. A party of attackers will approach its objective in happy ignorance of the fact that it is being heavily enfiladed the while, and will emerge from the Valley of the Shadow with strength unimpaired to inflict death and destruction on the defenders. A goes through the motions of bayonetting B, only to be told that he has already been shot by C. To this A replies that while he was doing his bayonet exercises, C was pinned down by covering fire from D. 'But no,' says E. 'With my B.A.R. I made a corpse of D as he was crossing yon wire fence.' And so on *ad infinitum*.[56]

There was also the related question of weapons proficiency. With limited range time and (in the case of older volunteers) variable eyesight, Home Guards were often not the best of marksmen. The average range score at 200 yards under good conditions in the Painswick platoon in Gloucestershire during 1941, for instance, was just under ten out of twenty.[57] In early 1943, the performance of two companies of the 6th Derbyshire battalion at the same distance was even worse. 'The conditions for shooting were not ideal,' the adjutant wrote, 'but this should not account for one third of the shots missing the target.'[58]

What was more, due to a mixture of poor training, a desire to experiment, and defects in ammunition, there were a fair number of accidental injuries and deaths in the handling of grenades and sub-artillery.[59] By the end of 1944, eight Home Guard officers and nine other ranks were officially listed as having been killed in training, a figure which does not include the fourteen officers and sixteen other ranks listed as killed in bomb disposal and other duties and in any case does not appear to be complete. In all 1,206 Home Guards were to die on duty.[60] The average on-duty death rate for the Home Guard was about 0.7 per thousand, as against an average rate of about 0.05 per thousand among regular troops in the UK. If we bear in mind that members of the Home Guard were on duty far less frequently and for shorter lengths of time than regular troops given their civilian work commitments, the difference becomes even more striking. In very approximate terms, the chances of a Home Guard dying on duty from causes that had nothing to do with the enemy were at least four times those of a regular soldier.[61]

Of more immediate concern than efficiency, however, was how the Home Guard felt about itself. For despite the best efforts of the War Office and GHQ Home Forces, morale was begining to slip again by early 1943. First and foremost, as one Allied victory followed another from November 1942 onward, the chances of a German invasion, even raids, seemed to grow ever more slim and the Home Guard—at least in its original role—appeared increasingly redundant.[62] And though the authorities proved reluctant to prosecute in civil court Home Guards who failed to show up for the minimum monthly duty period (for fear of generating a hostile public response),[63] many conscripts were still understandably keen to see the burden of Home Guard service lifted from their shoulders. Even some of the volunteers were also feeling that the hour of need was passing. When in February 1943 the GOC London District, Lieutenant-General Sir Arthur Smith, made comments which were misconstrued to suggest that the force would continue after the war, there were sharp questions from both sides of the House of Commons on behalf of alarmed Home Guards.[64]

Morale, furthermore, appeared to be particularly low among Home Guard AA units. Volunteers disliked being forced into AA units; creature comforts on many sites were minimal and the regulars hostile. As for those directed into the Home Guard, General Pile later recorded that many of the conscripts were so lacking in motivation that they were next to useless. 'They never turned up when they were wanted,' he noted, 'and, in fact, many units learned not to expect them.'[65]

Even among general service units there were problems, not least that the introduction of new types of weapons was starting to prove counter-productive. Increasingly, there were complaints of units being over-whelmed by the task of having to train for three separate pieces of sub-artillery, a variety of machine guns, and a host of grenades and bombs.[66] There was also continuous grumbling over supposed slights such as a proposal to get Home Guards to engage in fire-watching, the lack of officer privileges for Home Guard officers in military hospitals, and, above all, Home Guard officers being forced to travel third class on trains while regular officers travelled first class. 'It can so happen,' a petition from the Suffolk TA Association ran, 'that a Battalion Commander of the Home Guard will travel 3rd Class whilst his [regular] Adjutant will travel 1st Class.'[67]

There was also the lingering issue of women in the Home Guard. Dr Summerskill had doggedly continued to press the War Office on behalf of women who wanted to join the Home Guard, forming her own lobby group—Women's Home Defence—in 1941 and constantly arguing her case with P. J. Grigg (successor to Margesson as Secretary of State for War in the cabinet shuffle of February 1942).[68] By 1942 she had gained important allies in the shape of the formidable Dame Helen Gwynne-Vaughan, former Director of the ATS, and the Inter-Parliamentary Home Guard Committee. The fact that the War Office had from 1941 encouraged the Home Guard to continue to make use of the (civilian) Women's Voluntary Service for clerical tasks, cooking, and other support work only made it more difficult to argue against some type of formal association with the force.[69]

And, as always, the Prime Minister had his own views as to the future of the Home Guard. In the course of 1942, it had become clear after the introduction of compulsory enrolment that there were not enough un-committed men to raise the strength of the Home Guard much beyond 1,750,000, let alone the 2,500,000 postulated at the start of the year.[70] Indeed, as the likelihood of invasion and raids further diminished in the course of the year, the Prime Minister became concerned that the morale of the Home Guard might be being undermined by the con-scripting of men who did not want to be in the force and were not really necessary given that, as he put it in November, future 'invasion or large-scale airborne attack are unlikely'. Why not, Churchill reasoned, trim the force by 500,000 or so by creating a Home Guard reserve? That way both those who wanted to be free of the burden of service and those who feared the Home Guard was being short-changed would be satisfied.[71]

Within the War Office, the D-GHG made it clear that both the C-in-C Home Forces and GOC AA Command were not in favour of any cuts in the size of the force. Allowing women to serve in the Home Guard, however, was a good idea. 'The subject has attracted much political attention,' Lord Bridgeman wrote, 'and its settlement would be beneficial to the public relations of the Home Guard.' A scheme was drawn up for a volunteer women's auxiliary of about 100,000, whose members would not be armed or given uniforms, but would be given an identification badge.[72]

P. J. Grigg agreed with the views of his senior advisers. As, however, the allocation of human resources had by this point in the war become one of great potential friction between competing users of man- and woman-power, especially the War Office and the Ministry of Labour, he thought it prudent to consult other interested parties before responding to Churchill's idea or making a final decision about the enrolment of women. Meetings were set up with the Minister of Labour and the Home Secretary to discuss the situation.

Ernie Bevin, the down-to-earth chief of a ministry which had assumed almost totalitarian powers as far as the allocation of human resources was concerned, was opposed to the proposal on the grounds that it did not go far enough. The Minister of Labour was 'most disappointed' that more was not being done to ease the burden on workers who already put in long hours at factories. Surely the needs of arms production ought to have priority over compulsory service in a force whose utility seemed increasingly remote?[73]

Herbert Morrison, the Home Secretary, was more disturbed by the proposal to form a special unarmed women's auxiliary for the Home Guard. This would be cheap, but would it satisfy the critics? Grigg himself had doubts, yet thought it was the only way that a substantial increase in the size of the Home Guard would be accepted by the Treasury. Morrison was also worried that allowing women into the Home Guard would mean friction with other women's voluntary organizations, above all the WVS, as well as a Ministry of Labour keen to maximize the output of women factory workers. There would, in short, be 'competition for a dwindling source of supply'.[74]

Dr Summerskill, meanwhile, was trying to force the government's hand on the issue of women in the Home Guard by learning of, and then leaking, the details of the proposed scheme to the press in December 1942 complete with her own embellishments. This infuriated Grigg, who characterized his opponent as 'Amazonian'; but Morrison pointed out that a degree of co-opting might be more effective in future dealings than outright hostility. 'Your critic', he reflected, 'wants a gun, not a dishcloth. This proposal will appeal to her only if she sees it as a stepping stone to manlier things.'[75]

In any event, Grigg, Bevin, and Morrison, with the assistance of Sir John Anderson (Lord President), were eventually able to reach a consensus on how to respond to the Prime Minister. There was general agreement that the reserve idea would not in fact free up much manpower for other tasks, as the Home Guard were already engaged in a fair amount of Civil Defence work. Moreover, having calmed his colleagues' fears about potential conflicts over human resource allocation by pointing out that as many as 50,000 women were already serving as unofficial volunteers in support of the Home Guard and promising to limit enrolment where the need for labour in factories and other services was greater, Grigg was able to obtain agreement to the women's auxiliary plan.[76]

On 23 February 1943 the War Minister summarized their conclusions in a note for the Prime Minister. The idea of a Home Guard reserve was superficially attractive, but there were drawbacks. While at present the danger of attack was minimal the tide of war could still swing against the Allies, and it was the view of the C-in-C Home Forces that if the Home Guard was seriously reduced in size or readiness it would be difficult to revive 'in time to meet a renewed threat'. There was also the increasing need to employ the Home Guard on AA duties to be considered.

In addition, to reduce the size of the Home Guard would be a public admission that it was no longer so necessary for national defence, and that, as Grigg pointedly put it in reference to one of the PM's overriding preoccupations, would lead to widespread 'loss of keenness and morale'. The other tasks for which reserve Home Guards were supposedly needed, such as fire-watching and other civil defence duties, were already being carried out by the same men while active in the force, so there would be no real savings in manpower. 'For these reasons,' Grigg concluded, 'we do not recommend that the proposal for a Reserve be proceeded with.'[77]

The idea of forming a women's auxiliary for the Home Guard, however, could be viewed in a much more positive light. It would involve only volunteers, would not exempt them from civil defence duties, and would not be a financial drain (since the women involved would not be clothed, armed, or equipped beyond an identification badge). Preference for those over 45 years of age would minimize potential conflict with factories and other services making more active use of part-time womanpower. The scheme would, in fact, simply give official acknowledgement to the tens of thousands of women who were already working as clerks, typists, cooks, and messengers.[78]

The need for manpower was too great to allow disenchantment to interfere with the direction of Home Guards into AA Command; and calls for first-class travel allowances and medical treatment, despite the TA associations being in favour and a motion passed in the House of Lords, were difficult to meet in view of Treasury parsimony. P. J. Grigg, furthermore, believed that while allowing first-class travel would please the officers of the Home Guard, it would also alienate the more numerous other ranks. He would only agree to 'give further consideration to the question'.[79] There was, however, general agreement within the War Office that the women's auxiliary idea would pass Treasury scrutiny and show that the government was responsive to public concerns.

The Prime Minister, it turned out, was not quite satisfied with the joint reply to his own proposal sent to him by Grigg. He passed it on to his long-time confidant and scientific adviser, Lord Cherwell (now serving as Paymaster-General). With typical asperity, Cherwell chose to differ. 'I do feel', he minuted to Churchill on 4 March, 'that it is rather hard to keep 1.8 million men under an obligation to do 48 hours a month drill and sentry duty lest they and the Army should think the danger of invasion had dwindled and lose keenness.' Making one of the statistical comparisons for which he was notorious, Cherwell announced that '48 hours a month for 1.8 million men is equivalent to 350,000 full-time workers'.[80]

Churchill nevertheless decided not to challenge the ministers' conclusion, perhaps because of the reference to Home Guard morale. As it was, he merely forwarded a note to Grigg, Bevin, and Anderson repeating Cherwell's points and stressing that 'Commanders should be instructed not to insist on too many exhausting exercises and to release men who have reached a reasonable degree of proficiency if they are engaged in agricultural or industrial work'.[81]

As the third anniversary of the Home Guard approached, the War Office, far from allowing the force to begin fading away, was engaged in expanding it through the introduction of a women's auxiliary. Home Forces, meanwhile, was continuing to upgrade the training of units to meet potential raids, and General Pile at AA Command was contemplating drafting in even more Home Guards.[82]

How long this sort of thing could go on, however, was unclear. With the Germans reeling from the Stalingrad débâcle and the Allies clearing the last Axis forces from North Africa in early 1943, maintaining a sense that an enemy invasion of the British Isles was still a possibility for which a force of over 1.7 million men was needed would be increasingly difficult. While in 1941–2 some Home Guards may have felt a trifle redundant, with the enemy threat receding ever further in 1943–4 the potential existed for many members of the Home Guard—especially the directed men—to become more and more hostile towards the official policy of maintaining the force at full capacity. As always, both the nature and effectiveness of official policy towards the Home Guard would depend on the mood of the men themselves.

8 An Uncertain Future
1943–5

The Home Guard has built up a tradition of service and devotion to duty. I am confident that the coming year will add to that tradition and to the debt that my people owe to you.

Message of HM George VI to the HG, 14 May 1943[1]

The Home Guard is the unpaid, part-time, part-worn, couponless, sockless and breathless Army. . . . They are supposed to know the weight, killing power, mechanism and working parts of the rifle, several machine-guns, countless grenades, and a number of strange artillery weapons, to say nothing of truncheons, toggle-ropes, shot-guns and pikes . . . know all about extermination, decontamination, detonation, consolidation, to say nothing of salvation . . . recognise and describe aeroplanes and tanks of all nations at sight, and know how to deal with them . . . support the regulars. . . . Incidentally they are supposed to earn their own living if time permits.

Marquis of Donegall, A Tribute to the HG, 1943[2]

I regard it as the height of folly at a period when the country is virtually free from bombing . . . that millions of workers are called out night after night . . .

Walter Citrine, TUC General Secretary, Nov. 1943[3]

As in the past, though now to an even greater degree, a principal concern of the authorities in the lead-up to the third anniversary of the Home Guard was morale. Allied successes in the field, paradoxically, could increase the number of volunteers and conscripts who felt that their services were no longer necessary.

At the very end of 1942, as the extent of Allied successes was starting to become clear, General Paget had felt it necessary to issue a memorandum to senior Home Guard commanders assuring them that the force was still needed. The military situation was improving overseas, the C-in-C admitted, but war 'is a chancy business' and at some point in the future the threat might reappear. 'In fact,' he concluded, 'until the war is won, the security of the United Kingdom must be constantly assured; and we must allow none of our essential defence measures to deteriorate through a false and self-satisfying sense of safety.'[4]

A desire to banish thoughts of redundancy was expressed by other figures in this period. The GOC London District, for example, Lieutenant-General Sir Arthur Smith, sounded a similar note in a speech he made in February. 'It would be foolish', he claimed, 'to think that all risk of invasion is over, and even more foolish to suppose that Hitler will not attempt maybe a raid on this country and probably on London.'[5] During the Army estimates debate in March, P. J. Grigg himself took care to state that 'the effective protection of the home base is an integral part of the plans for offensive action elsewhere, and the Home Guard can well be proud of the contribution it is making.'[6]

The Prime Minister, though the decline in his personal popularity evident in 1942 had been halted and partially reversed by the summer of 1943,[7] was also becoming anxious about the morale of the Home Guard in light of the receding threat of enemy action. He had grown increasingly worried about a new commercial film, *The Life and Death of Colonel Blimp*, which—among other things—portrayed the Home Guard as a haven for redundant Old Buffer types. This was not the kind of image calculated to boost Home Guard morale, and Churchill was personally offended by the way in which cavalrymen of his own generation were treated in the film. He tried and failed to have *The Life and Death of Colonel Blimp* suppressed.[8] On a more constructive note he urged the War Office to play up the image of the Home Guard.

'Are we making enough of them?' the PM wrote to P. J. Grigg on 4 April 1943. 'Ought there not to be a Home Guard Week or a Home Guard Day? Ought they not to receive public recognition in some way or other, and to be made to feel that the nation realizes all it owes to these devoted men, who are our standby against seaborne invasion and descents from the air by paratroops?' In Churchill's view something would have to be done. 'They require,' he concluded, 'to be nursed and encouraged at this stage in their life.'[9]

The anniversary of the formation of the Home Guard had, as we have seen, been the occasion for much orchestrated praise in previous years; but the third anniversary celebrations would be bigger than ever. Evidently suspecting that not enough was being done by way of preparation, the Prime Minister raised the matter in a War Cabinet meeting on 12 April. There should be ceremonial parades throughout the country, and as much publicity as possible should be arranged. Everything should be on a grand scale.[10]

P. J. Grigg was not entirely happy with such exhortations as—in response to Churchill's earlier desire to cut down on unnecessary training—the C-in-C Home Forces had already issued orders that Home Guard commanders should dispense with all but the most necessary parade-ground drill.[11] It might look rather odd if the Home Guard was suddenly called upon to prepare for, and participate in, high-profile ceremonial parades. On the other hand the precedent of marking the anniversary had been set, and doing without some form of public recognition would be even more damaging than doing too much. 'This is one of the rare occasions', an instruction from GHQ Home Forces announced, 'which justifies time taken from the normal battle training of the Home Guard.'[12]

The Prime Minister, meanwhile, had been thinking of ways to make the most of the occasion. Why not, in addition to the King's message, have the Home Guard mount guard again at Buckingham Palace? And why should not he as Prime Minister make a personal contribution by making a radio speech on the evening of 14 May? As he would be in the United States by this date a live BBC broadcast would be more difficult to arrange; but the important thing was to make sure that the Home Guard knew that they were still wanted and needed.[13]

Planning for a massed parade in London illustrates the manner in which everything connected with the anniversary was geared, as Grigg wrote, to help 'stimulate the morale of the Home Guard'.[14] The idea of holding the main events in Wembley Stadium was rejected by the public relations directorate on the grounds that 'the public would be unlikely to turn up in large numbers', and that without admiring background crowds and weapons displays the press photographs would be insufficiently flattering. A ceremonial parade would be 'very dull', and the press 'would much prefer to have pictures of battle training display'.[15] Instead, there would a march of 5,000 Home Guards through central London, beginning in Hyde Park, passing through Stanhope Gate, past Hyde Park Corner, down to Piccadilly Circus, along Shaftesbury Avenue to Cambridge Circus, and from there down Charing Cross Road and Oxford Street to Marble Arch. The presence of the King, who had offered to take the salute, would be kept secret as a surprise.[16]

By the third week in April the preparations were complete. The King, as well as reviewing the London parade, would issue a special message (once again drawn up in draft form by the War Office for final modification by the monarch himself) and the Home Guard would mount guard at Buckingham Palace on 14 May. The Prime Minister would the same evening make a special radio broadcast from Washington, where he would be attending Anglo-American staff talks on future war strategy. The main activities, however, would have to wait until the weekend, when the public would be free to participate and observe. Sunday, 16 May, would be regarded as 'Home Guard Sunday', with parades organized for the afternoon not just in London but throughout the country to be followed by weapon and field-craft demonstrations. Props, such as bands and tanks, would be provided by the regular army. In addition, as P. J. Grigg noted in a Cabinet paper outlining the plans, 'the Minister of Information is arranging in conjunction with me for the fullest publicity to be given all activities in connection with the celebrations'.[17]

The King's message, as one might expect, concentrated on how important the Home Guard still was and the admiration in which it was held. 'On this, the third anniversary of the formation of the Home Guard,' the message began, 'I, as your Colonel-in-Chief, would like you to know how greatly I appreciate the regularity with which, in spite of many difficulties, you keep up your attendance at parades, and how gratified I am by the high standard of proficiency to which you have attained.' The force had done much in the way of valuable training of those young men subsequently called up into the regular forces, and was serving admirably 'side by side' with the Army in defence of the country. Moreover, as the Army moved overseas, so the Home Guard would be called upon to take over more tasks. 'The importance of your role', the message went on, 'will therefore inevitably continue to increase.'[18]

The Prime Minister, despite the fact that he and the Chiefs of Staff were overseas, had taken the time to produce quite a lengthy speech for the Home Guard, designed to restore a sense of pride and self-importance within the force. 'I have felt for some time', he began, 'a great desire that a tribute should be paid throughout Great Britain and in Ulster to the faithful, unwavering, and absolutely indispensable work done by the Home Guard month after month, and year after year.' After running through a swift but uplifting history of the force, Churchill got down to business. 'People who note and mark our growing mastery of the air, not only over our islands but penetrating into ever-widening zones on the Continent, ask whether the danger of invasion has not passed away,' he related. 'Let me assure you of this: That until Hitler and Hitlerism are beaten into unconditional surrender the danger of invasion will never pass away.' The likelihood of invasion also depended on the strength of the forces deployed to meet it, and of these the Home Guard was a vital component. Harkening back to the rhetoric of 1940, Churchill expressed his faith in the force.

And if the Nazi villains drop down upon us from the skies, any night . . . you will make it clear to them that they have not alighted in the poultry run, or in the rabbit-farm, or even in the sheep-fold, but that they have come down in the lion's den at the Zoo! Here is the reality of your work; here is that sense of imminent emergency which cheers and inspires the long routine of drills and musters after the hard day's work is done.

What was more, soon the Allies would be crossing the Channel, leaving the Home Guard with an even greater responsibility for the defence of the homeland. 'It is this reason which, above all others,' Churchill concluded, 'prompted me to make you and all Britain realize afresh . . . the magnitude and lively importance of your duties and of the part you have to play in the supreme cause now gathering momentum as it rolls forward to its goal.'[19]

In the short term the speeches and celebrations honouring the third anniversary of the Home Guard appear to have been more or less successful in convincing the public that the Home Guard was still very much a going concern. The government was demonstrating, as an editorial in *The Times* concluded at the time, that the Home Guard was still 'a most important piece on the national military chessboard'.[20] An anniversary, however, could only be celebrated once a year, and in the months after May 1943 concern over Home Guard morale continued to manifest itself in official circles.

More weapons and training were seen as a partial answer to the problem of flagging interest. Periodically egged on by the Prime Minister, the War Office sought to increase the supply of practice ammunition and personal weapons to the general service battalions, and by August 1943 only 150,000 men remained without rifles (and would shortly be issued Sten guns instead—in all 40 per cent of the Home Guard got Stens instead of rifles).[21]

By this point there were no more sub-artillery curiosities dating from 1940 to draw upon, but it remained War Office policy to keep introducing 'new' weapons to the Home Guard (while keeping as much existing equipment in service as long as possible) for the sake of appearances.[22] Hence the allocation of 100,000 obsolete Boys anti-tank rifles in July 1943, and then a relatively small number of 'special' Home Guard 75 mm anti-tank guns. The 75 mm gun was a hybrid, consisting of the shortened barrel of the now-obsolete 3" anti-aircraft gun mounted on the modified carriage of a First-World-War-vintage 4.5" Howitzer. It had a maximum range of 10,450 yards, a muzzle velocity of 2,500 ft/sec., and was mostly used for coastal defence.[23] Only when very obsolete weapons (such as the Northover Projector and the dreaded pikes) could be replaced at once with marginally less ineffective cast-offs from the Army (such as the 18-pounder field gun or 2-pounder anti-tank gun) was anything taken out of service.[24]

The attitude of the Home Guard, however, was not the only consideration in this policy of continual support. Churchill, who chided the Chiefs of Staff for seeming to rule out the possibility of enemy raids, believed that the anniversary celebrations would also give the enemy pause. 'I am anxious', he noted in a minute to the War Office on 11 April, 'that the enemy should have a vivid impression of the strength of our Home Guard. This will no doubt be conveyed to him by photographs of reviews, and will act as a deterrent on paratroop descents or oversea raids.'[25]

Those responsible for strategic deception were also keen to see the Home Guard built up publicly. To deceive the Germans into thinking that a cross-Channel invasion was scheduled for 1943, the strength of forces in the United Kingdom was deliberately overstated. Hints of an expeditionary force of three armies were put about, its fictional size in part a result of the supposed strength and battle-worthiness of the Home Guard in home defence. It was, in short, to the strategic advantage of the Allied war effort for the Home Guard to be portrayed as a keen and well-equipped fighting force.[26]

For all these reasons it was considered important to cultivate the aggressiveness of the Home Guard. At a meeting between Lord Bridgeman and Major-General J. A. Sinclair (MGGS Home Forces) in August, it was agreed that all those concerned should do everything possible in the way of 'maintaining Home Guard morale and not letting them gain the impression that their operational role is not taken seriously'.[27]

In practical terms this meant allowing for more aggressive mobility than had been considered safe in the past. In a memorandum issued to commands in late August 1943, GHQ Home Forces let it be known that 'where their state of equipment and training make it practicable', Home Guards were to be allowed to launch counter-attacks in the event of enemy raids.[28] 'The extension of their present role to include limited counter attack', a senior staff officer in Southern Command calculated, 'will undoubtedly be welcomed by H. G. Bns and provide a valuable tonic to enthusiasm.'[29] In addition, training was being upgraded to include the new battle-drill techniques being introduced into the Army, thus further emphasizing the degree to which the Home Guard was positively equated with the regular forces.[30]

Unfortunately all the efforts were not entirely successful. For one thing, despite the best will in the world, the War Office could not always produce weapons, and above all ammunition, on a scale the Home Guard thought its due. There were problems in getting production facilities for items no longer used by the Army, and, as always, the needs of the regular forces came first. A proposal to equip the Home Guard with the PIAT anti-tank weapon, for example, had to be abandoned due to the needs of the Army, while production delays in anti-tank ammunition for Smith guns meant that there were only about six or seven rounds per weapon in service. And, as always, there were those who remained dissatisfied with what was being issued. Despite the fact that the 2-pounder anti-tank gun had been requested repeatedly by Home

Guard units, when it was finally introduced in late 1943 there were complaints that, as the Home Guard commander of the Hampshire sub-district put it, it was 'not an anti-personnel weapon'.[31]

The emphasis on more aggressive training also caused some difficulties. The more enthusiastic units were, as in the past, going beyond what was considered realistic, demanding more transport, and roaming up to thirty miles afield in search of the enemy. There were complaints about the lack of mobility of the Northover Projector and Spigot Mortar, and orders had to be issued to stop the Home Guard towing the Smith gun behind cars, its unsprung wheels never having been designed for more than local manhandling.[32] Sir Smedley Crooke (Conservative MP for Birmingham Deritend and a leading member of the Home Guard lobby) in January 1944 even proposed in parliament that there were many Home Guards who were 'anxious to serve on the Continent in the forthcoming assault and who feel that as they are now so well trained and prepared they should be given the opportunity'.[33]

At the same time, however, there were those who thought the Home Guard was being overloaded. With the younger volunteers being continuously called up into the regular forces, the Home Guard was tending to become more middle-aged. The average age may have been statistically as low as 30, but with more conscripts and the effects of age the number of enthusiastic veterans had declined (possibly to as low as 7 per cent) and many Home Guards were finding it tough going.[34] Battle drill had been designed for fit men in their late teens or early twenties, and given all the duties the Home Guard was now expected to perform there was a feeling that the pace was now too much. Polls indicated that Home Guard duty was increasingly becoming an inconvenience, and the Ministry of Labour, as well as the Trades Union Congress, affiliated trade unions (such as the NUR), and certain MPs, all suspected that too much time was being put into Home Guard training that could have been used for more important work or needed rest. 'The tendency to keep on keeping with the same old thing over and over again', an internal TUC memorandum argued, 'is certainly not conducive to maximum energy for production purposes.'[35]

Friction was also growing over cases where the Home Guard was allegedly interfering in civil trades disputes. Jock Haston, a member of the Workers' International League, had alleged as early as April 1941 that during a strike in Scotland 'the Home Guard was used in a number of factories to intimidate the striking apprentices', and argued that the intervention of works Home Guards to prevent two sacked shop stewards getting back into a factory in Middlesex was clear evidence that the force was being used as a coercive arm of the bosses.[36] Complaints emanating from a Trotskyist splinter group could be ignored, and in most cases labour as well as management bore a share of the blame for such incidents; but by 1943–4 the situation was such that the Communist Party (which had pursued a much more conciliatory line towards the Home Guard since the German invasion of Russia) and even the TUC itself were expressing alarm at the zealousness of some Home Guard commanders in, for example, interfering with applications for service exemptions by union members and officials. 'Instances where employers have not hesitated to use the Home Guard against organized trade unionists and shop stewards have occurred,' the *Daily Worker* darkly warned.[37]

The War Office, meanwhile, while trying to placate organized labour, was having to contend with actions of other government departments which would have an impact on the outlook of the Home Guard. The first clash had come just prior to the third anniversary, when the Home Office had pressed for the visitors ban in coastal areas to be lifted now that the chances of invasion were so remote. The War Office had opposed the idea, largely on the grounds that 'the suspension of the restrictions would convey the impression that there was no longer any risk of invasion, and this might have a serious effect, not only on public morale, but on the morale of the Home Guard'.[38] The Home Office thought this a fairly lame excuse, and when the matter was referred to the Lord President's Committee in April a continuation of the blanket ban was not supported.[39]

A more serious threat emerged from the Lord President's Committee itself in the summer. Like everything else, material and labour for the manufacture of clothing was by the summer of 1943 growing scarcer, and the Lord President's Committee (the central directing body for production and supply matters) was considering ways in which the civilian clothing ration could be further cut. As the civil defence services and the Home Guard received uniforms free of charge and wore them while on duty, it was thought that perhaps their normal clothing ration could be pared down, thus generating savings.

Word of the proposed cut set off alarm bells in the War Office, and a memorandum arguing against the move was prepared for discussion at a meeting of the Lord President's Committee on 19 July which Lord Croft (Under-Secretary of State for War) would attend. The general thrust of the memorandum was that 'to deprive the Home Guard of a percentage of their clothing coupons would be a grave injustice and there would be serious repercussions in many directions'. Morale would slump, and with fewer clothing coupons men would tend to wear their uniforms more than at present—which would mean the War Office would end up paying for the savings made on the coupons. The Home Guard, 'a uniformed force which may be needed for operational duty at any moment and in parts of the country [AA Command] is now carrying out normal operational duty', *had* to be properly clothed and shod.[40]

The Committee, and in particular Sir John Anderson, the Lord President, was not impressed by Croft's enthusiastic but perhaps overly emotional exposition of the War Office case. Possessed of little romantic imagination but considerable reasoning ability and administrative talent, Anderson could not see why the Home Guard should get special treatment. The Home Secretary was allowing the clothing ration of civil defence personnel to be cut, so why should not all volunteer forces be required to give up coupons? The plain fact of the matter was that shortages had reached crisis proportions, and if something was not done in the near future the whole rationing system would break down. To his mind, the arguments put forward by Lord Croft 'entirely failed to carry conviction'.[41]

P. J. Grigg, however, was not about to concede defeat when he learned what had happened at the meeting. What needed to be done now was to take the case to higher authority, which in this case could only mean the War Cabinet and the Prime Minister. Writing to Churchill on 21 July, the War Minister made plain his opinion of the decision to cut the Home Guard clothing ration. 'I can imagine few things', he argued, 'which will do more to make the Home Guard feel that we set little store by their services and that they are ceasing to play an important role in our general defence arrangements.' And that, to judge by past experience, would generate 'the very strongest political objections in the House and in the country'.[42]

Churchill proved receptive to such arguments. He had recently received a letter of complaint from Lieutenant-Colonel Geoffrey Crump, commander of the Petersfield Home Guard, complaining of the way in which the civil defence services were apparently being given priority over the Home Guard.[43] The Prime Minister was therefore already primed to reject anything which might give cause for further offence. Instead of letting the matter be resolved in Cabinet, he decided to intervene personally. In a letter to Anderson dated 23 July, Churchill made clear his view that 'it would be most harmful to the Home Guard if they were subjected to the measures proposed'. Indeed, he took them as a personal affront. 'I do not see what is the use of my trying to work up the Home Guard,' the Prime Minister angrily dictated, 'if they are going to be slapped down like this.' The matter, Churchill concluded, should be reconsidered.[44]

Anderson, however, was not one to be bullied. In a lengthy reply some days later, he laid out in detail his reasons for not making an exception and suggested that in any case the War Office was exaggerating the potential reaction of the Home Guard. 'I should be reluctant to assume without argument', the Lord President wrote in classic civil-service style, 'that, if the matter were presented to them properly by their own Chiefs in a co-operative and not resisting spirit, their loyalty would not be equal to the strain of surrendering four coupons.'[45]

Irritated by the tone of Anderson's letter and believing his own reputation as a supporter of the Home Guard—reaffirmed on the third anniversary—might be damaged, the Prime Minister refused to accept that there was nothing more to say. He wanted the Lord President's Committee to re-examine the question, bearing in mind that 'I have stressed the great importance of the part they play'. Churchill clearly thought that too much was being made of the need to cut four coupons. 'Mere tightening of the screw for its own sake,' he wrote back to Anderson on 1 August, 'though very agreeable to some minds, will not necessarily increase the optimum war effort.'[46]

The Prime Minister also asked P. J. Grigg if he would be willing to present the War Office case again before the Lord President's Committee, but the War Minister proved reluctant. A former civil service mandarin himself, Grigg knew he could make a better case than had Croft (not the most subtle of advocates), but that logic was still on the side of the cost-cutters and that in that particular forum logic would prevail. A mixture of 'politics and psychology' demanded that the proposal be resisted, and the War Cabinet would tend to be more receptive to such considerations.

The Home Guard [Grigg wrote in reply to the Prime Minister] is going through a very difficult phase. It isn't easy to keep a Home Defence organization keen and prepared. It would be disastrous to the contentedness of the Force, and indeed the country as a whole, to allow it to be thought for one moment that we no longer have much use for the Home Guard. You know, and I think members of the War Cabinet know too, how loosely knit this force is in essentials, how readily its spirit might evaporate under discouragement and what seeds of trouble might be planted for future harvest. It is my earnest belief that a principle of this kind is dangerous and ought not to be risked.[47]

The Prime Minister was quite willing to go along with this, but the War Cabinet, meeting on 2 August, merely came to the conclusion that the matter should be referred back to the Lord President's Committee.[48]

News of the affair, meanwhile, had leaked out to the public—possibly from a source within the War Office. The reaction within the Home Guard was hostile in the extreme. Letters of protest were sent to MPs, and the *Sunday Express* ran a sympathetic story in its 1 August edition. It was Anderson who had done most to promote the idea of the Home Guard giving up coupons, but for unknown reasons (and much to his dismay) it was another member of the committee, Hugh Dalton (President of the Board of Trade), who was made out to be the villain in the press and became the hapless recipient of a barrage of angry notes from the Prime Minister. Best known in the public mind as the man who had tried to introduce a highly unpopular fuel rationing plan in 1942, Dalton probably seemed the obvious candidate as author of such a niggardly scheme.

Unwilling to serve as a public scapegoat, Dalton began writing to the Prime Minister protesting his innocence, and by 3 August was making it clear that he no longer supported the idea—'I quite appreciate the War Office objections.'[49] When Sir Thomas Moore (another leading member of the Home Guard lobby) asked in the House why the Board of Trade had decided to deduct the four coupons, the Parliamentary Under-Secretary, Captain Charles Waterhouse, stressed on 5 August that no final decision had been taken.[50] Thus when the question of cutting down on clothing coupons was discussed again by the Lord President's Committee on 17 August, the War Office representative was not alone in calling for the plan to be scrapped.

The Secretary of State for War, who this time was there in person to defend the interests of the Home Guard, noted that the circumstances of the force differed markedly from those of the other part-time services. But his real argument, he explained, was the effect the proposal to cut the clothing ration would have on Home Guard morale. It was difficult enough already to preserve a sense of keenness and efficiency; to go ahead with the proposed plan would be 'certain to produce widespread dissatisfaction'. The potential damage to the morale of the Home Guard outweighed whatever minor advantage there might be in cloth savings.

Dalton spoke next, pointing out that while the plan had merit, he could not but be 'impressed by the criticisms evoked'. Indeed, the reaction had been so negative that if the plan went ahead the credibility of the government in terms of fair administration might be seriously undermined. On balance, he favoured dropping the plan entirely.

Most other members of the committee now agreed that it would be 'inexpedient' to go ahead. The Lord President, rather annoyed, could only accept the majority decision while arguing that no further uniforms should be provided for any future part-time civilian services.[51]

A potential crisis in Home Guard morale over the question of clothing coupons was therefore avoided, and the Home Guard lobby happily concluded that raising a stink could still force the government's hand.[52] But in the following months it became apparent that in spite of measures taken to keep up the enthusiasm of the force, the realities of the strategic situation were by the autumn of 1943 beginning to seriously erode morale. It had still been possible in early 1943 to envision some sudden reversal in Allied fortunes: victory instead of defeat was still a rather novel phenomenon. But by the closing months of the year it was clear to all but the most optimistic volunteers that the Germans, now minus their Axis partner Italy, were well on the road to defeat. It was the Allies, after all, who were now launching oversea invasions. This in turn meant that there was less of a sense of purpose within the Home Guard, and—especially among the conscripts—a feeling that the amount of time they were being asked to devote to drills and musters was too great.

As early as July 1943 the home intelligence division of the Ministry of Information had been reporting evidence of increasing resentment at compulsory Home Guard service, and there were soon to be questions in parliament from left-wing MPs concerning the fairness of asking men who spent long hours working to take on additional duties of questionable value.[53] Caught between the need to prevent loss of confidence among committed volunteers by prosecuting absentee directed men in the civil courts and a desire not to appear too heavy-handed in public, the War Office introduced measures to enforce attendance at Home Guard drills which only managed to alienate all concerned by prosecuting nobody in 1942 and over 238 absentees the following year. There was frustration in some AA units (where absenteeism was greatest) over the inability to get solid convictions *pour encourager les autres*, while the Home Office, responsible for the civil prosecutions and therefore liable to be the partial focus of any public outcry, complained that the military authorities were being overzealous in bringing cases to the courts.[54] By October 1943, Lord Bridgeman had become alarmed enough to get the matter of Home Guard morale taken up by the Army Council.[55]

When the Army Council met to discuss the question of Home Guard morale on 30 October, they had before them a paper drawn up by the Director-General Home Guard outlining the perceived problems and what steps might be taken to alleviate them. The C-in-C Home Forces, whom Bridgeman had consulted and who had in turn consulted his army commanders, recommended that an important first step would be for the War Minister, or possibly the Prime Minister himself, to issue some authoritative pronouncement on the continuing importance of the Home Guard. In addition other confidence-building measures could be taken, including the reimposition of an invasion warning scheme involving the ringing of church bells. The decision taken in the spring of 1943 to scrap the ringing of bells as a warning signal along with the relaxation of the visitors ban in coastal areas had tended to suggest to the public that there simply was no possibility of future invasion or raids. To bring back the old scheme would have the reverse effect and boost the *esprit de corps* of the Home Guard. It was also recommended that those Home

Guards who had reached a certain level of proficiency should be given leave to attend fewer training periods and that greater efforts should be made to punish those who were failing to turn up (and thereby lowering the morale of the force as a whole).[56]

The Army Council, and in particular the Secretary of State for War, were not entirely convinced that the situation was as serious as Bridgeman made out, or that the measures proposed in his paper were necessarily practicable. The plain fact of the matter was that it was now virtually impossible to convince anyone that there was a possibility of enemy invasion, and any official attempt to do so would only make matters worse. On the other hand, as Grigg noted after having talked the matter over with Churchill, the Prime Minister 'was anxious that nothing should be said or done to lead the Home Guard to think that their operational role was any less important today than it has always been'. It might therefore be best simply to stress—without any great speech from the PM—that the role of the Home Guard lay in preparing to take over the defence of the country when the cross-Channel invasion of Europe began. As for the business of Home Guards being asked to do too much, it was Grigg's view that the best thing would simply be to make sure Home Guard commanders acted in a responsible and sympathetic manner towards those working long hours in factories or on farms. The only one of Bridgeman's proposals that was fully accepted was the need to stiffen penalties for those who were shirking their duties.[57]

In the meantime, problems continued to manifest themselves as the conscripts grew more restive. 'They judged their military duties by civilian standards based on their experience in civil employment,' Major-General L. A. Hawes noted, 'that is to say by factory regulations, trade unions, home life, daily civil contacts, and by the knowledge that they were unpaid and their punishments were limited.'[58] There was indeed a trade union mentality among many Home Guards, and it was probably inevitable that the TUC—despite the efforts of Lord Bridgeman to maintain a private consensus with senior officials[59]—would eventually make public their concerns over unnecessary service.

On 6 November 1943, Sir Walter Citrine, the General Secretary of the TUC, made a highly critical speech on the Home Guard in Manchester, subsequently reported by the BBC and in detail in the papers. In Citrine's opinion, the Home Guard had been formed to meet an imminent threat back in 1940; but 'now no amount of publicity or scaremongering can convince the average British worker at this stage of the war that invasion is a practicability'. Time spent on 'useless drills' would be better used in relaxation; and workers should not be subject to 'savage penalties' simply because they did not always turn up for parade.[60]

The more patriotic Home Guard commanders were outraged by this speech and similar grumblings in the press. As the minutes of a conference between the GOC Southern Command and senior Home Guard commanders held at this time record, 'vigorous protests' were voiced concerning the 'ill-informed, mischief-making articles' appearing in the press and sometimes even relayed over the wireless. Such articles, the commanders complained, 'have a subversive effect and are extremely discouraging to those who have the interests of the H.G. at heart'.[61] The Prime Minister too, reading of Citrine's speech in the *Sunday Express*, was worried that the morale problem would only be aggravated. 'Surely the speech of Sir Walter Citrine reported in today's papers', he anxiously minuted to Grigg on 7 November, 'will do a great deal of harm?'[62]

He himself certainly thought so, and took steps to try and undo Citrine's work. Churchill had at first been slightly reluctant to associate himself directly with what was, at best, a view shared by only part of the public, but by the second week in November had decided—much as Bridgeman had wanted—that he would have to make a speech defending the need to keep up the Home Guard. To have remained silent would have been to renege on the commitment he had made personally to oversee the fortunes of the force back in 1940. What was more, Churchill believed that the Home Guard still had a vital role to play as a garrison force when regular troops crossed the Channel the following spring. There was also the matter of Hitler's promised 'revenge' weapons to consider. On 8 November, the day after the press reported Citrine's remarks, the Prime Minister referred to the Home Guard in a speech at Mansion House. It was true, Churchill conceded, that the war was running in favour of the Allies:

We cannot, however, exclude the possibility of new forms of attack upon this island. We have been vigilantly watching for many months past every sign of preparation for such attacks. Whatever happens they will not be of a nature to affect the final outcome of the war. But, should they come, they will certainly call for the utmost efficiency and devotion in our fire watchers and Home Guard, and also for a further display of firmness and fortitude for which the British nation has won renown. This is no time to relax our precautions or discourage our splendid auxiliary services.[63]

Three days later in the House of Commons, in response to a question from Sir Ian Orr-Ewing (Conservative MP for Weston-Super-Mare) concerning the contents of Citrine's speech, Churchill again affirmed the need for preparedness. 'His Majesty's Government', he stated, 'attach the highest importance to the work of the Home Guard . . . who have played and continue to play so important a part in our home defence.'[64]

Having decided in light of Citrine's speech that counter-measures were after all necessary, Grigg got the Army Council to agree to have portions of the Prime Minister's Mansion House address and his comments in the House of Commons circulated to Home Guard units.[65] Senior Home Forces commanders also did what they could, Lieutenant-General H. C. Lloyd (GOC Southern Command), for example, sending a special message to Home Guard battalion commanders on 13 November assuring them that 'I regard the Home Guard as being every bit as important to the defence of this country today as it has been in the past' and that 'there is no telling what the Germans may do in the future, particularly when they become desperate'.[66]

On the other hand the question of overly long hours raised by Citrine could not be entirely brushed aside. Lord Cherwell, never really reconciled to the need to balance political expediency against production needs, warned the Prime Minister at the end of 1943 that if something were not done to cut down duties for the Home Guard there would be labour problems. Citrine's speech as TUC chairman, and the general sympathy shown for those charged with non-attendance at parades, were straws in the wind, and Cherwell urged Churchill to do something before more trouble ensued. Churchill was sufficiently concerned at what Cherwell predicted about the future to ask him to draw up a memorandum on possible changes, a document which he then passed on to the War Office with his signature. 'Home Guard duty', the memorandum stated, 'should be officially reduced and not left to the discretion of the Unit Commander.'[67]

P. J. Grigg, however, believed that existing efforts to keep the time spent on Home Guard duties within reasonable bounds were adequate. As he pointed out in a reply to the Prime Minister dated 20 January 1944, the C-in-C Home Forces had at the end of 1943 advised Home Guard commanders that every effort should be made to cut down on training for those in key industries and agriculture, and that subsequent training instructions had reinforced this message. Forty-eight hours training per month, the War Minister added, had always been the maximum permissible, and the average amount of time spent on Home Guard duties was now down to somewhere between twelve and sixteen hours per month. Churchill asked Cherwell if the matter ought to be pursued further. Either having lost interest or feeling satisfied with the figures Grigg had presented, the Paymaster-General responded in the negative and no more was said.[68]

Home Guard morale, unfortunately, did not significantly improve in the first months of 1944. The Ministry of Information was receiving new reports of public dissatisfaction with compulsory service, and among the general service Home Guard units there was the problem of good men being siphoned off by the Ack Ack units. 'The consequence', as Sir Ralph Glyn put it in canine terms in a letter of complaint to Lord Bridgeman dated 3 March, 'is that General Service Battalions are becoming considerably depleted and feel lost and sad just at a time when it is important that they should have their tails well up.'[69] Recruiting for the women's auxiliary, meanwhile, was yielding results far below expectations. The ceiling had been set at 80,000, but by March 1944 only 28,000 women—most of whom had already been working unofficially with the Home Guard—were enrolled.[70] Especially within the Ack Ack units, moreover, low morale and absenteeism remained a major problem: in one Glasgow rocket battery the average rate of absenteeism was 20 per cent.[71] Efforts to shame conscripts into turning up more often through a poster campaign showing Hitler congratulating a shirker as 'Mein Pal' only caused public annoyance.[72]

It was under these conditions that the question of the fourth anniversary was first discussed by the Army Council executive committee on 19

February. Ceremonial parades on the scale of previous years would, it was admitted, involve potential strain on transport facilities and might require additional hours of drilling in preparation. But it was also clear that 'the absence of any recognition of the Home Guard might have an adverse effect upon their morale'. The executive committee there-fore concluded that planning for another series of anniversary cel-ebrations should go ahead, to be held around 14 May at the discretion of GOCs.[73]

The Secretary of State for War, however, now had doubts. In his view the question of taking up transport space at a time when everything was being used in the build-up to D-Day ought not to be underrated, nor should the reaction of Home Guards to spending extra time practising the parade drill. It would certainly be in order to give the force a pat on the back, but why not later in the year?

The executive committee, however, was not certain that this was such a good idea, as was made evident at a meeting on 26 February. Given how much had been made of the 1943 anniversary, to pass over the fourth anniversary might 'give rise to some feeling that the military authorities did not appreciate the Home Guard at its proper value'. The Home Guard might be a little disgruntled over the amount of time spent on training and other duties, but this was at least in part simply a consequence of uncertainty over whether or not they had a continuing military role of importance. To fail to observe the fourth anniversary in some significant way would simply confirm these suspicions and produce low morale and a rise in dissatisfaction.[74]

Grigg remained unconvinced, and the executive committee decided to consult the Home Command GOCs on the matter. The majority of generals, it turned out, were in favour of celebrating the anniversary. Lieutenant-General H. A. Schrieber (GOC Western Command) even suggested a long-service medal be issued. 'Human nature being what it is,' Schrieber had written, 'there is no doubt that the presentation of something like a medal gives enormous satisfaction, and it is a cheap and most efficacious method of keeping up morale.'[75] The medal idea came to nothing, but at a meeting of the full Army Council on 4 March the Secretary of State for War reluctantly agreed to let parades and weapons demonstrations be held as long as men working long hours were not involved and no strain was put on the transport network.[76]

The array of events organized for the 1943 anniversary was more or less repeated in May 1944. A special guard was mounted at Buckingham Palace; a march-past was held in Hyde Park; there were parades and mock battle displays all over the country; and, as always, there were special messages of appreciation from the King and other luminaries.[77]

As in previous years, the King's message, drafted in the War Office, was carefully tailored to address current difficulties. After stressing that 'the duties assigned to you have a very special importance', and that the Home Guard would make a 'full contribution' to the upcoming cross-Channel invasion, the message focused on those who might think that too much was being asked of hard-working men. 'The burden of training and duty, dependent as it is on the needs of war, cannot fail to fall more heavily on some than on others,' the message read. 'To that great number of you who combine proficiency and enthusiasm in Home Guard work with responsible work of national importance in civil life, I would send a special message of thanks and encouragement.'[78]

Other messages also touched on the theme of how important the Home Guard still was. 'Never before', General Lloyd (now GOC London) announced forcefully in a special Order of the Day, 'has the Home Guard been so necessary to the safety of the nation.' Everyone had a duty to put his shoulder to the wheel. 'The great mass of the Home Guard are showing a spirit of keenness which is inspiring,' he continued. 'A few and only a few are not supporting their comrades: let them brace themselves before it is too late, and before men and women can say that they did not do their duty.'[79] Generals Schrieber (now GOC South-Eastern Command) and Franklyn (GOC Southern Command) spoke in a similar vein on the growing need for the Home Guard. As Schrieber put it:

We shall shortly be starting a great offensive campaign which we hope will bring final victory over the Germans. The Home Guard will then have placed upon it a greater responsibility than ever before, as the defence of Britain will rest almost entirely on its shoulders. Our Armies overseas will be depending on the Home Guard for the safety of their main base and I know they will not be let down.[80]

All this talk of increasing responsibilities was by no means mere propaganda. The number of men from the Home Guard taking the place of regular troops was continuing to increase. By late summer 141,676 Home Guards were on anti-aircraft sites, 7,000 were manning coastal batteries, and another 7,000 were engaged in bomb disposal work, not to speak of the tens of thousands engaged in more mundane garrison duties and civil defence work.[81] During the Buzz Bomb attacks on London, indeed, local general service Home Guard units (prodded by Home Forces) helped a good deal in clearing rubble, traffic control, and other tasks. And while general service units were (curiously) ordered not to fire at Buzz Bombs, Home Guard heavy and light Ack Ack batteries (the latter manned by factory units) played a part in combating the menace.[82]

On the other hand the talk of a role for the Home Guard in defending Britain against enemy air- or sea-borne counter-attacks was for public relations purposes only. The chances of enemy parachute raids designed to disrupt Operation Overlord, the Allied cross-Channel operation, were in reality non-existent. The Allies had near-total command of the air, and what remained of the German parachute corps after the battle for Crete was fully committed to ground operations in Italy and elsewhere.[83] But in the public mind there really did seem to be a danger of spoiling raids. 'It is plausible to lots of English people', Mollie Panter-Downes reported for the *New Yorker* on 21 May, 'that the Germans may stage a token invasion or series of parachute raids.'[84]

The authorities certainly seemed to be preparing the Home Guard for such a contingency. Thanks in part to pressure from Churchill, ammunition supplied to the force was greatly increased, and units were allowed to participate in 'battle inoculation' exercises involving the copious use of explosives and live ammunition. The Home Guard seemed to be being prepared for 'the real thing', and on D-Day and the following nights units of the force in southern regions were put on full alert complete with night patrols and security-checks.[85]

In some units, at least, all this gave rise to a renewed sense of excitement and enthusiasm. Predictably, however, morale quickly declined once it became clear the enemy was not going to respond. There was an almost palpable sense of disappointment among the more dedicated members of the Home Guard, and a general renewal of complaints about being forced to dedicate long hours to a pointless cause. 'Hitler can't possibly invade us now, even if he wanted,' one disgruntled member was overheard complaining, 'so why should we be forced to play soldiers?'[86]

With the Allied invasion of France going well and Buzz Bomb launch sites being overrun, the War Office began to contemplate shutting down the Home Guard. A preliminary plan had in fact been drawn up toward the end of 1943. The general idea was for an order to be issued at the appropriate time that would bring to an end compulsory enrolment and drills. The formal dissolution of the force, however, was left unresolved. When the Army Council executive committee discussed the plan on 23 November, they generally agreed with the proposed action but, very conscious of the potential damage to Home Guard morale, directed that all discussion of the final demise of the force be kept strictly confidential.[87]

Unfortunately, keeping the matter confidential meant not informing GHQ Home Forces, which had its own ideas about the future of the Home Guard. General Sir Harold Franklyn (who had succeeded Paget as C-in-C Home Forces) made it plain that he thought the force would continue in being until Germany had surrendered. 'The risk [of enemy attack] is now very small indeed,' he admitted in an address to the 10th (Essex) Battalion Home Guard in August 1944, 'but why should we run any risk at all?'

I am responsible for the defence of this country, and I am not going to run any risk. Continuing the Home Guard is nothing more than continuing to pay the premium on an insurance policy. Everyone will agree that this is worth doing. People will say that there are plenty of Regular soldiers about, but there are not. I can tell you that they are all on the other side of the Channel. It is unlikely that the Home Guard will be stood down until the war with Germany ends, which may or may not be many months.[88]

Similar sentiments were expressed by other senior Home Forces commanders such as Lieutenant-General Kenneth Anderson (GOC Eastern Command). Franklyn himself thought that the Home Guard ought to continue even after the war in Europe had ended, and was not reluctant to say so. 'The C-in-C is convinced that the HG will be continued after the war in some form or other,' a member of his staff wrote. 'It may not be called the HG and it may not be in the present shape, but he is certain that a citizen force will be part of our defence requirements.'[89]

In the War Office, meanwhile, planning was proceeding on the basis of other assumptions. P. J. Grigg was against continuation of the Home Guard in any form as a military force, and as early as 17 June was arguing the need to relax Home Guard duties. A campaign by the *Daily Mail* in August in favour of such a course of action, in which it was suggested that 90 per cent of the Home Guard wanted an end to the present level of duties, confirmed to Grigg that something would have to be done.[90] The Home Guard directorate agreed, and suggested a two-stage stand down involving the end of compulsory service and the suspension of many duties at least a month prior to a formal stand-down announcement. This would effectively bring the force to an end, but no actual disbandment order would be given, 'thus avoiding political discussions on the ultimate fate of the Home Guard'.[91] By this point even Churchill had no objection, minuting on Grigg's proposed relaxation order, 'It seems sensible.'[92] Again, however, nothing was said to anyone outside the corridors of Whitehall. 'These were clearly not subjects suitable for formal announcement,' the Army Council agreed.[93]

It therefore came as something of a shock to some when Grigg suddenly announced over the radio on 6 September that Home Guard operational duties were being suspended and that all parades would from now on be voluntary. Most members of the Home Guard, particularly the directed men, were heartily relieved.[94] The more keen volunteers, however, were rather upset by the suddenness of it all. 'Naturally the Home Guard had been hurriedly called into being,' the chronicler of the 4th Buckinghamshire Battalion noted bitterly, 'but no one felt the need to dismiss it so hurriedly by broadcast.'[95] It was the same in other units where Franklyn's views had been made known. 'The general feeling in the Battalion', a CO wrote, 'was one of surprise that any alteration could have been thought of before the war was over.'[96]

All in all it suggested that the days of the Home Guard were numbered, that the future 'held promise of an ignominious fade away', despite the fact that a *News of the World* poll released in January 1944 had shown that 55 per cent of the Home Guard were in favour of continuation after the war.[97] To some it seemed to make a mockery of the talk about how the Home Guard had brought people of diverse backgrounds together and forged a functional comradeship of enduring proportions ('an extraordinary getting together of all classes,' as General

Eastwood, then DGHG, had put it in 1941, 'creating a sympathetic understanding of how the other fellow lives and the realization of the good there is in each other regardless of class');[98] talk which had led many to assume that the Home Guard would have a future after the war.

Sir Ralph Glyn, for example, had submitted a plan to the Ministry of Information in July 1944 in which the Home Guard administrative structure could be used to ease the transition to civilian working life for those soon to be demobilized from the forces, and it was not only the C-in-C who assumed that somehow or other the force would continue after hostilities had ceased. 'We have in the Home Guard a disciplined body composed of the finest elements in this country drawn from every walk of life and distributed throughout the entire countryside down to the remotest village,' the GOC South-Midland District enthusiastically wrote in a letter to Southern Command on 17 July. 'These character-istics, which were the natural consequence of the war time role of the Home Guard, can, if suitably applied, be of great value during the period of re-settlement and re-construction.'[99]

To people who shared such views, the follow-up announcement in late October that the Home Guard would stand down in early November was confirmation of the worst.[100] 'We learned that, like the grin on Alice's Cheshire Cat,' one volunteer bitterly wrote in a letter to *The Times*, 'we were to fade out, leaving no trace of our existence.'[101]

A particular source of annoyance was the announcement that Home Guard uniforms were to be returned for reissue to the Army. This, as Churchill recognized, could be—and was—interpreted as a mean-spirited act toward volunteers who had served their country faithfully for years. On 19 September the Prime Minister, although then in the United States heavily occupied with talks on future strategy, took time out to send a cable to Grigg making clear that he thought the decision ought to be reversed: 'there can be no question of the Home Guard returning their boots or uniform.'[102] The matter was then discussed in various committees and finally brought before the War Cabinet at the end of September. The evidence of a clothing shortage was undeniable, but the general feeling was that the Home Guard should be allowed to retain their uniforms and even, if possible, their greatcoats.[103] News of the proposed withdrawal of uniforms had meanwhile leaked out to the public, and along with letters of protest the Secretary of State for War had to face a barrage of questions on the matter in parliament. It was therefore with some relief that on 10 October, Grigg was able to announce that the Home Guard would be able to retain all of its issue clothing.[104]

Planning for the stand-down, meanwhile, continued, the War Office trying to make the occasion more palatable by organizing various events for 3 December along the lines of previous anniversaries. The central event would be a march of over 7,000 Home Guards, drawn from units all over Britain, through the West End of London, culminating in a parade in Hyde Park to be reviewed by the Colonel-in-Chief and a host of other military and civil dignitaries and a banquet given by the Lord Mayor. There were special orders of the day emphasizing the important role the Home Guard had played. General Franklyn, for example, wrote that the force 'for over four years has stood prepared to repel any invader of our shores' and that 'the reliance that has been placed on you during these years has been abundantly justified' insofar as the Home Guard had freed enough regular troops to make victory on the Continent possible.[105]

And, as always, there was to be a message of thanks from the King. In fact, there were two: a special written message issued on 14 November, and a radio broadcast on the evening of 3 December. The written message, however, a draft of which Grigg had submitted to 10 Downing Street for comments in October and which had been extensively revised by a distinctive hand before it was passed on to the Palace, was in all but name Churchill's final homage to the Home Guard.

For more than four years [the message began] you have borne a heavy burden. Most of you have been engaged for long hours in work necessary to the prosecution of the war or to maintaining the healthful life of the nation; and you have given a great portion of the time which should have been your own to learning the skills of the soldier. By this patient, ungrudging effort you have built and maintained a force able to play an essential part in the defence of our threatened soil and liberty. I have long wished to see you relieved of this burden, but it would have been a betrayal of all we owe to our fathers and our sons if any step had been taken which might have imperilled our Country's safety. Till very recently, a slackening of our defences might have encouraged the enemy to launch a desperate blow which could grievously have damaged us and weakened the power of our own assault. Now, at last, the splendid resolution and endurance of the Allied Armies have thrust back that danger from our coasts. At last I can say that you have fulfilled your charge.

The Home Guard has reached the end of its long tour of duty under arms. But I know that your devotion to our land, your comradeship, your power to work your hardest at the end of the longest day, will discover new outlets of patriotic service in time of peace.

History will say that your share in the greatest of all our struggles for freedom was a vitally important one. You have given your service without thought of reward. You have earned in full measure your country's gratitude.[106]

The King's broadcast was rather less grandiloquent, but nevertheless struck a chord. 'You have gained something for yourselves,' His Majesty asserted. 'You have discovered in yourselves new capabilities. You have found how men from all kinds of homes and many different occupations can work together in a great cause, and how happy they can be with each other. That is a memory and a knowledge which may help us all in the many peacetime problems that we shall have to tackle before long.'[107] Many listeners considered these words the best the King had ever delivered over the radio.[108]

Reaction among the Home Guard to the various messages of thanks and farewell reviews was, as the home intelligence division of the Ministry of Information found, generally positive. The weather was poor, but the public turned out in large numbers to cheer on the London marchers. 'H.M. the King's broadcast and the final parades', a report for the second week in December noted, 'have done a great deal to get rid of the previous ill-feeling about the stand-down, though familiar comment about this is still heard, as well as regrets at disbanding.' On the whole, therefore, this final effort to shape the opinion of the Home Guard and thereby avoid embarrassment had succeeded—so much so, indeed, that members of the civil defence services began to complain that proportionately too much praise was being heaped on the force.[109]

It only remained, therefore, to disband the force officially. Yet even at this stage there were worries about how the announcement would be received. The DCIGS, Lieutenant-General Sir Ronald Weeks, at a meeting of the Army Council executive committee on 30 December 1944, expressed concern that if War Office plans were leaked they might 'provide material for those ill-disposed to the Government and the War Office to make mischief'. Other members of the committee, however, believed that the 'political implications' of disbandment were less serious than the DCIGS feared. The stand-down order, after all, had been a clear indication that the Home Guard was no longer needed, and at this stage in the war a disbandment order would simply be regarded as the logical final step.[110]

Still, there were those who believed that the stand-down order had not been an irrevocable sign. 'I should like to emphasize', Brigadier G. W. Sutton had proclaimed to the 26th Sussex Battalion at its stand-down parade, 'that this does not mean that the HG is to disappear or that the HG is discharged or demobilized or disbanded or dismissed.'[111]

Either because of residual fears that a disbandment would be greeted negatively by the die-hards, or more likely because it was not seen as a particularly important step in the wake of the stand-down, victory in Europe and then against Japan passed without any formal announcement of the passing of the Home Guard. This silence proved to be a mistake.

On 3 September 1945, Citrine wrote to the new Secretary of State for War, John Lawson, stating that 'the delay in disbandment is giving rise to some suspicions that it is proposed to use [the Home Guard] in the event of industrial unrest'.[112] Lawson assured the General Secretary in writing some days later that 'there is no intention whatsoever to use the Home Guard in the event of industrial unrest'; adding on the subject of disbandment that 'as soon as it is possible an announcement will be made'. Citrine, however, with the support of the TUC Finance and General Purposes Committee, continued to press the War Office, writing to the Prime Minister directly on the matter on 26 November.[113] This seemed to do the trick. On 12 December it was officially announced that as of 31 December 1945 the Home Guard would cease to exist even as an inactive reserve.[114]

The Home Guard, then, like the old soldiers many of them were, had faded away after September 1944. And for the majority of the public who recognize the name, either from personal experience or, more often these days, the immensely popular *Dad's Army*, the Home Guard was born, lived, and died in the Second World War. The disbandment in 1945, however, was not in fact quite the end of the story.

9 Epilogue: Red Scare
1948–57

We are a most extraordinary people. If anybody said, 'Don't let us have special constables' there would be an outcry. And after all the Home Guard are super-special constables and the 'criminals' they may have to meet far worse than special constables have to meet. If only people realised that we would be more successful.

Maj.-Gen. Sir Guy de Courcy Grover, CO Plymouth & South Devon HG Sector, 1954[1]

In the immediate aftermath of the Second World War, the chances of another major armed conflict in the foreseeable future must have seemed to most people in Britain remote in the extreme. Yet within a matter of forty-eight months, deteriorating relations between the Western Allies and the Soviet Union had raised once more the spectre of war in Europe—and with it interest in a volunteer home defence force.

As the government's attitude toward the Soviet Union had hardened, so too had that of most MPs and those they represented.[2] There remained, however, the alarming spectre of growing Communist influence in the trade unions, and thus the possibility of communist agents fomenting strikes and sabotaging industrial activities in order to disrupt a future war effort.[3]

It was in this context, in March 1948, that Lieutenant-General Sir Gerald Templer, Vice-Chief of the Imperial General Staff, put forward the idea of resurrecting the Home Guard. Templer argued that the regular forces and Territorial Army would have their hands full coping with the initial Soviet thrusts in the event of war. Ordinarily the police were responsible for maintaining law and order, but they were unarmed and might easily be unable to maintain control. Civil administration and government might easily break down under the pressure of massive

Soviet air attacks, and Communist-led rioters might try to fill the power vacuum. 'This latter threat', the VCIGS argued, 'must be countered from the very outset of the war.' A new Home Guard would provide the military stiffening necessary to help the civil authorities cope with any attempts at subversion that might occur.

Templer's argument struck a chord among generals and ministers increasingly worried about the threat from within, and in June 1949 a working party of representatives from the service ministries and the Home Office was set up to study the Home Guard option in detail.[4] By the summer of 1950 a draft plan had been formulated.

In the event of war a volunteer force of 1,730,000 men for both internal security and anti-invasion defence purposes would be needed. But financial and other constraints made it prudent for only the 200,000 or so men who could be immediately issued with arms and equipment to be called out at the start of any future war. (The remainder of the Home Guard would take over six months of wartime production to equip properly.) The plan was endorsed by the appropriate service committees, and in the second week of November 1950 the Minister of Defence, Emanuel Shinwell, briefly announced the government's intention to lay the foundations for the raising of a new Home Guard in time of war.[5]

The government's step-by-step strategy, however, appeared unacceptably lackadaisical to the more militarily inclined Tory backbenchers, who saw the Korean War as clear proof of the expansionist tendencies of world Communism and a warning that Western Europe could become the next battleground. Tories such as Brigadier Sir Ralph Rayner (MP for Totnes), Sir Ian Fraser (MP for Lonsdale), and Brigadier Sir Frank Medlicott (National Liberal MP for Norfolk East) had been pushing for the resurrection of the Home Guard for many months, and Shinwell's announcement did little to appease them. In their view the Home Guard was needed at once, while there was still time to make it an effective force in being, ready to meet the Communist onslaught.[6]

The Labour government, therefore, came under pressure to raise a new Home Guard at once—pressure that could not easily be ignored in view of the fact that in the general election of February 1950 the Conservatives had made substantial gains while Labour's majority had shrunk to six seats.

Shinwell, echoing the initially defiant mood of his colleagues, at first dismissed the Home Guard Now lobby. But when, over the winter of 1950–1, a general war seemed to loom closer as Chinese forces inter-vened in Korea to devastating effect, the Minister of Defence began to waver. Might there not, after all, be some merit in preparing a Home Guard? 'If war were to break out this year or next,' he suggested to his Defence Committee colleagues, 'we must assume that the Russians would over-run Western Europe in a matter of weeks.' Soviet forces would therefore acquire very quickly the forward bases from which to launch airborne and seaborne attacks on the United Kingdom. A Home Guard raised when war broke out, Shinwell worried, would not have sufficient time to train and equip itself before the emergencies the force was designed to face were upon it.[7]

The Chiefs of Staff as a whole remained convinced that the original plan was sound. 'Although it would be highly desirable to build up the Home Guard now so that it will be ready for its main tasks immediately in an emergency,' they responded in a report to the Minister of Defence, 'it would be impracticable to do so at present except at the expense of the preparations for war of the Regular and Reserve Armies.'[8]

Yet growing concern over the Fifth Column threat—no doubt fuelled by the unmasking of Soviet spies Burgess and Maclean[9]—had by the summer of 1951 led to a reassessment of the situation within UK Land Forces and sections of the War Office. Lieutenant-General Sir John Whiteley, the DCIGS, reporting to the Army Council in July and speak-ing on behalf of home commanders, argued that the next war would begin with heavy Soviet air attacks, supported by airborne landings and Fifth Column activities designed to interfere with the operation of British air defences. If the Home Guard was to cope with these threats and maintain order, then at least 200,000 men would have to be armed and ready to act at once rather than weeks after hostilities had begun. 'Strategic considerations', Whiteley concluded, 'suggest that the Home Guard should be enrolled, armed and trained before the autumn of 1952.'[10]

However, even as military opinion—though not that of the Chiefs of Staff as a whole—was swinging in favour of a peacetime Home Guard, the Minister of Defence was once more turning against the idea. Shinwell by July 1951 had been convinced by his service minister colleagues that the political risks of this course of action in fact outweighed any marginal gains in national security.

A peacetime Home Guard would please opposition critics but would in turn alienate left-wing backbenchers and precipitate calls by a new Home Guard lobby in parliament and the press for more weapons and equipment than were currently available—with calamitous consequences for the morale of the force and possibly causing the diversion of resources needed more urgently by the regular and reserve forces. With a wafer-thin majority in the Commons and a Chancellor of the Exchequer insisting on a stringently limited military budget, embodying the Home Guard in peacetime seemed an act of political folly. A force which continued to exist and evolve only in War Office memoranda would, in contrast, be figuratively—if not literally—a paper tiger.[11]

The new Home Guard, therefore, continued into the autumn of 1951 to be merely a subject for endless inter-departmental discussion and argument. War plans were drawn up, and staff officers appointed to Commands; but wrangling continued to delay completion of the administrative infrastructure.

There was, for example, great difficulty in settling on how to prevent undesirables from volunteering and getting hold of weapons. The War Office, as we have seen, had become greatly concerned over the 'threat from within'. If the Home Guard was to be effective in countering Fifth Column activities, it would itself have to be free from Communist influence. And that meant each volunteer would have to undergo a security vetting. Who, though, would carry out such a task? The security service seemed an obvious candidate, but MI5 recoiled at the prospect of having to examine the personal history of hundreds of thousands of men—a task far beyond its manpower capabilities. MI5 claimed that as the Home Guard would not have access to secret material the volunteers would fall outside their jurisdiction: the matter was one for the Home Office and police to handle.

The War Office therefore approached the Home Office in September 1951 with a request that regional police forces should on the basis of criminal records vet potential Home Guards. The Home Office proved no more eager than MI5 to take up the job. 'It is quite clear', one senior official minuted on 18 September, 'that this proposal cannot be accepted.' MI5 was responsible for security in the armed forces, and the

Home Guard would form part of these forces. Thus, logically, 'it is the Security Service who must take the responsibility'.[12]

Real progress was difficult to achieve, a state of affairs which proved beneficial to a government too enmeshed in the financial crisis to favour anything but the status quo in defence matters. But in the wake of Labour's defeat in the general election of October 1951 and the return to power of Winston Churchill, the formation of the Home Guard suddenly gained a new urgency.

Possibly influenced by the recent writings of Liddell Hart, who theorized that the Soviet Union was quietly preparing for airborne operations against Britain, Churchill had come by the end of the 1940s to fear that the country was in serious danger of being taken by surprise through airborne assaults on key installations.[13] On 5 March 1951 he wrote to Lord Trenchard of his fears concerning the consequences of 'large-scale paratroop raids—twenty thousand or so—in our present defenceless condition, where our troops are out of the country, or to be sent away, and we have no Home Guard'.[14] The seriousness with which Churchill viewed the situation became public knowledge when a speech delivered to men of an RAF auxiliary squadron he had been invited to inspect and address in June 1951 was reported in the national press.

The dangers which will confront us should another war come—and we all earnestly hope it may be averted—would not only be those of bombing raids but also, I think very probably, of air descents—of landings by paratroop pilots [*sic*] and personnel on a larger scale than anything that has yet been conceived. In these circumstances we should need all our strength in the air, far more than we have at present. Also I trust that our Home Guard will be called into being so that some effective means of defending ourselves may no longer be denied us.[15]

At the start of 1951 the Home Guard played no part in Conservative campaign strategy. But by the time the second general election took place it had come to feature in the parliamentary questions of the party's high-profile heir apparent, Anthony Eden, and in the campaign guide-lines issued by Central Office to local party associations. 'Conservatives', candidates were urged to stress in speeches and debates on defence, 'recognise the important role the Home Guard must be ready to fill immediately hostilities break out.' Efforts had been made to get the Labour government to adopt a peacetime force, but—with their typical failure to properly understand national security needs—this sound advice had been rejected.[16] A peacetime Home Guard was thus very much on the Conservative defence policy agenda when the party came to power in October 1951.

The Speech from the Throne on 6 November made it clear to all that the new government intended to form a peacetime Home Guard. Within a week a new outline plan had been drawn up within the War Office based on the premiss that Soviet airborne forces—estimated some years later to number in the region of 70,000 men[17]—posed an immediate threat to the security of United Kingdom air bases, and that the best way to meet this threat would be to place the Home Guard in a state of greater readiness by forming a peacetime cadre force around 600,000 men strong (60 per cent of the proposed total wartime strength).[18]

The Chiefs of Staff, however, and in particular Marshal of the RAF Sir John Slessor, made it clear to the new War Minister, Anthony Head (MP for Carshalton), that they still did not think a large peacetime Home Guard was necessary. Granted, it might be useful to have some men at the ready, but once specific vulnerable points and key mobilization posts were identified and accounted for, only about 50,000 Home Guards would be required in peacetime. In any event they wanted time to discuss the matter further.

But time was something Head did not possess—a Home Guard bill having been scheduled for second reading in the Commons on 22 November 1951. Chairing the Army Council shortly after his meeting with the Chiefs of Staff, Head stated emphatically that it was 'essential that all decisions still outstanding [concerning a new Home Guard] should be taken in time for [me] to prepare for the debate'.[19] In effect this meant that the War Office would have to prepare a brief without benefit of any further advice.

As 22 November approached, difficulties began to multiply. Even when the peacetime strength was pared down to 125,000 men, the cost was still estimated to run in the region of £2,500,000 per year—a mere drop in the bucket in one sense, but potentially embarrassing for a government which had claimed in its election manifesto a uniquely Tory ability to get more defence value for the pound than Labour had managed. Rifles or Sten guns could be provided for the 125,000 Home Guards, but, it transpired, not any uniforms. An arm-band and old-pattern helmet would have to do for the time being. By 22 November, indeed, the Secretary of State for War was sufficiently worried to make a last-minute plea to Cabinet for extra funds to provide a Home Guard clothing allowance. A grant of £12. 12 *s*. per man was agreed to a matter of hours before Head was due to speak.[20]

Perhaps sensing that the government might be accused of going too far, the Secretary of State for War, in introducing the Home Guard bill in the House of Commons that afternoon, began by stressing that the new force would not be subject to military law, the only rules being that volunteers (between the ages of 18 and 65) would have to undergo fifteen hours of training four times a year and sign on for two years with the option of resigning on one month's written notice. Only in the more vulnerable eastern half of the country would full-strength units be formed to guard key installations and aerodromes and, in the event of air attack, help the Civil Defence services.

The response in the House to this statement was cautious, and far from unanimously favourable. True, old Home Guard commanders such as Sir Thomas Moore and other Tories were generally supportive in their comments, and Shinwell himself, the former Labour War Minister, stated that he would not vote against the bill. But the majority of speakers from both parties, and especially those on the Labour benches, had reservations. F. H. Hayman (Labour MP for Falmouth and Cranborne) argued that the Fifth Column threat the new force was supposed to combat was as illusory in 1951 as it had been in 1940; Wilfred Fienburgh (Labour MP for Islington North) adding that in any case foiling sabotage was a job for specialists and could not be carried out by simply placing Home Guards at factory gates. Lieutenant-Colonel J. B. White (Conservative MP for Canterbury), while asserting that there was indeed a danger of a Communist Fifth Column, added to the opposition case by arguing that anti-sabotage work was really the business of the police. Both Woodrow Wyatt (Labour MP for Aston) and—rather surprisingly in view of his earlier lobbying efforts—Ralph Rayner (Conservative MP for Totnes) prophetically suggested that without any immediately discernible danger of invasion it would be difficult to attract recruits.

Opposition backbenchers were also concerned at the social and political implications of a force designed to combat internal as well as external threats. The enthusiastic manner in which Anthony Head himself, as a member of the RIIA group studying the Soviet threat to Western Europe the previous year, had argued in favour of increased security measures designed to root out Fifth Column activities, did little to inspire confidence in the government's intentions. If the Home Guard became—as Fienburgh, James Simmons (Labour MP for Brierley Hill), and other Labourites feared it might—'a Praetorian Guard of elderly Tory buffers', then it could develop anti-democratic, anti-working-class attitudes in pursuit of sabotage prevention. Even Shinwell, in refusing to vote against the bill, stated that at the committee stage he would be introducing amendments 'to ensure that nothing is done by this Tory Government to increase militaristic fervour'.[21]

The press seemed equally divided over the need for a Home Guard in peacetime. The *Glasgow Herald* approved, but—no doubt to the government's consternation—*The Times* on 22 November devoted a leading article to demolishing the whole idea. That there would be a need for a Home Guard in the event of war was beyond dispute; 'but to restart it now on any large scale would clearly be an error in view of the strain represented by the rearmament of the first line'.[22]

Instead of being a shining example of the government's commitment to a strong national defence, the Home Guard bill—debate over which dragged on over nineteen hours amid fraying tempers at the committee stage[23]—had generated a sense that the Conservatives had rushed into a major reform without taking time to think through its implications and drawbacks. The omens thus far were not good. But, now that a commitment had been made, the War Office set about trying to repair the damage.

A special Home Guard co-ordinating conference, with representatives from various War Office departments present, was called on 13 December by Major-General E. O. Herbert, Director of the Territorial Army and, perforce, the man responsible for organizing and administering the new Home Guard. Herbert reminded his colleagues that the resurrection of the force had generated a good deal of public notice, and although there were more important projects, 'there was none which if not satisfactorily carried out would be likely to produce more hostile criticism'.[24]

At first the subsequently organized public relations campaign appeared to be going smoothly. The news in January 1952 that His Majesty the King had once more decided to assume the title of Colonel-in-Chief to the Home Guard was widely publicized, and media-consciousness was also present in the decision to reach the widest possible audience by having the War Minister explain the need for a new Home Guard and call for volunteers over the radio rather than just issuing a communiqué.[25] But it was not long before problems and criticism began to recur.

At the co-ordinating meeting on 13 December 1951, it had been agreed that the Home Office, despite its earlier lack of enthusiasm, should be approached again with a view to having the police vet potential recruits. To emphasize the importance attached to the request, Anthony Head was prevailed upon to write directly to Sir David Maxwell Fyfe, the Home Secretary, on 21 December. But the senior Home Office officials to whom Fyfe passed on the letter for comment were, if anything, even more adamant than before that the police should not become involved. Vetting would take up a lot of valuable police time, and if word that a volunteer of left-wing sympathies had been rejected on security grounds leaked out then public confidence in the police could be seriously eroded. The whole idea that it was necessary to screen the Home Guard was in any case ludicrous. Their work would not be sufficiently sensitive, and any attempt at sabotage by an individual would quickly be dealt with by other Home Guards. To make sure that police opinion matched that of the Home Office, a meeting of chief constables was called for 17 January. The chief constables, it transpired, thoroughly disliked the War Office proposal.[26]

The Home Secretary's response to the War Office request was therefore negative, pointing out that: (*a*) it was 'fundamental that the police do not "screen" people for security for any purpose'; (*b*) attempts during the last war to do so had been a public relations disaster; (*c*) despite what the War Office thought the police themselves were far from keen to take up the task; and (*d*) the Home Office had in any case no authority to instruct chief constables on their specific tasks. 'I am sorry to be unhelpful,' Maxwell Fyfe added, 'but you will appreciate that there are real difficulties both in principle and from the standpoint of the many duties which now fall on an under-manned Police Force.'[27]

Home Office suspicions that some of the more zealous Home Guard commanders could create trouble through over-enthusiastic attempts to keep out 'undesirables' seemed to be confirmed when in February 1952 it emerged that Colonel Ambrose Keevil, the CO of the Home Guard in Surrey, had stated at a local press conference that potential recruits would have to undergo a 'very severe' screening process. George Wigg, Labour MP for Dudley and previously private secretary to Shinwell at the Ministry of Defence, took up this statement in the Commons, asking Anthony Head if such vetting was to be War Office policy. Concluding that discretion was the better part of valour, the War Minister at this point decided to drop any idea of screening the Home Guard. The War Office had no intention of vetting recruits, he replied to Wigg's question on 19 February—Keevil had spoken without his knowledge or War Office consent. This, however, did not stop the opposition suspecting— sometimes rightly—that Home Guard commanders could at times exceed their authority in terms of who was, and was not, allowed into the force.[28]

Not that the public were exactly lining up to participate. In marked contrast to the overwhelming enthusiasm of 1940, the reaction to Anthony Head's radio appeal was largely one of indifference. In the age of the hydrogen bomb and successive crises which never actually resulted in full-scale war, the Home Guard appears to have struck the man in the street as both anachronistic and unnecessary. By 18 February 1952, only 28,120 men had registered to join, and by March recruiting was still yielding under 4,000 new volunteers per month—a far from encouraging response given the target figure of 125,000.[29]

Scenting failure and an issue with which to undermine the government's credibility, Labour backbenchers were not slow to attack. As early as 24 March, George Wigg, in the course of the Army Estimates debate, was arguing that the Home Guard 'meets no military need and, in fact, it is a colossal waste of money'. Woodrow Wyatt drove the point home the following month, placing the Secretary of State for War on the spot by comparing recruiting expectations with current results and asking: 'would it not be better to abandon this foolish scheme before further time and money is wasted on it?'[30]

At this stage, this was something the government was not willing to contemplate. Quite apart from the political fallout that would ensue from abandoning the Conservatives' first piece of legislation, Churchill, ageing but obstinate as ever, remained firmly convinced of the need for a peacetime Home Guard in the face of potential war with the Soviet Union. 'He is obsessed', his personal physician, Lord Moran, wrote in his diary on 16 January 1952, 'with the precarious existence of Britain.'[31]

Efforts to make the Home Guard viable were therefore stepped up rather than abandoned. In March, for example, the Cabinet, on the Prime Minister's recommendation, agreed to the formation of an additional ten cadre battalions for Northern Ireland. Field-Marshal Sir William Slim himself made a radio broadcast on 26 April, two days before the first units were to be raised, to try and counter the view that a Home Guard was an anachronism. 'Believe me,' the CIGS argued, 'if the horrors of atomic bombing fall on this island one of our first needs will be a force of steady, disciplined, armed men throughout the country—a Home Guard as well as a civil defence force.'[32]

Slim's broadcast was applauded by existing supporters of the Home Guard.[33] But in the face of widespread public indifference and an inability to spend lavishly on advertising and public relations—not to speak of uniforms and equipment—the War Office could do little to fundamentally improve the situation. Peacetime apathy and the opposition of the Labour Party to a Home Guard in being were usually blamed by army commanders as the cause of the disappointingly low recruiting figures; but whatever the reasons, within five months the total strength of the 567 Home Guard battalions had only managed to inch its way up to 22,000 men.[34]

By the autumn of 1952 the evidence of failure could no longer be ignored, and Anthony Head ordered the DCIGS to draw up a memorandum outlining what might be done to save the situation. The only option Head ruled out in advance was disbandment.

General Whiteley, a strong supporter of the peacetime Home Guard scheme, proposed two lines of action. On the one hand, he felt, if more money were given over to publicity—say, £50,000 or so—and uniforms provided for the cadre battalions, then the apathy and low morale which were handicapping recruitment could be overcome. 'Without such encouragement,' the DCIGS warned, 'the whole scheme may collapse.'

However, at the same time it was clear that the original battalion recruiting goals were unrealistic. A cadre of fifty men, sometimes spread over a very wide area, was proving too small to keep a battalion-sized administrative unit in order. The cadre battalions in western England, Wales, and Scotland should therefore be increased to 100 men. On the other hand, the active battalions in eastern England were clearly never, even under the best of circumstances, going to reach their peacetime target strength of 900 men. Active battalions should recruit to the more realistic total of 600 men.[35]

When the Army Council executive committee discussed these proposals on 26 September, a consensus quickly emerged that further retrenchment was necessary. Lieutenant-General Sir Nevil Brownjohn, the VCIGS, argued that while a full-strength peacetime Home Guard in the eastern half of England had made sense when first conceived, the Chiefs of Staff no longer considered large-scale airborne invasion to be a serious threat. Anti-sabotage forces would still be needed, but this task could be accomplished by far fewer men. His proposal that active and cadre battalions be cut and raised to a strength of 100 men respectively—reducing the establishment of the Home Guard by 91,000 officers and men—was accepted with alacrity. As for the publicity money Whiteley had asked for, the executive committee agreed that the cupboard was practically bare—a mere £10 per battalion could be spared for local efforts.[36]

Anthony Head, however, felt that this course of action would still be too dangerous politically. Less than a year previously the government had claimed that an active Home Guard was vital and practicable: how would it look if suddenly the bigger units (those in eastern England) were reduced to a size that really made them only cadres? Such a move would be interpreted as an admission of failure; an admission that, as the Opposition kept asserting, the government had rushed into a policy without thinking through the consequences.

On the other hand, the Minister knew full well that without some sort of reform the Home Guard issue could only become more embarrassing. Wyatt, Swingler, and even Shinwell were all by this point weighing in heavily on the issue. 'The right hon. gentleman,' Shinwell began a few days later as he groped for an adequate metaphor to express his contempt, 'has created an abortion!'[37] Meanwhile, counter-claims that Opposition criticism was 'both premature and unhelpful' sounded increasingly hollow and defensive.[38]

A compromise solution appeared the only viable option. Head managed to persuade a reluctant Prime Minister and General Sir Miles

Dempsey (C-in-C UK Land Forces) to concede that while 100 men per battalion was impossibly low, 300 men per battalion in eastern parts of the country might just be adequate as long as recruiting efforts were kept up.[39]

On 12 November 1952, Head announced the intended reforms in the Commons, explaining that 300-man units 'relying on rapid expansion on the threat of war to enable them to carry out their full tasks over a prolonged period' could do the job previously allocated to 900-man active battalions in peacetime. Trying to pre-empt criticism, the Minister blamed difficulties encountered thus far on the failure of the Opposition to support a vital part of the nation's defences. This attack drew angry retorts from the opposite benches, and prompted Attlee, not easily drawn, to speak out and expose the government's real motive for introducing changes. 'Does it not rather suggest', he returned frostily in reference to Head's statement, 'that the plans have been fitted to the men available rather than the number of men available being called up for particular plans which are being worked out?'[40]

There was, of course, a large element of truth in Attlee's comment. Unfortunately for the government, the Home Guard failed to attract even enough recruits to fill the new, smaller, battalions. People were just not convinced that the need existed, and by early 1953 one unit in Herefordshire was down to 10 per cent of its allocated manpower while the Home Guard as a whole now numbered a mere 20,000 other ranks. There were, to be sure, 9,000 Home Guard officers, but this only highlighted the manpower shortage.[41] Who ever heard of an infantry force in which for every five officers there were only eleven men to command?

Unwilling to concede defeat, Churchill decided to make a personal appeal on behalf of the Home Guard during a carefully prepared speech on defence matters delivered in the House of Commons on 5 March 1953. 'So far,' the Prime Minister admitted, 'its growth has not been in any way adequate to our needs.' The Home Guard still played a vital part in the defence of airfields and vulnerable points by allowing the Territorial Army to take up other tasks, and should be supported. 'I make my appeal to all parties in the House to help in every way in encouraging enlistment in the Home Guard,' Churchill continued, 'not as a measure of panic or alarm but as a bringing into play of a new, effective and necessary element in our system of home defence.'[42]

A central aspect of the renewed effort was the setting up of Home Guard factory sub-units in May 1953. Consultations between the Ministry of Labour and the TUC, however, revealed that while some trade unions were willing to go along with the idea, the more left-wing were totally opposed to the scheme. The National Union of Tailors and Garment Workers, for example, announced its 'deep hostility' to units whose function would in their view be to 'persecute and fight the militant Trade Unionist'.[43] Those who were already suspicious or critical of the Home Guard, in short, remained unconvinced by Churchill's appeal, and recruiting continued to fall far below War Office expectations.[44]

By the autumn of 1953 the total number of active Home Guard volunteers had only increased by approximately 2,800 over seven months: very disappointing, and even alarming when it was considered that those who had joined up in early 1952 would soon be coming to the end of their two-year commitment and might well decide not to re-enlist given how poorly the Home Guard had fared. The Opposition was pressing for abolition of the force, and with the economic situation making defence cuts likely in the near future, to keep spending large sums on the Home Guard would only increase criticism.

Head, perhaps regretting that he had not left well enough alone, was aware of all this; but he was also aware that the government had invested a substantial amount of political capital in the Home Guard. The question was, would it be better to bite the bullet now and concede that a mistake had been made, or renew his efforts to make the force viable? Unwilling to make such a choice alone, the Minister had a paper drawn up outlining the current situation for the Cabinet to consider.[45]

In late October 1953 the Cabinet discussed what to do. Head remained impartial, but stressed that if it was decided to press on, then 'the case for doing so must be effectively presented if recruiting were to be maintained'. Lord Alexander, the urbane Field-Marshal whom Churchill had appointed Minister of Defence in early 1952, said he had no doubt that 'there was a good case for retaining in peacetime the nucleus of an organization which in the atomic age might well have an invaluable part to play, particularly in assisting the civil defence services'. Taking their cue from Alexander (and quietly overlooking the fact that civil defence was only a secondary task in current Home Guard operational orders—in other words that it had been created with a different purpose in mind) others took up the civil defence theme. Churchill, obviously pleased at this, closed discussion by stating that it was 'clearly the view of the Cabinet that the Home Guard should be retained'.[46]

Thus in early November 1953, when Labour MP Woodrow Wyatt called on the government to disband the Home Guard—as he had been doing periodically for some time—the Secretary of State for War took the opportunity to reaffirm the Cabinet's commitment to the force. The Home Guard, Head explained to the House, would be able at short notice to take on (unspecified) duties which would otherwise have to be carried out by regular and reserve units needed elsewhere. 'Moreover,' he added, reflecting the new Cabinet rationale for the force, 'if atomic war should come, Home Guard support to our Civil Defence services is likely to be of vital importance.'[47] In Cabinet, Churchill had stressed that the decision to maintain the force 'should be announced boldly';[48] and Head, after enumerating the reasons for not scrapping the Home Guard, proceeded to do so. The force was 'an essential part of our preparedness', involved 'selfless voluntary service', and deserved un-wavering support. 'I sincerely hope and believe', the War Minister concluded, 'that the great majority of the House will give help and encouragement to recruitment and service in the Home Guard.'[49]

Fighting words: but the realities of the situation remained unchanged. Labour backbenchers continued to deride the government's efforts to rejuvenate the Home Guard, Wyatt contemptuously referring to it as a 'farce' and Ian Mikardo (the pugnaciously left-wing MP for Reading South) accusing the Secretary of State for War—with more accuracy than he knew—of 'merely continuing [the Home Guard] as a sort of face-saver'.[50] And, whatever truth there may have been in government charges of an 'unholy alliance' between parliamentary critics and the press, recruiting continued to be extremely sluggish.

Nigel Fisher, Tory MP for Hitchin and originally a supporter of the Home Guard, described to the House in March 1954 the plight of one typical battalion in his constituency. The money allocated for publicity in the autumn of 1953 had been welcome, but despite all efforts only two new recruits had come forward. Two years after the formation of the battalion, its CO found himself in dire straits: 'to defend 150 square miles of Eastern England this battalion commander has precisely 40 rifles, three Bren guns and 25 men.'[51] In Southern Command as a whole,

Home Guard units on average numbered only 60 per cent of their allocated strength in April 1954, and overall the force stood at just over a third of its active establishment.[52]

There were signs by this point that the government was beginning to have second thoughts. In the new defence estimates announced in March 1954, it was noted that expenditure on the Home Guard was to be cut by £86,000. But in the spring and summer a major national recruiting drive was launched, involving, among other publicity efforts, a radio appeal by Lord Alexander himself after the six o'clock news on 5 May. Yet again, however, the results were less than inspiring. In Southern Command the recruiting drive netted a grand total of 597 new volunteers, while in the subsequent campaign in Western Command— even more short of recruits—the figure dropped to a paltry 351.[53] The basic problem remained the same. 'It took a lot to convince the average Englishman that he was wanted in a defensive force in peace time,' Lieutenant-General Sir Francis Festing (GOC Eastern Command) was reported to have said after inspecting the Middlesex Home Guard, going on to add that the average man 'preferred to let it be understood that he was ready to serve when the emergency came'.[54] The argument that this might be too late fell largely on deaf ears.

By 1955 it was becoming clear to all that the new Home Guard was never going to attract enough recruits to make it viable. The total number of volunteers was now 37,000—more than ever before but still far short of requirements.[55] Hitherto it had been the determination of the ageing Prime Minister to keep the Home Guard going that had stiffened the resolve of Anthony Head and others when alternatives were discussed. Standing down the Home Guard would be an admission of failure, but the longer matters were left as they were, the more ridiculous the whole thing seemed. The decision to reduce expenditure on the Home Guard by another £22,000 in the 1955 Army Estimates was symptomatic of an increasing desire to cut losses. When Churchill finally retired in April 1955 to make way for Anthony Eden, it was only a matter of time before something happened.[56]

A major defence review under the new Eden government concluded that the advent of hydrogen weapons and delivery systems made large-scale conventional war in Europe unlikely. This provided justification for thinning the ranks of the regular army, substantially cutting the reserves, and—last but not least—standing down the Home Guard.[57]

On 20 December 1955, Head, now Minister of Defence, announced in the House of Commons that the Territorial Army was to be scaled down to two divisions, both of which would be assigned to home defence. The Home Guard would therefore no longer be needed unless an emergency arose, and would be stood down as an active force. Perhaps trying to soften the blow for those die-hards who had stayed the course and were already expressing feelings of betrayal, he emphasized that standing down did not mean actual disbandment.[58]

Some Home Guard units protested, but as by this point the Home Guard had ceased its slow and painful expansion and was actually getting smaller, public opinion was probably summed up by *The Times*, which tartly remarked that the move was long overdue.[59] In any event, despite Head's claims to the contrary, the writing was clearly on the wall.

The Home Guard, once again existing only on paper, was given the final *coup de grâce* in the summer of 1957. As of 31 July, John Hare (the new Secretary of State for War) explained to the House in June, the Home Guard would cease to exist entirely: an announcement which generated gales of derisive laughter on the Labour benches.[60] The Director of the Territorial Army might wistfully suggest that 'the future is unknown and the Home Guard may of course be needed again';[61] but in an age of supersonic jets and ballistic missiles there appeared to be no call for the kind of amateur volunteers who had come forward so often in the past.

Conclusion

It is nearly ten years now since [the war] ended. Yet there remains in one's memory the procession of those who passed through the corridors of the Home Guard Directorate: the VIPs, the politicians, the Blimps, armed to the teeth, the self-styled 'business men,' the inventors of potential Home Guard equipment, practical and otherwise.

Lord Bridgeman, 1954[1]

We were living in cloud-cuckoo-land, I suppose . . .

Ex-LDV Rex Harrison, 1974[2]

. . . a landing in England must be regarded as an act of sheer desperation which need only be risked in a hopeless situation . . .

General Alfred Jodl, OKW Chief of Operations Staff, Aug. 1940[3]

From its origins in the panic atmosphere of April–May 1940 to its formal disbandment in December 1945, the wartime Home Guard was an organization quite different in certain fundamental respects from the regular armed forces and even, in some ways, its volunteer predecessors (or indeed its 1950s incarnation). These differences help explain the curious evolution of the Home Guard, in which the desires of the men themselves (or at least their advocates), rather than the strict requirements of national defence, determined policy-making.

Very much like the VTC of the Great War and the Rifle Volunteers of the late nineteenth century, the more active members of the Home Guard were simultaneously critical and demanding of higher authority, taking the view that the force had been raised and expanded due to pressure from concerned citizens rather than through foresight on the part of the government or military authorities. Local initiative and organization were the keys to change, and actions on the part of central authority which ran counter to the interests of volunteers themselves ought to be vocally resisted. The attitudes and actions of enthusiasts like Ralph Glyn and Josiah Wedgwood—'slowly, with bitterness, the War Office can be shifted'[4]—mirror the thoughts and behaviour of earlier advocates of volunteer forces such as Alfred Richards and Lord Desborough. Another similarity was the tendency of officers and men to offer suggestions to, and question the orders of, their immediate superiors. They were proud volunteers, conscious of their patriotism, thinking they knew best, and—significantly—not subject to the array of imposing coercive measures contained in military law that maintained silence among the ranks in the Army and Navy. The result was that everyone from the Prime Minister down to the lowliest section commander could be inundated with suggestions, queries, and complaints; a phenomenon not too dissimilar from the pressures exerted by the VTC and the RVCs.

In one central respect, however, the wartime Home Guard differed from earlier manifestations of local defence initiative and the post-war force. It was infinitely larger in scale, which in turn allowed it much greater influence.

The Rifle Volunteers were never a genuinely popular movement, numbering as they did only a few hundred thousand in a generally anti-militarist age.[5] Much the same could be said of the VTC, overshadowed as they were by the patriotic appeal of the pals battalions in Kitchener's Armies.[6] As for the Home Guard of the 1950s, it was, as we have seen, only the influence of Churchill which kept it alive. The wartime Home Guard, in contrast, raised in time of national peril, really was popular. Whereas the Rifle Volunteers in 1861, at the height of their strength, made up 0.8 per cent of the total male population, and the volunteers of the VTC in 1917 about 0.7 per cent, in June 1941 the total membership of the volunteer Home Guard, in relation to the adult male working population not engaged in essential police or civil defence work, or in the regular armed forces, was 19.6 per cent. This meant that about one out of every five men not otherwise engaged was enrolled in the force (not to mention the thousands of women engaged in unofficial support duties).[7] Conversely, of course, not everyone agreed with what the Home Guard stood for or was inclined to join; there were parts of

Glasgow, for instance, where it was always hard to find recruits.[8] But in general terms the Home Guard came close to being the people in arms in a way that earlier corps had not, a fact which may explain in part why so little reference is made to the predecessors of the Home Guard—especially the VTC—in the literature of the time.

Of more consequence was the effect the size of the Home Guard had on its ability to influence policy. From the decision to raise the Local Defence Volunteers through to the question of when to announce disbandment, most major and many minor decisions concerning role, weapons, tactics, and a host of other matters were framed mainly in terms of how the public and members of the Home Guard (often treated as, *de facto*, synonymous) would respond. Political considerations, broadly conceived, often outweighed purely military considerations in the formulation and implementation of policy.

To alienate the Home Guard would be to alienate a significant portion of the population, and in the age of Total War it was recognized that national morale was a key component in sustaining a viable war effort. And what the people in arms wanted badly enough, they either got or appeared to get. The LDV had been formed, after all, in order to control the burgeoning demand for civilian defence that manifested itself in the spring of 1940 rather than because there was an overwhelming military need for such a force.

Once the LDV existed, furthermore, it quickly moved away from mere passive observation and traffic control toward an active fighting role—again largely in response to pressure in the press, parliament, and through letters to MPs, ministers, and generals. Once the fighting role had been established, there arose the issue of in what form the fighting units should approach their task (the people's militia/guerrilla army question) and the more general cry for more and better weapons (which would last into the middle of 1944).

In each case the authorities were faced with difficult choices. To come down hard against the guerrilla option might appear to many members of the Home Guard as typical Blimpishness and lead to embarrassing questions in parliament and the press; while simply to admit that the financial and industrial resources necessary to equip the Home Guard on a scale similar to the Army were lacking would produce a national outcry of frightening proportions. In both cases military needs (avoiding free-ranging Spanish Militia-style guerrilla bands and properly equipping the Army) dictated one course of action while political realities (the danger of undermining national confidence in the government and military establishment) dictated the opposite.

The authorities tried to solve these conundrums by employing subtle cunning and persuasion in controlling left-wingers while unveiling weapons which in reality were of dubious fighting value, but which in all probability would never have to be fired in anger and could be presented as worthwhile. It is significant that Churchill, always concerned to keep up national confidence and aware through secret and general intelligence sources of how unlikely invasion was, pushed through the production of Home Guard sub-artillery even though the Ordnance Board thought it worthless.

This approach could sometimes backfire, as the pike fiasco demonstrated all too vividly: but on the whole mass production of cheap, ineffective weapons such as the Northover Projector allowed the War Office to have its cake and eat it too. Maintaining the Home Guard from 1941 onward cost about £1,000,000 a month—a large sum in itself but a tiny fraction of what was being spent on equipping the regular army.[9]

Throughout the four years of its existence, furthermore, there was a manifest desire on the part of the Prime Minister and War Office to maintain public confidence in the usefulness of the Home Guard through public gestures such as anniversary parades and speeches. There was also a strong desire to avoid moves such as the withdrawal of clothing coupons which could be politically sensitive, no matter how rational such steps might seem in logistical terms.

To be sure, governments had succumbed on occasion to pressure from the VTC and Rifle Volunteer lobby in the past. But the rifle volunteers were for the most part concerned with keeping the War Office out of their affairs rather than giving it directions; and despite backers in the press and House of Lords, it was often an uphill struggle for the advocates of the VTC, supplicants as they were at the altar of that inscrutable oracle Lord Kitchener and subject to efforts by General Macready and others in 1917–18 to close them down.[10]

The much larger and more powerful Home Guard liked to pretend that it was hard done by, constantly short-changed, and put upon by higher authority—'when I was in the Home Guard,' Orwell wrote in

1944, 'we used to say that the bad sign would be when flogging was introduced'[11]—but in reality once a desire had been made evident in parliament, the press, or through private representation (and sometimes even if it had not) the War Office strove mightily in both rhetorical and concrete terms to show how responsive it was to Home Guard wants and needs. Instead of the defensiveness that often overtook earlier volunteer lobbying efforts once a force had been set up and running, the righteous aggressiveness characteristic of the period surrounding the creation of the LDV in 1940 continued right through to the Home Guard stand-down in 1944—and with telling effect. The Home Guard was simply too big to either ignore or completely control.

This was not a position with which all senior officers could cope. Despite the fact that it was part of the armed forces of the Crown, the Home Guard was a world apart from the Regular Army with its emphasis on discipline and obedience. (Indeed in this respect it more closely resembled the *laissez-faire* outlook and behaviour of the Rifle Volunteers and VTC.) General Pownall, landed with the unenviable task of trying to create some order out of the chaos of the spring of 1940, wanted another command within weeks and was 'mightily glad to go' when transferred to Northern Ireland in October. 'They are a troublesome and querulous party, the Home Guard,' he reflected in his diary. 'There is mighty little pleasing them, and the minority is always noisy.'[12] General Eastwood, the first Director-General of the Home Guard, was rather more keen on the force, commenting in 1941 that 'greater trust has been placed in the population. The Government is trusting the people.'[13]

In Major-General Lord Bridgeman, however, who had served as Deputy-Director Home Guard under Eastwood, the War Office found the perfect man for a job that was somewhere between that of a labour relations expert and a professional politician. Always, in the words of a Home Office official, 'helpful, reasonable and anxious to co-operate',[14] an infinitely patient listener who smoked a pipe and spoke with a disarming honesty and conciliatory manner, Bridgeman managed the difficult task of making those he talked and corresponded with in the Home Guard feel that he understood and cared about their point of view. He could publicly sing the praises of the force in lyrical terms—'we see on the chessboard of war the Home Guard as the Castle guarding the King, while the Knights of the Regular Army went overseas in search of the King's enemies'[15]—at the same time realistically coping with periodic forays by the Prime Minister into directorate affairs and dealing with Whitehall bureaucrats who did not always understand that the Home Guard could be coaxed and cajoled but never ordered about. Of the constant call for weapons and equipment, he stated candidly in 1941: 'We must not and cannot stop it. It would be wrong to try and stop it.'[16]

P. J. Grigg as War Minister did his best to adopt similar tactics, but coming from a civil service background was temperamentally unsuited for the job and occasionally gave vent to his true feelings in the House. 'In debate I was a bit out of my element perhaps,' he reflected in his memoirs, 'and I was apt to be more controversial than the circumstance warranted.'[17] Lord Croft as Under-Secretary of State was a true believer in the Home Guard—he himself had served in a volunteer regiment at the turn of the century—but could occasionally let his enthusiasm run away with him, as the 'Croft's Pikes' label demonstrated. Sir Edward Grigg, the other Under-Secretary and the man Eden had initially chosen to deal with Home Guard matters in parliament, was by late 1941 side-lined as the political importance of the force grew and questions in the Commons were handled by the Minister. Lord Bridgeman, therefore, became the point man in War Office relations with the Home Guard, and it is a measure of his success that, in a war in which senior posts were filled and vacated with dizzying rapidity, it was only in 1944, as the Home Guard was approaching stand-down, that he was transferred to become a deputy adjutant-general.

National morale, in short, determined the course of Home Guard development rather than strictly military considerations. This is not to suggest, however, that military considerations were absent. Once the force was in being military commanders from the C-in-C Home Forces downward sought to incorporate the Home Guard into their defensive plans, and from the middle of the war onward the force played an increasingly important part in filling in for regulars (particularly in AA Command) as the manpower shortage became acute.

Manning anti-aircraft batteries and helping in civil defence work, however, was not what the Home Guard itself saw as its primary role, and therefore not what the authorities promoted as its most important function. Both in the minds of its members and in official pronouncements, the Home Guard was, from first to last, meant for local defence against enemy seaborne and (above all) airborne invasion. In the event, the Home Guard was never put to the test, a fact which led many members to assume—and the War Office authorities to confirm—that their presence had been a major deterrent in launching an invasion.[18] But just how likely was an enemy assault? And what role did the Home Guard play—if any—in German calculations?

Public fears in Britain that an invasion was being prepared in the summer of 1940 were not without foundation. In mid-July, Hitler had issued Directive No. 16, which ordered planning to begin for a cross-Channel attack in September 1940 or in the spring of 1941. There was, however, a certain make-believe quality to the planning of Operation Sealion. Despite much bickering over a broad versus narrow-front approach, neither the Wehrmacht nor the Kriegsmarine had much confidence in the outcome of any cross-Channel operation at all, including the final quite limited assault agreed to in August.

Apart from a fleet of small fast motorboats for the first wave which was supposed to establish five beachheads, the invasion force of twelve divisions would have to rely principally on several hundred towed river barges collected from the Rhine and elsewhere to get across the treacherous English Channel. The main defence against attack by the ships of the Royal Navy during the eleven days needed to ferry the force across was to consist of a band of mines on either side of the narrow-front route from Boulogne–Ostend to Beachy Head–Folkestone. The Army had produced a few hastily improvised airscrew-driven catamarans and tanks fitted with snorkels, and eventually the Luftwaffe agreed to land elements of the 7th *Fliegerdivision* behind the beachhead in support, but the German armed forces remained critically short of transport aircraft after losses in Holland and possessed none of the specialized landing ships, armoured vehicles, and other craft which were such an essential component in the success of the Allied invasion of Normandy four years later.

Hitler, meanwhile, displayed very little interest in Sealion, seeing it more as a propaganda ploy to frighten the British into coming to terms with him than a real strategic option. The German High Command Chief of Operations Staff rightly concluded that even with total command of the air over the Channel and southern England (something the Luftwaffe was failing to achieve) the plan would be very risky, and Field-Marshal von Rundstedt, the principal Army commander, growled 'Sealion, rubbish!' every time the subject came up. After the Luftwaffe had failed to knock out the RAF, Hitler cancelled Sealion in October 1940. By the following spring Hitler had turned his attention to the problem of an invasion of the Soviet Union, and planning for a cross-Channel attack was never revived.[19] Though the German military authorities opened intelligence files on the Home Guard and the Propaganda Ministry indignantly claimed that the force was contrary to international law, there is no evidence to suggest its presence was much of a contributing factor in the decision to cancel Sealion.[20] The often quite accurate intelligence summaries issued to Wehrmacht units of the invasion force in August outlining expected British defences and resistance did not mention the Home Guard at all.[21]

If the RAF had fared less well in the Battle of Britain, and the decision had been taken to launch Sealion (either in the autumn of 1940 or spring of 1941), it is likely that the operation would have failed. In a war game organized at Camberley Staff College in 1974 to test the feasibility of Sealion involving many of the planners participating at the time, only the development of mist enabled the first wave to remain undetected until it landed—the weather could alternatively have turned so nasty as to swamp the barges—and once ashore the German Army was unable to establish a sufficiently strong beachhead to prevent local defences, the Mobile Column, and above all the Royal Navy from forcing an evacuation after three days.[22]

How would the Home Guard have done if Sealion had been launched? Apart from those units engaged with the coastal defences near the landing beaches along from Folkestone and on the path inland, the first clash of arms would have been between the Home Guards of villages such as Etchinghill, Postling, and Paddlesworth and parachute regiments of the 7th *Fliegerdivision*. Despite the burning desire of many volunteers to get to grips with the enemy—the sort of enthusiast General Adam met as GOC Northern Command who asked 'Do you think Hitler is coming, sir?', adding: 'It will be an awful pity if he doesn't.'[23]— in one sense it would have been no contest. Luftwaffe parachute troops were highly trained, well-armed professionals who would have been able to overwhelm the surrounding village platoons of more or less untrained

Home Guards in short order, as the more thoughtful volunteers came to realize. ('It really makes cold shivers run down my spine', one volunteer later remarked, 'at the thought of what we escaped.')[24] Older men hastily grouped together and armed with a few shotguns and rifles would have been no match for squads of élite *Fallschirmtruppen* armed with sub-machine guns.[25]

However, in order to link up with the main landing and to push inland, the airborne troops would have had to move through one village after another, and fight a series of short, sharp engagements with the local Home Guard. The local units would be unable to stop the advance, but—as Brooke planned—they could eventually slow it down and give time for units of the Field Force to arrive.

The cost, though, might have been high. The German government had claimed since May 1940 that the Home Guard were *francs-tireurs* and did not recognize them as members of the armed forces. Moreover, as operations in Crete in 1941 showed, German paratroops were not overly conscientious in observing the Geneva Convention when striving to establish landing sites. Battles with the Home Guard could easily have led to the killing of innocent civilians as well. There was the added possibility that regular units of the British Army and the Home Guard would come into contact without adequate recognition, thereby creating confusion and possibly a 'blue on blue' situation. If, furthermore, the main German landing force *had* established a viable beachhead and started to advance toward London, the actions of the auxiliary units, dressed like the Home Guard but carrying on a guerrilla campaign behind enemy lines, would probably have confirmed the *franc-tireur* image with predictable results for captured volunteers as well as the civilian population.

Given that none of the above came to pass or was likely to do so, can it be said that the Home Guard was a worthwhile undertaking? Was it not perhaps just a useful source of comic material for writers and cartoonists of the day and the ex-Home Guard creator of *Dad's Army*?[26] While the exploits of the Walmington-on-Sea platoon and other fictionalized Home Guard units accurately portray some of the more absurd aspects of the force, the Home Guard was nevertheless import-ant to Britain's war effort in a number of ways. In the early years, and especially in the spring and summer of 1940, it gave people a means of

direct participation in the defence both of the nation and of their immediate locality, and therefore a way of taking part, becoming truly
involved, in the tumultuous events of the day. Like the larger-than-life
rhetoric of the Prime Minister, the Home Guard gave ordinary citizens—or at least ordinary male citizens—a feeling that they were engaged in a great enterprise, a battle between the forces of light and
darkness (the latter taking the shape, even in children's nightmares, of
Nazi parachutists).[27] 'Whatever the fighting value of the Home Guard,'
as General (retd.) Sir John Burnett-Stuart, commander of the 1st
Aberdeenshire Battalion put it, 'it was a great national gesture and
a great tonic. It was the outward and visible sign of the spirit of
resistance.'[28]

There is the possibility that class distinctions became more evident
between officers and other ranks within the force as people of influence—the local squire, the factory manager, the retired majors, colonels, generals, and so forth—assumed command positions and wore
their old uniforms. But there is also much to suggest—making due
allowance for wartime propaganda—that many ex-generals and other
notables remained happily in the ranks, that higher authority and social
élites in general were often treated with a cheerful lack of deference,
and above all that the Home Guard experience (a reflection of more
general wartime shifts in social behaviour and class relations) often
involved a lot of cross-cultural social mixing, comradely mateyness,
and even on occasion the opportunity for quiet reflection and poetic
inspiration.[29]

No two units, of course, were quite the same, which makes generalizations hazardous. The urban and country units tended to mirror their
separate social structures, and the AA units were different again. Much
could also depend on the enthusiasm and initiative of local Home Guard
commanders, and a man transferring from one part of the country to
another could find himself in a different world.[30] On the whole, however,
taking account of the grumbles of directed men and the difficulties
encountered on AA sites, the Home Guard experience seems to have
been a positive one for most, and the force itself an integral part of the
fabric of wartime morale.

Moreover, even as the importance of the Home Guard declined in
this respect in proportion to the perceived invasion threat, the force

became more important in other ways. It was, to begin with, a useful observation tool in 1940–1, even if on occasion volunteers got carried away by their own fears and false alarms were reported. More importantly, as the war progressed and the manpower pool was depleted, the Home Guard provided a ready source of stand-in troops.

The force was particularly useful in the manning of anti-aircraft gun and rocket batteries—118,649 Home Guards had been seconded to AA Command by August 1944 and made up close to half all gun and rocket crews[31]—but also became involved in everything from coastal defence work and minefield maintenance to auxiliary bomb disposal and civil defence work.

It was rarely glamorous, was often uncomfortable, and its significance in freeing regulars to go overseas was sometimes exaggerated in order to boost Home Guard morale and deceive the enemy. Yet when all is said and done, the alternate duties performed by the Home Guard were important, and did allow at least 100,000 assorted gunners, signallers, and other specialist troops to be transferred to more aggressive tasks.[32] The Home Guard of the 1950s, a mere shadow of its former self, was embarrassingly lacking in real function. But of the wartime Home Guard it is fitting to quote the passage from Milton adopted as a motto by more than one Home Guard unit: 'They also serve who only stand and wait.'[33]

Note on Sources

Source material from which to gather information on the Home Guard is nowadays plentiful. However, as little has been written on the subject, a brief summary of the main sources on which I have drawn would seem in order.

There are a number of categories of documentary evidence available to scholars interested in the Home Guard. The first, and most important in understanding how the force was viewed and treated by the military and civil authorities, are the relevant—and quite extensive—War Office, Cabinet Office, Prime Minister's Office, Ministry of Information, and (to a lesser extent) Home Office, Ministry of Defence, and Ministry of Labour files available at the Public Record Office, Kew and—for the Ulster Home Guard—Cabinet papers at the Public Record Office of Northern Ireland, Belfast.

A second important category is made up of private papers of members of the Home Guard and the politicians and senior officers who oversaw the development of the force.

The third major form of documentary evidence, mostly to be found in county and local record offices and, for the Home Guard north of the border, the National Library Scotland, consists of the records of individual Home Guard units and higher formations, deposited when the Home Guard stood down or in subsequent years. Though generally not catalogued in any detail and varying in quality—everything from the odd platoon roll-call sheet to the administrative files of entire zones—these records taken as a whole have proved invaluable in building up a picture of how the force saw itself and its relations with higher authority. County Territorial Army Association minutes have also occasionally been of use.

A further documentary source consists of Home Guard-related letters and articles published in newspapers and journals, as well as letters sent to trade unions and other organizations. These are quite useful in providing details of certain events and in gauging popular opinion on a variety of subjects related to the activities of the force.

The very large number of local unit histories written during or shortly after the war, though they sometimes make rather tedious reading, have proved inestimable as a source. Unlike current recollections—in which the passage of time has sometimes blurred details to a considerable extent—these histories vividly convey local developments and attitudes shortly after they happened. Moreover, unlike histories of Regular Army units subject to direct or indirect military censorship, the authors of Home Guard unit histories often did not flinch from pointing out controversial issues and conflicts with higher authority. Like the Home Guard itself, they were sometimes quite outspoken.

The attitudes and opinions expressed in unit histories are, to be sure, usually those of the more committed and enthusiastic officers and NCOs; but taken in conjunction with Ministry of Information files, private papers, letters to the editor, and unit documents which concentrate on the less committed ranker, such histories can play a vital part in building up an overall picture of the Home Guard. There are, in addition, many published memoirs and diaries of those involved with the force, not least those of senior generals, which have proved useful.

The only major potential source of primary material which has not been tapped in this study is oral testimony—an omission which perhaps warrants some explanation. An interesting sample of solicited recollections has been collated and published by Frank and Joan Shaw under the title *We Remember the Home Guard*; but given the size of the force—well over 1,500,000 men (and later tens of thousands of women as well)—any firm conclusions would require testimony from literally hundreds of thousands of former Home Guards, and would encompass only the younger portion of the force (bearing in mind that those already getting on in age in the 1940s have mostly passed away). A specifically social history of the Home Guard would doubtless benefit from such a Herculean endeavour, assuming it were feasible; though comparison of what is said in *We Remember the Home Guard* with War Office and other records illustrates the extent to which the passage of time has blurred memories of (say) what weapons were used and when particular events happened. 'The best historical evidence', as C. P. Stacey put it, 'is evidence recorded *at the time*.'[1] In any event, as is made clear in the introduction, this book is

---

[1] C. P. Stacey, *A Date with History* (Ottawa, 1983), 229–30.

primarily a history of the Home Guard in the political and military context, for which the documentary and published sources outlined above (and listed in detail in the bibliography) have generally proved quite adequate—though the reader will of course be the ultimate judge of that.

Notes

Introduction

1. G. Macdonald Fraser, *The Hollywood History of the World* (London, 1988), 232.
2. See PRO, WO 199/402, encl. 11A, MA to C-in-C, Mar. 1943, Secret; IWM, Carden Roe Papers, 77/165/1, Kirke to Carden Roe, 18 June 1943; C. Graves, *Great Days* (London, 1944), 139, 152, 190, *passim*.
3. A brief but fairly typical example of the idealization of the Home Guard is contained in Arthur Bryant's *The Lion and the Unicorn* (London, 1969), 73. The 'Home Guard ethos' can be seen as part of a more general myth surrounding public attitudes and behaviour in 1940. See A. Calder, *The Myth of the Blitz* (London, 1991).
4. IWM, Carden Roe Papers, 77/165/1, Editor, *Army Quarterly*, to Carden Roe, 25 Feb. 1946.
5. See PRO, CAB 140/118, *passim*.
6. I. F. W. Beckett, *The Amateur Military Tradition, 1558–1945* (Manchester, 1991).
7. Ibid., introduction.

Chapter 1

1. The poem of the same name was published in *The Times* on 9 May 1859.
2. This derived from an incident in Wandsworth Park where an over-zealous volunteer mistakenly shot a dog. See H. Cunningham, *The Volunteer Force: A Social and Political History 1859–1908* (London, 1975), 78.
3. The term is taken from I. F. W. Beckett's *The Amateur Military Tradition, 1558–1945* (Manchester, 1991), a meticulous and comprehensive study of part-time military service in Britain and the only single-volume work on the subject. See also A. Babington, *Military Intervention in Britain: From the Gordon Riots to the Gibraltar Incident* (London, 1990), 1–2.
4. See L. G. Schwoerer, *'No Standing Armies!'* (Baltimore, 1974), ch. 4.
5. Beckett, *Amateur Tradition*, chs. 3–4; see also H. T. Dickinson, 'Popular Conservatism and Militant Loyalism 1789–1815', in H. T. Dickinson (ed.), *Britain and the French Wars* (London, 1989), 114, 117–18; J. R. Western, 'The Volunteer Movement as an Anti-Revolutionary Force, 1793–1800', *English Historical Review* 71 (1956), 603–14.

6. Beckett, *Amateur Tradition*, 103; see also C. Emsley, *British Society and the French Wars, 1793–1815* (London, 1979), 38, 102–4; R. Glover, *Britain at Bay: Defence against Bonaparte, 1803–14* (London, 1973), 44–6.

7. E. M. Spiers, *The Army and Society 1815–1914* (London, 1980), 79–80, 163; M. S. Partridge, *Military Planning for the Defense of the United Kingdom, 1814–1870* (New York, 1989), 138ff.; Babington, *Military Intervention*, ch. 5, 99–100, 108, 112–13.

8. A substantial number of merchants and professionals were eager to do their bit, but felt shut out of the normal avenues of voluntary military service either by location or social standing. The (now voluntary) militia remained low in public esteem, while the predominantly rural yeomanry appeared socially exclusive. As Ian Beckett has pointed out, neither force necessarily matched its stereotype: but the popular image of both was enough to generate widespread calls for a third approach. See Beckett, *Amateur Tadition*, 139–40, *passim*.

9. *The Times*, 19 Apr. 1859, 9; see I. F. W. Beckett, *Riflemen Form: A Study of the Rifle Volunteer Movement 1859–1908* (Aldershot, 1982), ch. 2.

10. Spiers, *Army and Society*, 165–6.

11. Beckett, *Riflemen Form*, ch. 5.

12. The militia, increasingly an alternative route for both officers and men on their way into the Army, was by the last decades of the nineteenth century really more of an unofficial reserve than a true local volunteer force.

13. Beckett, *Amateur Tradition*, 180ff. For an overview of the changes taking place in warfare which made the amateur tradition obsolescent, see M. van Creveld, *Command in War* (Cambridge, Mass., 1985), ch. 4; id., *Technology and War: From 2000 B.C. to the Present* (New York, 1989), chs. 11–12.

14. Glover, *Britain at Bay*, 44–5; Beckett, *Amateur Tradition*, 106–7.

15. See, e.g., H. Strachan, *The Reform of the British Army, 1830–54* (Manchester, 1984); B. Bond, *The Victorian Army and the Staff College, 1854–1914* (London, 1972); E. M. Spiers, *Haldane: An Army Reformer* (Edinburgh, 1980).

16. About forty MPs were volunteers. See Spiers, *Army and Society*, 253–6; Beckett, *Amateur Tradition*, ch. 8; id., 'H. O. Arnold Forster and the Volunteers', in I. Beckett and J. Gooch (eds.), *Politicians and Defence: Studies in the Formulation of British Defence Policy 1845–1970* (Manchester, 1981), ch. 3.

17. Spiers, *Haldane*, ch. 5, 276–9.

18. J. Gooch, *The Prospect of War: Studies in British Defence Policy 1847–*

1942 (London, 1981), 10, 12–13, 14; see also A. J. Marder, *From Dreadnought to Scapa Flow, 1: The Road to War, 1904–1914* (London, 1961), 358.

19. Ibid., chs. 6–7, 345–8.
20. See I. F. Clarke, *Voices Prophesying War: Future Wars 1763–3749* (Oxford, 1992), ch. 4; D. A. T. Stafford, 'Spies and Gentlemen: The Birth of the British Spy Novel', *Victorian Studies* 24 (1981), 489–509.
21. D. French, 'Spy Fever in Britain, 1900–1915', *Historical Journal* 21 (1978), 355–8; see A. M. Gollin, 'England is No Longer an Island: The Phantom Airship Scare of 1909', *Albion* 13 (1981), 43–57.
22. French, 'Spy Fever', 364–70.
23. P. Dennis, *The Territorial Army 1906–1940* (Woodbridge, 1987), 18–31.
24. *The Times*, 6 and 8 Aug. 1914, 9.
25. I. F. W. Beckett, 'Aspects of a Nation in Arms: Britain's Volunteer Training Corps in the Great War', *Revue Internationale d'Histoire Militaire* (1985), 28–9; *The Times*: 8 Aug. 1914, 9; 10 Aug. 1914, 9; 13 Aug. 1914, 9; 17 Aug. 1914, 4; 18 Aug. 1914, 7; 19 Aug. 1914, 7.
26. Central Association of Volunteer Training Corps [CAVTC], *The Volunteer Force and the Volunteer Training Corps during the Great War* (London, 1920), 3.
27. Ibid., 3, app. II.
28. *The Times*, 31 Oct. 1914, 9; Beckett, 'Aspects', 29; see *The Times*: 5 Nov. 1914, 9; 3 Nov. 1914, 9; 8 Nov. 1914, 4.
29. CAVTC, app. IV; PRO, CAB 106/1188, 'The Volunteer Force during the Great War', 1–2.
30. See J. M. Osborne, 'Defining Their Own Patriotism: British Volunteer Training Corps in the First World War', *Journal of Contemporary History* 23 (1988), 67–8; CAVTC, 7, 10–11.
31. 68 HC (Deb.) 5s, cols. 775, 782–3, 1302; 69 HC (Deb.) 5s, cols., 96–7, 102, 301, 502, 505–8, 516, 608, 621–2, 626, 1129; 70 HC (Deb.) 5s, cols. 33, 625–35; 71 HC (Deb.) 5s, cols. 493, 505, 527.
32. See 20 HL (Deb.) 5s, cols. 343–4; PRO, CAB 106/1188, 'Volunteer Force', 2; CAVTC, 14–15.
33. 80 HC (Deb.) 5s, col. 244; see also 23 HL (Deb.) 5s, cols. 793–5; 80 HC (Deb.) 5s, col. 63; 76 HC (Deb.) 5s, cols. 184, 1775; 74 HC (Deb.) 5s, cols. 154, 1489; CAVTC, 19.
34. 80 HC (Deb.) 5s, col. 876.
35. Beckett, 'Aspects', 30; 84 HC (Deb.) 5s, cols. 151–3; PRO, CAB 106/1188, 'Volunteer Force', 3, 5.
36. Osborne, 'Defining Their Own Patriotism', *passim*.

37. 23 HL (Deb). 5s, cols. 786–8; PRO, CAB 106/1188, 'Volunteer Force', 3–4; CAVTC, 23–4.

38. PRO, WO 32/5048, Précis of AC meeting, 23 July 1917; see ibid., Gibbon to WO Secretary, 3 Dec. 1917; Beckett, 'Aspects', 31–2.

39. See PRO, WO 32/5049, Report of a meeting of representatives of the Volunteer Force, 27 May 1918; CAB 106/1188, 'Volunteer Force', 9–10.

40. Ibid., Conference on the Organization of the Volunteer Force, 21 Dec. 1917, *et al.*; ibid., Maj.-Gen., GS HF, to DSD, 24 July 1917; ibid., Volunteer Force return of Strength, 31 May 1917; ibid., Note from DMO to DCIGS, 29 Sept. 1917.

41. Beckett, 'Aspects', 37.

42. Ibid., 32.

43. Osborne, 'Defining Their Own Patriotism', 72. Volunteer Motor Transport units were kept on the books until March 1921 as an emergency reserve in case of strikes. See PRO, CAB 106/1188, 'Volunteer Force', 10; WO 32/5050, *passim.*

44. During the Abyssinian Crisis of 1935, for example, Sir Percy Harris (now MP for Bethnal Green Southwest and Liberal Chief Whip) and Sir John Smedley-Crooke (Tory MP for Birmingham, Deritend) approached the War Minister, Duff Cooper, proposing a new volunteer force in the event of war. Cooper was polite but cool, taking the view that modern fighting conditions made the concept of calling out the people to defend their homes rather out of date. See PRO, WO 199/3236, encl. 4A, Proposed National Defence Force memo, 1935; 309 HC (Deb.) 5s, col. 2409.

45. B. H. Liddell Hart, *The Defence of Britain* (London, 1939), 134. See Cmd. 5381/1937, 9; 344 HC (Deb.) 5s, col. 2174; 351 HC (Deb.) 5s, col. 1183; 315 HC (Deb.) 5s, col. 228; *'We Also Served': The Story of the Home Guard in Cambridgeshire and the Isle of Ely 1940–1943* (Cambridge, 1943), 75.

46. See 351 HC (Deb.) 5s, cols. 580, 1183, 1804, 2099–100; M. S. Gilbert, *Finest Hour: Winston S. Churchill*, VI (London, 1983), 59–60.

Chapter 2

1. B. H. Liddell Hart, *The Defence of Britain* (London, 1939), 133.

2. CCC, Croft Papers, CRFT 1/14, Hore-Belisha [War Minister] to Croft, 7 July 1939. This was in response to a proposal from Sir Henry Page Croft to the War Office that a 'Veteran Army Corps' be formed for defensive purposes [ibid., Croft to Hore-Belisha, 10 May 1939].

3. J. Gooch, *The Prospect of War: Studies in British Defence Policy, 1847–1942* (London, 1981), 9–24.

4. See I. F. Clarke, *Voices Prophesying War: Future Wars 1763–3749* (Oxford, 1992), 159–60; U. Bailer, *The Shadow of the Bomber: The Fear of Air Attack and British Politics, 1932–1939* (London, 1980). The 1936 film version of the H. G. Wells novel *The Shape of Things to Come* provides a graphic depiction of what people thought aerial bombing would be like.

5. See PRO, WO 190/879, app. A, MI3 minute, 1 Nov. 1939; WO 193/697, encl. 1A, minute 5, Balfour-Davey to MO3, 26 Sept. 1939.

6. PRO, CAB 65/1, WM 55(39)2; ibid., WM 66(39)5; CAB 65/2, WM 75(39)9; LHC, Kirke Papers, 20/3, 6–9.

7. M. Gilbert, *Finest Hour: Winston S. Churchill, VI* (London, 1983), 59–60.

8. PRO, CAB 106/1188, 'L.D.V. and Home Guard', memo by Lord Cobham, 9 Mar. 1945.

9. See A. Calder, *The People's War: Britain 1939–45* (London, 1969), ch. 2.

10. Clive Ponting, in his book *1940: Myth and Reality* (London, 1990), has argued that the apathy characteristic of the Phoney War in fact continued right through the summer of 1940. Private accounts, letters in the press, as well as the Ministry of Information and Mass-Observation files he himself cites, all suggest that while apathy did exist, there was a definite increase in interest in the war and concern over developments once the *Blitzkrieg* began. See, e.g., M. Panter-Downes, *London War Notes 1939–1945* (New York, 1971), 51 ff. The huge response to the call for the LDV (see below) is clear evidence that apathy was the exception rather than the rule by June 1940. A rather more balanced view of the myths surrounding the summer of 1940 can be found in A. Calder, *The Myth of the Blitz* (London, 1991).

11. See L. de Jong, *The German Fifth Column in the Second World War* (Chicago, 1956), 95 ff. For reactions to the Belgian surrender, see M. Allingham, *The Oaken Heart* (London, 1941), 202; Panter-Downes, *London War Notes*, 64–5. It may be, as Roger Keyes suggests in his book *Outrageous Fortune: The Tragedy of King Leopold III of the Belgians 1901–1941* (London, 1984), that Churchill and others deliberately cast doubt on Leopold's patriotism to make him the scapegoat for the failure of Allied strategy. His obvious lack of enthusiasm for the Allied cause, however, made it easy to suspect him of fellow-traveller sympathies of one sort or another.

12. PRO, INF 1/264, Public Opinion on the Present Crisis, 30 May 1940. See Allingham, *Oaken Heart*, 207; B. Porter, *Plots and Paranoia: A History of Political Espionage in Britain, 1790–1988* (London, 1989), 176; P. and L. Gillman, *'Collar the Lot!': How Britain Interned and Expelled its Wartime Refugees* (London, 1980), 73 ff.

13. PRO, FO 371/25189, 'Fifth Column Menace', Neville Bland, May 1940.

14. PRO, CAB 65/7, WM 141(40)9, 27 May 1940.

15. A. O. Bell (ed.), *The Diary of Virginia Woolf, V: 1936–1941* (London, 1984), 14 May 1940, 284; see J. Langdon-Davis, *Parachutes over Britain* (London, 1940), 20, 26, 30; P. Donnelly (ed.), *Mrs Milburn's Diaries: An Englishwoman's Day-to-Day Reflections 1935–45* (London, 1979), 37; IWM, H. R. V. Jordan, 'Military Security Intelligence in the Western Command 1939–1946: A Personal Memoir', 23.

16. *The Times*, 11 May 1940, 7.

17. IWM, H. R. V. Jordan, 'Military Security', 24; C. Graves, *The Home Guard of Britain* (London, 1943), 10.

18. CCC, Croft Papers, 2/4, An Appreciation of Present Defence Needs, 30 May 1940.

19. Bod. L., Dawson diary, 15 May 1940. For a more detailed discussion of the public and official hysteria surrounding the Fifth Column scare, see A. W. B. Simpson, *In the Highest Degree Odious: Detention without Trial in Wartime Britain* (Oxford, 1992), 105 ff.

20. See O. Mosley, *My Life* (London, 1968), 401. It is likely, given his Great War service, that Mosley meant what he said, though understandably the authorities thought it best to play it safe and intern him.

21. F. H. Hinsley and C. A. G. Simkins, *British Intelligence in the Second World War, 4: Security and Counter-Intelligence* (HMSO, 1990), 41–2; A. J. Sherman, *Island Refuge: Britain and Refugees from the Third Reich* (Berkeley, Calif., 1973).

22. R. Wheatley, *Operation Sea Lion: German Plans for the Invasion of England, 1939–1942* (Oxford, 1958), 156, n. 4; V. Kuhn, *German Paratroopers in World War II* (London, 1978), 48 ff.; A. Ausems, 'The Luftwaffe's Airborne Losses in May 1940: An Interpretation', *Aerospace Historian* 32 (1985), 184–8.

23. Gillman, *'Collar the Lot!'*, 75 ff.

24. J. W. Wheeler-Bennett, *John Anderson: Viscount Waverley* (New York, 1962), 239, 240 ff.; Gillman, *'Collar the Lot!'*, 80.

25. Ibid., chs. 10–13; Wheeler-Bennett, *John Anderson*, 240 ff.; *Manchester Guardian*, 13 May 1940. See Hinsley and Simkins, *British Intelligence*, 47 ff.; Simpson, *Highest Degree Odious*, 105 ff.

26. NLS, MS 3816, 167, cutting from *Daily Sketch*, 31 Oct. 1944.

27. CAB 65/7, WM 116(40)1; 116 HL (Debs.) 5s, col. 329; see *Sunday Pictorial*, 12 May 1940.

28. 361 HC (Debs.) 5s, col. 8; J. Wedgwood, *Memoirs of a Fighting Life* (London, 1941), 245–6.

29. HLRO, Harris Diary, HAR1/1, 13 May 1940.

30. *Daily Mail*, 17 May 1940, 4; *Sunday Pictorial*, 12 May 1940, 11; *Sunday Express*, 12 May 1940, 6.

31. *British Legion Journal* 19 (1940), 335; see also *Daily Telegraph*, 11 May 1940, 7.

32. See, e.g., CCC, Spears Papers, 1/278, letters in response to *Sunday Express* article; PRO, WO 199/1885, encl. 1–3A, May 1940; J. G. Mountford, *Halesowen Home Guard* (Shrewsbury, 1944), 5.

33. *The Times*, 12 May 1940, 7.

34. See Hinsley and Simkins, *British Intelligence*, ch. 3.

35. HLRO, Beaverbrook Papers, BBK/D/359, Beaverbrook to Eden, 19 May 1940; ibid., Eden to Beaverbrook, 24 May 1940; see CCC, Hankey Papers, 10/9, 'Home Defence' memo, 27 May 1940, 22; see also B. Collier, *The Defence of the United Kingdom* (HMSO, 1957), 123.

36. Langdon-Davies, *Parachutes*, 35–6.

37. *The Times*, 11 May 1940.

38. NLS, MS 3816, 167, cutting from *Daily Sketch*, 31 Oct. 1944; L. A. Hawes, 'The First Two Days: The Birth of the L.D.V. in Eastern Command', *Army Quarterly* 50 (1945), 186; H. L. Wilson, *Four Years: The Story of the 5th Battalion (Caernarvonshire) Home Guard* (Conway, 1945), 19.

39. CCC, Spears Papers, 1/278, Mulholland to Spears, 16 May 1940; see IWM, Carden Roe Papers, 77/165/1, 'Birth Pangs of the Home Guard', 1.

40. PRO, CAB 66/8, WM 199(40)2, 10 July 1940.

41. Sir Percy Harris in his diary entry for 13 May not only mentions the rather embarrassing welcome given to Chamberlain and the silence from the Tory benches that met Churchill when he entered the House for the first time as PM (noted by other observers), but also describes how he had talked with the Speaker 'who did not have much confidence in Winston's character and was convinced he was unreliable'. [HLRO, HAR1/1, 13 May 1940.]

42. N. Nicolson (ed.), *Harold Nicolson: Diaries and Letters 1939–1945* (London, 1967), 7 May 1940, 76.

43. Graves, *Home Guard of Britain*, 15, 280.

44. Northants RO, HGb/1, Shillito notes, n/d.

45. P. Finch, *Warmen Courageous: The Story of the Essex Home Guard* (Southend-on-Sea, 1951), 8.

46. E. R. Murrow, *This is London* (New York, 1941), 98; K. Martin, *Editor: A Second Volume of Autobiography, 1931–45* (London, 1968), 280; B. G. Holloway (ed.), *The Northamptonshire Home Guard 1940–1945* (Northampton, 1945), 43; 'We Also Served': The Story of the Home Guard in

Cambridgeshire and the Isle of Ely 1940–1943 (Cambridge, 1944), 31–2; Bucks RO, Basden Papers, D113/77, 'The Home Guard of Farnham Royal', 2; Mountford, *Halesowen Home Guard*, 5; Northants RO, HGb3, 'The Story of the Peterborough Home Guard', 1.

47. IWM, Hawes Papers, 'Formation of the L.D.V.', encl. Anderson to Hawes, 26 June 1941.

48. LHC, Kirke Papers, 20/3, 4, 11; WO 166/1, app. B, Provision of Military Protection for Vulnerable Points, 7 Feb. 1940; see D. J. Newbold, 'British planning and preparations to resist invasion on land, September 1939–September 1940', Ph.D. thesis (London, 1988), 23–4, 58–61.

49. PRO, WO 199/3236, 'Home Guard (Local Defence Volunteers) Origins' memo by Maj. J. Maxse, encl. 20/Misc./1745, 7 May 1940.

50. PRO, CAB 65/7, WM 116(40)1, 9 May 1940.

51. PRO, CAB 79/4, COS(40)123, 11 May 1940.

52. IWM, Carden Roe Papers, 77/165/1, 'Birth Pangs of the Home Guard', 1.

53. Ibid., 1–2.

54. Ibid., 2–5; LHC, Kirke Papers, 20/3, 12; see also PRO, WO 199/3236, 'Home Guard (Local Defence Volunteers) Origins', memo by Maj. J. Maxse.

55. IWM, Carden Roe Papers, 77/165/1, 'Birth Pangs', 7.

56. P. J. Grigg, *Prejudice and Judgement* (London, 1948), 340; LHC, Kirke Papers, 20/3, 12–13. Grigg, then PUS at the War Office, was admittedly no great admirer. See CCC, Grigg Papers, 9/6/8, Grigg to Grigg, 15 July 1940.

57. Lord Avon, *The Reckoning* (London, 1960), 103.

58. IWM, Carden Roe Papers, 77/165/1, 'Birth Pangs', 8–9.

59. Ibid., 9; Hawes, 'First Two Days', *passim*; IWM, Hawes Papers, 'Formation of the L.D.V.', encl. Anderson to Hawes, 26 June 1941; see PRO, HO 45/25113, sub-file 863601/1.

60. NLS, MS 3819, f. 39, Notes on Conference held at Headquarters, Home Forces, on 16th May 1940.

61. LHC, Pownall Diary, 20 June 1940; see IWM, J. K. Howard and H. W. Endicott, *Summary Report, British Home Guard* (1941), 10–11.

62. IWM, Carden Roe Papers, 77/165/1, 'Birth Pangs', 9.

Chapter 3

1. *'We Also Served': The Story of the Home Guard in Cambridgeshire and the Isle of Ely 1940–1943* (Cambridge, 1944), 32.

2. Berks. RO, Glyn Papers, D/EGL/0149, Bisgood to Glyn, 21 Aug. 1940.

3. A. Eden, *Freedom and Order: Selected Speeches 1939–1946* (2nd edn.,

New York, 1971), 71–3; see B. G. Holloway (ed.), *The Northamptonshire Home Guard 1940–1945* (Northampton, 1949), 16.

4. M. Panter-Downes, *London War Notes, 1939–1945* (New York, 1971), 60; see NRO, HGb36, H. Banks, 'Jordan's Lot: A Saga of the Home Guard', 1; see CCRO, CR528/13, typescript history of 22nd Bn, 1; G. Beardmore, *Civilians at War: Journals 1938–1945* (London, 1984), 53, 59.

5. *The Times*, 18 May 1940, 3. See C. Graves, *The Home Guard of Britain* (London, 1943), 14 ff., 21; A. Rootes, *Front Line Country* (London, 1980), 25; F. and J. Shaw (comps.), *We Remember the Home Guard* (Oxford, 1990), A. Lawrie recollection, 81–2.

6. See PRO, HO 186/1512, HSWR no. 66, Home Secretary to Regions, 16 May 1940; INF 1/264, Public Opinion on the Present Crisis: Points from Regions, 24 May 1940, Leeds; *Daily Mail*, 17 May 1940, 3; GLRO, HG1, London Civil Defence Region circular no. 154, 8 June 1940; Glos. RO, 2095/2, L.D.V. 1/40, Conference at Cheltenham, 22 May 1940; Northants RO, HGb/1, V/722/4, County Cmdr to Group Cmdrs, 27 May 1940; Wilts. RO, 2999/4, Chief Warden to Hoore, 15 Nov. 1940; E. Raymond, *Please You, Draw Near: Autobiography 1922–1968* (London, 1969), 71; S. Ward, *War in the Countryside 1939–45* (London, 1988), 129; *The Times*: 16 May 1940, 3; 27 May 1940, 3.

7. Graves, *Home Guard*, 64 ff.; MRC, MSS. 200/F/3/51/22/66, Federation of British Industries correspondence on factory units, May–Aug. 1940; see E. D. Barclay, *The History of the 45th Warwickshire (B'Ham) Battalion Home Guard* (Birmingham, 1945), 7.

8. See HLRO, Beaverbrook Papers, BBK/D/359, *passim*; LHC, Alanbrooke Papers, 3A/IV, 230; PRO, AVIA 15/706, *passim*.

9. *The Times*, 27 May 1940, 3.

10. BUL, Avon Papers, AP/12/2/33C, 'Survey of the Position', BBC broadcast 14 Aug. 1940; Central Statistical Office, *Statistical Digest of the War* (HMSO, 1951), 13, table 15; NLS, MS 3816, f. 400, extract from *Scotsman*, 11 Oct. 1940, quoting letter from Croft to Sir Samuel Chapman, MP; PRO, T 162/864/E1628/1, Humphreys-Davies to Crombie, 14 May 1940; J. Brophy, *Britain's Home Guard: A Character Study* (London, 1945), 17.

11. PRO, WO 199/3237, entry 3, WO telegram 8560 (A.G. 1A), 15 May 1940; Graves, *Home Guard*, 15.

12. PRO, HO 199/264, HSWR no. 66, Home Office to Regions, 16 May 1940.

13. PRO, WO 199/3237, entry 1, Order in Council, Defence (Local Volunteers) Regulations, 17 May 1940.

14. Ibid., entry 6, 27/Gen./2694 (A.G. 1A), Lambert to GOCs, Area Cmdrs, 18 May 1940.
15. B. Collier, *The Defence of the United Kingdom* (HMSO, 1957), 123–4; IWM, J. K. Howard and H. W. Endicott, *Summary Report, British Home Guard* (1941), 10–11.
16. Glos. RO, D2338/2/4, Minutes of the General Purposes Committee, 2 Oct. 1940.
17. Northants RO, HGb1, file 5, Shillito handwritten notes, n/d [*c*. May 1940]. See Graves, *Home Guard*, 15–16.
18. A. G. Street, *From Dusk Till Dawn* (London, 1947), 11; R. D. Brown, *East Anglia 1940* (Lavenham, 1981), 88; P. Lewis, *A People's War* (London, 1986), 31; see J. W. Ogilvy-Dalgleish, *The Rutland Home Guard of 1940– 44* (Oakham, 1955), 5–7.
19. Graves, *Home Guard*, 17; *The Times*, 16 May 1940, 3.
20. See, e.g., J. Lee, 'Early Days in the Home Guard', *The Back Badge* 1 (1946), 61; '*We Also Served*', 63–4; J. Brady, *The History and Record of 'B' Company 10th (Torbay) Battn. Devonshire Home Guard* (Torquay, 1944), 12; *35th City of London Battalion Home Guard* (London, 1946), 1– 2; J. C. Spence, '*They Also Serve': The 39th Cheshire Battalion Home Guard* (London, 1945), 19; Shaw, *We Remember*, L. Jackson recollection, 7; N. Longmate, *How We Lived Then* (London, 1971), 109; D. E. Jackson, *East Anglia at War 1939–1945* (Norwich, 1978), 30; R. D. Brown, *East Anglia 1940* (Lavenham, 1981), 85.
21. H. Gough, 'The Home Guard—Its Early Troubles—How They were Met and Overcome', *Household Brigade Magazine*, Summer 1944, 64; see D. Brownrigg, *Unexpected: A Book of Memories* (London, 1942), 157; H. Gough, *Soldiering On* (London, 1954), 239 ff.; LC, J. Walker Papers, OC 2nd (Staincross) Bn, West Yorks HG to Group Cmdr, 18 Nov. 1940; PRO, INF 1/264, Public Opinion on the Present Crisis, 20 May 1940, 18 May 1940.
22. NLS, MS 3816, f. 268, cutting from *Sunday Graphic*, 29 June 1941; 365 HC (Deb.) 5s, col. 1245; H. L. Wilson, *Four Years: The Story of the 5th Battalion (Caernarvonshire) Home Guard* (Conway, 1945), 34; IWM, Howard and Endicott, *Report*, 15; *Sunday Graphic*, 18 May 1941, 5.
23. Northants RO, HGb3, 'The Story of the Peterborough Home Guard', 2.
24. Ibid., HGb1, file 5, Northamptonshire HG order of battle, 30 Nov. 1940.
25. IWM, PP/MCR/208, Memoirs of J. Farley, 2.
26. I. F. W. Beckett, *The Amateur Military Tradition 1558–1945* (Manchester, 1991), 269; WYAS(H), KC 113/8, OC 1 Platoon to OC 'B' Coy, 2 (West Riding) Bn HG, 6 Nov. 1942; Northants RO, HGb1, file 5, cutting

from *Chronicle & Echo*, 4 Dec. 1944; Suffolk RO (Ipswich), IA1/411/15, roll of 6th Bn Suffolk HG.

27. *Picture Post*, 17 May 1941, 26; see also Northants RO, HGb1, file 5, Northamptonshire HG order of battle, 30 Nov. 1940.

28. GLRO, HG1, LDV—London Area: Provisional List of Inner Zone Organizers.

29. Lewis, *People's War*, 31; L. Mosley, *Backs to the Wall: London Under Fire 1939–45* (London, 1971), 55; see R. Harrison, *Rex: An Autobiography* (London, 1974), 67.

30. LHC, Pownall Diary, 20 June 1940; see F. Law, *A Man at Arms: Memoirs of Two World Wars* (London, 1983).

31. NLS, MS 3816, p. v; HLRO, Beaverbrook Papers, BBK/D/359, Beaverbrook–Eden correspondence, 1940; ibid., HG/1, Record of Service book, Palace of Westminster HG; GLRO, HG1, LDV—London Area: Provisional List of Inner Zone Organizers.

32. 361 HC (Deb.) 5s, col. 9.

33. Berks. RO, Glyn Papers, D/EGL/0149, Glyn to Eden, 22 May 1940.

34. See PRO, HO 199/264, Kerr to Parker, 16 May 1940; WO 199/1886, encl. 121A, DPR to C-in-C HF, 24 May 1940.

35. Wilson, *Four Years*, 22; see PRO, CAB 69/1, DO(40)5, 20 May 1940.

36. 361 HC (Deb.) 5s, col. 331; see PRO, WO 199/3248, Trg Instruction No. 1; PRO, CAB 69/1, DO(40)15, 10 June 1940.

37. Berks. RO, Glyn Papers, D/EGL/0149, Macmillan to Foss, 28 May 1940.

38. PRO, WO 199/3237, encl. 6, Lambert to GOCs, 18 May 1940; see Raymond, *Please You*, 89.

39 PRO, WO 199/3237, entry 54, 54/misc./4454 (O.S.7), 28 June 1940; CAB 106/1202, Notes on Home Defence for Secret Debate in House of Commons, 8 June 1940, sec. H; LHC, Pownall Diary, 20 June 1940.

40. B. G. Holloway (ed.), *The Northamptonshire Home Guard 1940–1945* (Northampton, 1949), 59; Dalgleish, *Rutland Home Guard*, 12.

41. L. W. Kentish, *Bux 4: Records and Reminiscences of the 4th Buckinghamshire Battalion Home Guard* (1945), 20; see Bucks. RO, D113/77, Basden Papers, 'The Home Guard of Farnham Royal', 5; Northants RO, HGb36, H. Banks 'Jordan's Lot: A Saga of the Home Guard', 3; Shaw, *We Remember*, R. Rowberry recollection, 36; Street, *From Dusk*, 17; Holloway, *Northamptonshire Home Guard*, 30; Wilson, *Four Years*, 32; B. Boothby, *Home Guard Goings-On* (London, 1941), 29–30; Ashford Home Guard *O.C.A. Magazine* 1 (3), June 1947, 5; H. Smith, *Bureaucrats in Battledress: A History of the Ministry of Food Home Guard* (Conway, 1945), 23–4; 'We Also Served', 81; Spence, 'They Also Serve', 44.

42. LHC, Pownall Diary, 20 June 1940; see PRO, CAB 106/1202, Memorandum on Preparation for Defence, CRHF 1/2556, 8 June 1940, 3(f).
43. H. J. Wiltsher, *'Ever Faithful': The 1st (Loyal City of Exeter) Battalion, Devon Home Guard, 1940–1945* (Exeter, 1946), 17.
44. K. Martin, *Editor: A Second Volume of Autobiography* (London, 1968), 279.
45. Holloway, *Northamptonshire Home Guard*, 59–60.
46. Gough, *Soldiering On*, 243; see Brophy, *Britain's Home Guard*, 35.
47. PRO, INF 1/264, Public Opinion on the Present Crisis, 15 June 1940.
48. PRO, WO 199/3243, History of the Formation and Organization of the HG, 1.
49. Graves, *Home Guard*, 13.
50. PRO, WO 199/3248, Trg Instruction No. 2, 1; see LC, J. Walker Papers, CRHF 1/1147(G), Notes on German Parachute Troops, HQ HF, 6 June 1940; 361 HC (Debs.) 5s, col. 241.
51. PRO, PREM 3/223/1, Notes on LDV; see Hants RO, 286M87/2, CRAC No. 5/11283/30(G), 7 June 1940.
52. Brady, *History and Record*, 12; Street, *From Dusk*, 14; 'The Watch on the Braids', 6; Kentish, *Bux 4*, 7–9; P. Hallding, 'Early Days', *Choughs Annual Register* 2 (Truro, 1945); *History of the Cheshire Home Guard: From L.D.V. Formation to Stand-Down 1940–1944* (Aldershot, 1950), 69, 96; CPL, LOC 319, Slack Papers, Hints for Home Guards, Aug. 1940; Glos. RO, D5023/3/1, LDV (Painswick Coy), general instructions, n/d [summer 1940].
53 Dalgleish, *Rutland Home Guard*, 8; see Glos. RO, 2095/2, LDV South Midland Area, LDV/D/1, 20 May 1940; Shropshire RO, 3974/173, Official History of 'D' Coy, 3; S. W. Wayman, *With the Home Guard: The History of 'A' (Winchester City) Company 5th Hampshire Battalion* (Winchester, 1945), 16; W. A. D. Englefield, *Limpsfield Home Guard 1940–1945* (London, 1946), 3; see A. Boyd, *A Brief History of the 1st Moray Battalion Home Guard* (1945).
54. Hants RO, 268M87/2, Aldershot Cmd Memo No. 1 on the Duties of the LDV, encl. to CRAC No. 5/11283/2(G), 25 May 1940; IWM, Hawes Papers, 'G' Ops No. 3/336, Eastern Cmd to Regional Commissioners, 20 May 1940; NLS, MS 3819, f. 39, Notes on a Conference, HQ HF, 16 May 1940; see LC, J. Walker Papers, Notes on the Employment of LDV, 21 May 1940, SO LDV, Yorks. Area; J. Jellen, 'The Home Guard', *Journal of the Royal United Services Institution*, May 1944, 127.
55. *The Story of No. 2 Company of the 7th Battn. Somerset Home Guard* (1944).

56. LHC, Liddell Hart Papers, 1/112/35, Brophy to Liddell Hart, 15 Aug. 1940.

57. Northants RO, HGb1, Mellows to Wake, 27 June 1940; see Boyd, *Brief History*, 8; Spence, *'They Also Serve'*, 55.

58. PRO, WO 199/3243, History of the Formation and Organization of the HG, 2; Gough, *Soldiering On*, 243; Brownrigg, *Unexpected*, 157; Wiltsher, *Ever Faithful*, 21–2.

59. Gough, *Soldiering On*, 243; J. Wedgwood, *Memories of a Fighting Life* (London, 1941), 248.

60. *'We Also Served'*, 51. Gough was teaching the Chelsea LDV to throw imaginary hand grenades in the expectation that the real thing would eventually be issued as an offensive weapon. See Harrison, *Rex*, 67.

61. Leics. RO, DE 3620/17, 6/SECRET L.F./44, 22 June 1940.

62. 116 HL (Debs.) 5s, cols. 467–86.

63. 362 HC (Debs.) 5s, col. 62.

64. PRO, CAB 106/1202, Speech by J. C. Wedgwood, June/July 1940; see also C. Mackenzie, *My Life and Times, Octave 8, 1938–1946* (London, 1969), 95.

65. 361 HC (Debs.) 5s, col. 757; 362 HC (Debs.) 5s, cols. 281–3, 458, 645, 686, 1052–7, 1105; 376 HC (Debs.) 5s, col. 2136.

66. *Picture Post*, 20 July 1940, 34.

67. Hants RO, 286M87/2, Memo to Platoon Cmdrs, ref. to CRAC 5/11283/2(G), 11 June 1940.

68. PRO, PREM 3/223/3, HG, Weekly Return for week ending 1 Aug. 1940; ibid., Weekly Return for week ending 13 July 1940.

69. J. R. Colville, *Man of Valour: The Life of Field-Marshal The Viscount Gort* (London, 1972), 231; PRO, WO 199/3237, entry 68, 54/Misc./4448 (F1), 8 July 1940.

70. 116 HL (Debs.) 5s, cols. 486–7.

71. 362 HC (Debs.) 5s, col. 686.

72. PRO, WO 199/3234, Trg Instruction No. 8, July 1940; ibid., Trg Instruction No. 10, July 1940; see LC, J. Walker Papers, SO, LDV, Yorks. Area, to County Cmdrs, 15 July 1940; CCRO, CDX/429/2, OPs Orders, 'A' Coy, 3 (Carmarthenshire) Bn HG, 20 Apr. 1941.

73. T. Holman, 'Looking Back', *Choughs Annual Register* 2 (1945); see Englefield, *Limpsfield Home Guard*, 5; Brophy, *Britain's Home Guard*, 16; Shaw, *We Remember*, A. Lawrie recollection, 83; N. R. Bishop, *'An Honour to Serve': A Short History of the 8th Surrey (Reigate) Battalion Home Guard May 1940–December 1944* (n/d), 11.

74. PRO, PREM 3/223/3, HG weekly returns for 13 July, 1 Aug. 1940.

75. N. Nicolson (ed.), *Harold Nicolson: Diaries and Letters 1939–1945* (London, 1967), 103–4; see LHC, Pownall Diary, 8 July, 13 July 1940.
76. PRO, PREM 3/223/3, Morton to Churchill, 13 June 1940; see Berks. RO, Glyn Papers, D/EGL/0149, Glyn to Morton, 23 May 1940.
77. Wedgwood, *Memories*, 248.
78. PRO, CAB 67/7, WM 170(40)9, 17 June 1940; ibid., PREM 3/223/3, Bridges to Churchill, 18 June 1940; see W. S. Churchill, *The Second World War, II: Their Finest Hour* (London, 1949), 235.
79. PRO, PREM 3/223/3, Churchill to Eden, 22 June 1940.
80. Ibid., 26 June 1940; H. Morrison, *An Autobiography* (London, 1969), 185; see M. Gilbert, *Finest Hour: Winston S. Churchill, 1939–1940* (London, 1983), 600.
81. N. Longmate, *How We Lived Then: A History of Everyday Life during the Second World War* (London, 1971), 103.
82. Bod. L., Woolton Papers, Diary, Box 2, 30 Nov. 1940; see Beardmore, *Civilians*, 109–10; Chandos, *The Memoirs of Lord Chandos* (London, 1972), 99; D. Reynolds, 'Churchill in 1940: The Worst and Finest Hour', in R. Blake and Wm. R. Louis (eds.), *Churchill* (New York, 1993), 254; I. Berlin, *Mr. Churchill in 1940* (Boston, 1950), 24, 26–7; L. Thompson, *1940: Year of Legend, Year of History* (London, 1966), 138–40.
83. J. Colville, *The Fringes of Power: Downing Street Diaries, 1939–1955* (London, 1985), 275.
84. See E. Barker, *Churchill and Eden at War* (London, 1978), 17–20; LHC, Kirke Papers, 20/3, 13.
85. PRO, PREM, 3/223/3 [also BUL, AP/20/8/20], Churchill to Eden, 27 June 1940; Ismay, *The Memoirs of Lord Ismay* (London, 1960), 187.
86. PRO, PREM 3/223/3 [also BUL, AP/20/8/30], Eden to Churchill, 28 June 1940.
87. Ibid., Churchill to Cooper, n/d; see also BUL, Avon Papers, AP/20/8/43A, Eden comments on PM's letter to Cooper.
88. Ibid., Cooper to Churchill, 3 July 1940.
89. Ibid., Seal to Edwards, 16 July 1940; Churchill to Cooper, 6 July 1940.
90. See, e.g., *The Times*, 29 July 1940, 5; Wiltsher, *Ever Faithful*, 21; Street, *From Dusk*, 42; Dalgleish, *Rutland Home Guard*, 12; Wilson, *Four Years*, 36; see also Ismay, *Memoirs*, 187; H. Agar, *Britain Alone: June 1940–June 1941* (London, 1972), 67.
91. LHC, Pownall Diary, 29 July 1940.
92. PRO, INF 1/208, LDV Film Scenario and notes, 20 July 1940; see D. Lindsay, *Forgotten General: A Life of Andrew Thorne* (London, 1987), 80.
93. BUL, Avon Papers, AP/20/1/20A, diary entry 22 July 1940.

94. PRO, CAB 69/8, 190(40)4, 1 July 1940.

95. Churchill, 235, 237; BUL, Avon Papers, AP/20/8/68, Churchill to Eden, 20 July 1940.

96. PRO, PREM 3/223/3, Churchill to Eden, 11 Aug. 1940; ibid., Churchill to Ismay, 2 Aug. 1940; ibid., Morton to Ismay, 9 July 1940.

97. Id., 15 July 1940, 5; id., 16 July 1940, 5.

98. BUL, Avon Papers, AP/8/91, Churchill to Eden, 11 Aug. 1940. In the end it was decided to stick to the idea of county regiment badges.

99. Ibid., AP/20/8/68, Eden to Churchill, 22 July 1940.

100. LHC, Pownall Diary, 12 Aug. 1940; see Gough, *Soldiering On*, 243; Wedgwood, *Memories*, 248.

101. Vt. Bridgeman, 'The Home Guard', *Journal of the Royal United Services Institution* 87 (1942), 141.

Chapter 4

1. H. L. Wilson, *Four Years: The Story of the 5th Battalion (Caernarvonshire) Home Guard* (Conway, 1945), 36.

2. *Daily Herald*, 6 July 1940, 2.

3. LHC, Pownall Diary, 20 June 1940; Vt. Bridgeman, 'The Home Guard', *Journal of the Royal United Services Institution* 87 (1942), E. Grigg comment, 151.

4. B. Collier, *The Defence of the United Kingdom* (HMSO, 1957), 123–4.

5. See, e.g., J. Leasor (ed.), *War at the Top: Based on the Experiences of General Sir Leslie Hollis* (London, 1959), 97; S. Milligan, *Adolf Hitler: My Part in His Downfall* (London, 1971), 38; W. P. Crozier, *Off the Record: Political Interviews 1933–1943*, ed. A. J. P. Taylor (London, 1973), 184.

6. PRO, CAB 106/1202, Ironside to Dill, 11 June 1940.

7. R. Macleod and D. Kelly (eds.), *The Ironside Diaries 1937–1940* (London, 1962), 343.

8. Hants RO, Aldershot Cmd Memo No. 1 on the Duties of the LDV, encl. to CRAC No. 5/11283/2(G), 25 May 1940; IWM, Hawes Papers, 'G' OPs No. 3/336, Eastern Cmd to Regional Commissioners, 20 May 1940.

9. Northants RO, HGb1, LDV Instruction No. 2; see Glos. RO, 2095/2, LDV/D/1, South Midland Area instruction, 20 May 1940.

10. D. Lindsay, *Forgotten General: A Life of Andrew Thorne* (London, 1987), 139–40, 143.

11. *The Times*, 24 July 1940, 9.

12. LHC, Alanbrooke Papers, 5/3/1, Diary, 29 June 1940.

13. LHC, see Pownall Diary, 27 Aug. 1940.

14. J. Connell, *Auchinleck* (London, 1959), 167 ff.; Glos. RO, D2095/2, Southern Cmd Ops Instruction No. 27, 7 Sept. 1940.

15. Interview with R. Parkinson, quoted in *The Auk: Auchinleck, Victor of Alamein* (London, 1977), 57.

16. J. Colville, *The Fringes of Power: Downing Street Diaries, 1939–1955* (London, 1985), 192–3.

17. See N. Hamilton, *Monty: The Making of a General 1887–1942* (London, 1981), 424–5, 444.

18. F. Morgan, *Peace and War: A Soldier's Life* (London, 1961), 140.

19. LC, J. Walker Papers, GOC 44th Div. to County Commander, West Riding HG, 3 Sept. 1940.

20. B. Horrocks, *A Full Life* (London, 1974), 96; see F. Law, *A Man at Arms: Memoirs of Two World Wars* (London, 1983), 169, 180; IWM, PP/MCR/182, Memoirs of Major-General Douglas Wimberley 2, 13; Glos. RO, D2095/1, Bn Order 2, 14 June 1940, para. 12; *The Times*, 24 July 1940, 9.

21. Leasor, *War at the Top*, 97.

22. See, e.g., n. 9; ch. 3, n. 53, n. 54; NLS, MS 3816, HG Branch HQ, Scottish Cmd May 1940–Mar. 1945: Brief Account, 1; Connell, *Auchinleck*, 343.

23. PRO, WO 199/3248, LDV Trg Instruction No. 2, June 1940; see ibid., INF 1/208, Seaton Section LDV: Standing Orders; Northants RO, HGb1, LDV Zone Instruction No. 2, May 1940; Glos. RO, 2095/2, Local Defence Volunteers, South Midland Area, LDV/D/1, 20 May 1940. A sense of the continuing anxiety over the Fifth Column can be gained from the brief written by the novelist Dennis Wheatley for the Joint Planning Staff on likely German tactics in June 1940. See D. Wheatley, *Stranger Than Fiction* (London, 1976), 65.

24. *Sunday Express*, 19 May 1940, 7; see *Sunday Pictorial*, 9 June 1940; *Daily Herald*, 20 May 1940, 5; *Daily Express*, May–June 1940, *passim*; F. and J. Shaw (comps.), *We Remember the Home Guard* (Oxford, 1990), H. K. Burnet recollection, 30.

25. *Daily Mail*, 15 May 1940, 4; see *Daily Herald*, 8 June 1940, 8, *passim*; *Daily Express*, 22 May 1940, 1, *passim*; *News of the World*, 9 June 1940, 6, *passim*.

26. E. R. Murrow, *This is London* (New York, 1941), 102; see also M. Panter-Downes, *London War Notes, 1939–1945* (New York, 1961), 63, 66.

27. M. Allingham, *The Oaken Heart* (London, 1941), 206.

28. Murrow, *This is London*, 210–11.

29. PRO, INF 1/264, Public Opinion on the Present Crisis: Morale in the Regions, 22 May 1940; see ibid., 24 May 1940; ibid., INF 1/254, Home Morale Emergency Committee, 4 June 1940.

30. Glos. RO, D5023/3/1, LDV (Painswick Coy) General Instructions, June 1940.

31. Ibid., D2095/2, Adj., Gloucester Bn to Coy, Platoon and Section Cmdrs, 4 Nov. 1940.

32. Ibid., D2095/1, Bn. Order 13, 18 Sept. 1940.

33. GLRO, HG1, LDV Area Organizer, London Area, to manufacturers and utility companies, encl. B, para. 8, 30 May 1940.

34. Hants RO, 286M87/2, Notes of a Meeting between the C-in-C, HF, and the Leaders of the LDV, June 1940 [printed]. Ironside, it should be noted, was by no means alone in official circles in expressing such sentiments. See Wheatley, *Stranger Than Fiction*, 92, 101.

35. H. Smith, *Bureaucrats in Battledress: A History of the Ministry of Food Home Guard* (Conway, 1945), 12; NLS, MS 3818, f. 93, Record of Zone I (City of Glasgow) HG, Glasgow Area; ibid., MS 3816, HG Branch, HQ, Scottish Cmd, May 1940–Mar. 1945: Brief Account, 2.

36. PRO, HO 45/25113, Extracts from a memorandum made at General Ironside's LDV Conference at York, 6 June 1940; see also IWM, Ingram Papers, 84/7/1, Lecture to Beneden Coy, 22 June 1940.

37. P. Hallding, 'Early Days', *Choughs Annual Register* 2 (1945); see J. Burke, *Rights and Powers of the Home Guard* (London, 1940), 4–5.

38. PRO, HO 45/25113, sub-file 863601/22, Egan to Baker, 13 June 1940.

39. G. Beardmore, *Civilians at War: Journals, 1938–1946* (London, 1984), 69; see Shaw, *We Remember*, K. Palmer recollection, 163.

40. K. Macksey, *Armoured Crusader: A Biography of Major-General Sir Percy Hobart* (London, 1967), 179; NLS, MS 3816, cutting from *Scottish Daily Express*, 15 Aug. 1940; see PRO, INF 1/264, Public Opinion on the Present Crisis: Points from Regions, North-East, 3 July 1940; *Sunday Pictorial*, 2 June 1940, 7; N. Gelb, *Scramble: A Narrative History of the Battle of Britain* (London, 1985), 82–3; D. E. Johnson, *East Anglia at War 1939–1945* (Norwich, 1978), 28; F. Archer, *When Village Bells Were Silent* (London, 1975), 74–5.

41. See *Daily Herald*, 16 Aug. 1940, 3.

42. Reproduced in *British Legion Journal* 20 (1940), 64.

43. Bucks. RO, Basden Papers, D113/77, 'The Home Guard of Farnham Royal', 4.

44. H. Scott, *Your Obedient Servant* (London, 1959), 134; PRO, CAB 79/6, COS(40)304, 10 Sept. 1940; see LC, J. Walker Papers, Walker to Ridley-Smith, 4 June 1940; ibid., YA 7517/11, SO HG (Yorks. Area) to Group Cmdrs, 7 Sept. 1940.

45. PRO, MEPO 2/7013, encl. 1B; LC, J. Walker Papers, Vaughn to Walker,

15 June, 6 Aug. 1940; *Daily Herald*, 13 July 1940, 3; J. Jellen, 'The Home Guard', *Journal of the Royal United Services Institution*, May 1944, 128; *The Watch on the Braids: The Record of an Edinburgh Home Guard Company 1940–1944* (Edinburgh, 1945), 9; S. Schiminski and H. Treece (eds.), *Leaves in the Storm: A Book of Diaries* (London, 1947), 68.

46. Bn Order 12, quoted in A. St. H. Brock (ed.), *7th Hertfordshire Battalion Home Guard: A History of the Battalion, 1940–44* (1945), 3; see Northants RO, HGb1, County Instruction no. 8, 11 June 1940, para. 3; Shaw, *We Remember*, L. C. Jeffries recollection, 80–1; BRL, MS 1383/2/11, 2 Platoon report, 17 Aug. 1940; A. G. Street, *From Dusk Till Dawn* (London, 1947), 35–8; 'We Also Served': The Story of the Home Guard in Cambridgeshire and the Isle of Ely, 1940–1943* (Cambridge, 1944), 78–9; *The Story of the First Berkshire (Abingdon) Battalion Home Guard* (Manchester, 1945), 16; P. Hallding, 'Early Days', *Choughs Annual Register* 2 (1945); see also *Sunday Pictorial*, 25 Aug. 1940, for the Gort episode.

47. See PRO, HO 45/25113, sub-file 86360/22, James to Baker, 13 June 1940; B. G. Holloway (ed.), *The Northamptonshire Home Guard 1940–1945* (Northampton, 1949), 67.

48. P. Fleming, *Invasion 1940: An Account of the German Preparations and the British Counter-measures* (London, 1957), 68, n. 2.

49. PRO, INF 1/264, Public Opinion on the Present Crisis: Points from Regions—North-East, 10 June 1940.

50. LC, J. Walker Papers, CRNC 2/18259/G/LDV, Northern Command circular 14 June 1940.

51. *Daily Herald*, 22 June 1940, 5.

52. *Daily Worker*: 29 June 1940, 2; 26 June 1940, 2.

53. Johnson, *East Anglia*, 28–9.

54. See LC, J. Walker Papers, CRNC 2/18259/G/LDV, Northern Cmd to Area HQs, 14 June 1940; ibid., Chief Constable to County Cmdr, 10 June 1940; *News of the World*, 4 Nov. 1940, 3; Northants RO, HGb1, County Instruction no. 18, 2 July 1940; J. C. Spence, 'They Also Serve': The 39th Cheshire Battalion Home Guard* (London, 1945), 44; Street, *From Dusk*, 34, 32; M. Glover, *Invasion Scare 1940* (London, 1990), 3; 'We Also Served', 78; *Ashford Home Guard O.C.A. Magazine* 3 (2) Aug. 1949, 6–7; N. R. Bishop, 'An Honour to Serve': A Short History of the 8th Surrey (Reigate) Battalion Home Guard, May 1940–December 1944* (Reigate, 1945), 21; R. D. Brown, *East Anglia 1940* (Lavenham, 1981), 92; A. W. B. Simpson, *In the Highest Degree Odious: Detention without Trial in Wartime Britain* (Oxford, 1992), 108; Shropshire RO, 3974/173, History of 'D' Company: Incidents.

55. R. Hough and D. Richards, *The Battle of Britain: The Jubilee History* (London, 1989), 195. Nicolson was awarded the Victoria Cross.

56. Northants RO, HGb48, County Cmdr to Group and Bn Cmdrs, 10 Oct. 1940.

57. H. J. Wiltsher, *'Ever Faithful': The 1st (Loyal City of Exeter) Battalion, Devon Home Guard, 1940–1945* (Exeter, 1946), 18; see Shaw, *We Remember*, L. Jackson recollection, 7; ibid., B. McGill recollection, 266–7; *Sunday Pictorial*, 1 Sept. 1940, 16; Wilson, *Four Years*, 50; J. R. Williams, *A Record of Service, No. 1 Battalion (Denbighshire) Home Guard* (Conway, 1943), 20; J. W. Ogilvy-Dalgleish, *The Rutland Home Guard of 1940–44* (Oakham, 1955), 19–20; *The Story of No. 2 Company of the 7th Battn. Somerset Home Guard* (1944), 18; J. Brady, *The History and Record of 'B' Company 10th (Torbay) Battn. Devonshire Home Guard* (Torquay, 1944), 19–20, 25; C. Browne, *12th Battalion Northumberland Home Guard, 'C' Company 1940–1944* (Gateshead-on-Tyne), 8; Smith, *Bureaucrats*, 8; PRO, INF 1/264, Points from Regions—Bristol, 5 July 1940; Northants RO, HGb36, H. Banks, 'Jordan's Lot: A Saga of the Home Guard', 96–7; Hants RO, 268M87/1, Binstead LDV Log Book, 8 Sept. 1940; WYRS(H), KC 113/13, Orderly Officer Report, B Coy, 2Bn, 29 Aug. 1940; Wilts. RO, 2099/4, Brown to Knoll, n/d; CRO, DDX 445/1, Log Book, 29 July 1940, *passim*; BRL, MS 1383/2/1, 11, power station reports, *passim*; N. Longmate, *The Real Dad's Army* (London, 1974), 34.

58. See n. 1, above.

59. Chester City RO, CR 528/1, Memo: Reported Parachute Landing by Enemy Troops, 11 Sept. 1940; ibid., No. 1 Coy, Memo no. 6, 27 Sept. 1940.

60. C. Mackenzie, *My Life and Times, Octave 8, 1938–1946* (London, 1969), 100–1; Collier, *Defence*, 223–4; *Evening Dispatch*, 9 Aug. 1940, 1; Spence, *'They Also Serve'*, 47; CCRO, CDX/429/2, circular, OC 3Bn Carmarthenshire HG, 2 Dec. 1940.

61. *Daily Herald*, 9 Sept. 1940, 1.

62. See W. Ansel, *Hitler Confronts England* (Durham, NC, 1960); *Daily Express*, 15 Aug. 1940, 1.

63. Chester City RO, CR 528/1, No. 1 Coy, Memo no. 6, 27 Sept. 1940; Hough, *Battle of Britain*, 195; see Schiminski, *Leaves*, 50; J. Lehmann, *I am My Brother* (New York, 1960), 68–9.

64. Northants RO, HGb1, Instruction no. 2, n/d; see ibid., no. 6, 10 June 1940; Glos. RO, D2095/1, Bn Order no. 3, 24 June 1940; LC, J. Walker Papers, YA 7517/7, SO HG (Yorks Area) to Group Cmdrs, 6 Sept. 1940.

65. Suffolk RO (Ipswich), HD 1012/1, Summary of HF/1/422/2 by OC 8th Bn, 6 Nov. 1940.

66. Leics. RO, DE 3620/24, LF/3/40/159, SO to Group Cmdrs, 1 July 1940; Glos. RO, D2095/1, Bn. Order no. 11, 5 Sept. 1940; Northants RO, HGb1, Instruction no. 8, 11 June 1940; GLRO, HG/1, H.F./192/OPs., L.D.V. 113, LDV HQ to Zone Cmdrs, 24 July 1940.

67. LC, J. Walker Papers, County Cmdr to Group Cmdrs, 14 June 1940.

68. GLRO, LCC Bn. Instruction no. 5, app. B; see Northants RO, HGb1, Instruction no. 18, 2 July 1940.

69. IWM, Ingram Papers, Orders for 14 July 1940, f. 37; Northants RO, HGb1, Instruction no. 31, 3 Aug. 1940.

70. Collier, *Defence*, 223–4.

71. PRO, MEPO 2/7013, encl. 1B, Police Federation, 'V' Division, New Maldon Station, resolutions passed 25 June 1940.

72. See Berks. RO, Glyn Papers, D/EGL/0169, Glyn to Legge, 29 Aug. 1940; Wilson, *Four Years*, 23; *Evening News*, 14 Oct. 1940, 3.

73. PRO, MEPO 2/7013, encl. 3A, Whitehead to Game, 3 July 1940; ibid., Game to Sergison-Brooke, 1 July 1940.

74. Ibid., encl. 6B [or GLRO, HG/1], London Area LDV HQ to Zone Cmdrs, 6 July 1940; ibid., encl. 5B, Game to Whitehead, 6 July 1940; encl. 4A, Game to Sergison-Brooke, 4 July 1940; ibid., Game to Whitehead, 4 July 1940.

75. See, e.g., LC, J. Walker Papers, correspondence between Chief Constable, Yorks West Riding and County HG Cmdr, June–Sept. 1940.

76. P. Sillitoe, *Cloak without Dagger* (London, 1955), 146–7.

77. *Daily Express*, 16 Aug. 1940, 2; see Morgan, *Peace and War*, 140.

78. LC, J. Walker Papers, OC 2Bn Otley Group HG to Otley Group HQ, 16 Dec. 1940; see ibid., Chief Constable, Yorks West Riding to County Cmdr, 23 Nov. 1940.

79. PRO, WO 199/360, minute 33, Lt.-Gen. H. G. Lloyd to BGS (Ops), 3 March 1941.

80. P. Mayhew (ed.), *One Family's War* (London, 1985), 69; see IWM, PP/MCR/208, J. Farley memoir, 2; Northants RO, HGb36, H. Banks, 'Jordan's Lot: A Saga of the Home Guard', 72.

81. W. F. Stirling, *Safety Last* (London, 1953), 191.

82. See Chester City RO, CR 501/1, Western Cmd HG Orders, no. 2, 7 May 1941 (ACI 544/1941); NLS, MS 3818(I), f. 338; *Illustrated London News*, 24 Aug. 1940, 250.

83. T. Hopkinson, *Of This Our Time* (London, 1982), 179; HLRO,

Beaverbrook Papers, BBK/D/359, Beaverbrook to Eden, 3 Oct. 1940; ibid., Eden to Beaverbrook, 2 Oct. 1940.

84. Ibid.
85. LHC, Alanbrooke Papers, 3A/IV, Notes on My Life 4, 230; see PRO, AVIA 16/656, PAS(MF) minute, 1 July 1940, *passim*. Only in early 1941 were MAP armoured cars passed over to the Army.
86. Berks. RO, Glyn Papers, D/EGL/0151, Glyn to Wells, 27 June 1940; see ibid., D/EGI/0155, Glyn to Currey, 25 July 1940.
87. See LHC, Pownall Diary, 19 Aug. 1940; WO 199/1889, encl. 1130A.
88. BUL, Avon Papers, AP/20/8/76, Churchill to Eden, 27 July 1940.
89. PRO, PREM 3/223/13, Churchill to Eden, 13 Aug. 1940; see ibid., Eden to Churchill, 21 Aug. 1940; ibid., Sandys to Churchill, 7 Aug. 1940.

Chapter 5

1. G. Orwell, 'The Home Guard and You', *Tribune*, 20 Dec. 1940, 8.
2. PRO, WO 163/414, Report of a Sub-Committee of the AC to consider questions relating to the HG, Oct. 1940, para. 42.
3. See *Picture Post*, 17 May 1941, 26.
4. *Daily Worker*: 29 May 1940, 3; 17 May 1940, 3. This was also the line taken by other far-left parties such as the Trotskyist Workers' International League. [MRC, MSS. 75/3/2/2–3.]
5. *Volunteer for Liberty* 7, July 1940, 1.
6. See 'Cato' [W. Charlton, M. Foot, P. Howard], *Guilty Men* (London, 1940); *Daily Express*, 21 June 1940, 4.
7. Quoted in H. Agar, *Britain Alone: June 1940–June 1941* (London, 1972), 79.
8. PRO, INF 1/264, Public Opinion on the Present Crisis: Points from Regions, North-East, 18 June 1940; see ibid, May–Aug., *passim*.
9. F. Warburg, *All Authors are Equal* (London, 1973), 36–7.
10. Orwell, 'Home Guard and You', 9; see M. Sheldon, *Orwell: The Authorized Biography* (New York, 1991), 326–7.
11. T. Wintringham, 'The Lessons of Spain', *Picture Post*, 15 June 1940, 24.
12. Id., 'The Home Guard Can Fight', *Picture Post*, 21 Sept. 1940, 10.
13. T. Hopkinson, *Of This Our Time* (London, 1987), 177–8.
14. See D. Fernbach, 'Tom Wintringham and Socialist Defence Strategy', *History Workshop* 14 (1982), 76; *Picture Post*, 21 Sept. 1940, 9, *passim*; *Daily Herald*: 26 Aug. 1940, 3; 10 Sept. 1940, 3; *Illustrated London News*, 10 Aug. 1940, cover; *Sphere*, 10 Aug. 1940, 172–3; Chester City RO, CR 528/1, Notes on a Course for HG Instructors at Osterley Park, 8–10 Oct. 1940; *British Legion Journal*, 20 (1940), 92–3.

15. See J. Langdon-Davies, *Parachutes over Britain* (London, 1940); id., *Fifth Column* (London, 1940).

16. *Sunday Pictorial*: 6 Oct. 1940, 17; Sept.–Mar. 1941, *passim*.

17. *Picture Post*: 13 July 1940, 3; 6 July 1940, 43–5; 27 July 1940, 5.

18. Ibid., 12 Oct. 1940, 3; see Berks. RO, Glyn Papers, D/EGL/0149, Glyn to E. Grigg, 4 Sept. 1940; D. Wheatley, *Stranger Than Fiction* (London, 1976), 187.

19. H. Smith, *Bureaucrats in Battledress: A History of the Ministry of Food Home Guard* (Conway, 1945), 29.

20. PRO, WO 199/3243, History of the Formation and Organization of the HG, 4; HO 45/25009, ref. 700.169/62, minute, 18 Sept. 1951; WO 199/ 3238, encl. 125A. Though see 364 HC (Deb.) 5s, col. 975.

21. PRO, WO 165/92, LDV Inspectorate meeting 8, 16 July 1940, item 14; see ibid., meeting 7, 12 July 1940, item 18.

22. F. H. Hinsley and C. A. G. Simkins, *British Intelligence in the Second World War, 4: Security and Counter-Intelligence* (HMSO, 1990), 57, 65 ff.

23. Hopkinson, *Of This*, 178–9; Fernbach, 'Tom Wintringham', 73.

24. Warburg, *All Authors*, 37.

25. *Picture Post*, 21 Sept. 1940, 10; PRO, WO 199/3237, encl. 303, circular to all officers HG Inspectorate, 3 Aug. 1940.

26. See LHC, Pownall Diary, 12 Aug. 1940.

27. LC, J. Walker Papers, YA 7517/7, encl. 27/LDV/10 (TA1), 6 July 1940; ibid., YA 7517/5, encl. TA 2/BM/941, 5 July 1940.

28. PRO, CAB 140/118, Latham to Butler, 12 May 1949; WO 165/92, HG directorate meeting 21, 10 Sept. 1940; WO 199/3237, encl. 371, MT 7 circular, 12 Sept. 1940; T 162/864/E41628/1, Ottley to Crombie, 11 Sept. 1940, 26 Sept. 1940; see *Picture Post*: 21 Sept. 1940, 10; 14 Sept. 1940, 32.

29. J. Langdon-Davies, *Home Guard Warfare* (London, 1941), ix.

30. See Smith, *Bureaucrats*, 42.

31. Langdon-Davies, *Home Guard Warfare*, ix; see id., *The Home Guard Training Manual* (London, 1940), publisher's note.

32. PRO, WO 199/3248, HG Instruction No. 20, Nov. 1940; ibid., HG Instruction No. 26, Mar. 1941; 364 HC (Deb.) 5s, col. 975; 365 HC (Deb.) 5s, cols. 1355, 1426. Books not on the list of approved titles included *The Art of Guerrilla Fighting and Patrol* (London, 1940) and *The Home Guard Handbook* (London, 1941) by Alfred Kerr, *Rights and Powers of the Home Guard* (London 1940) by John Burke, and *The Home Guard Encyclopedia* (London, 1941) by Andrew G. Elliot. John Brophy, on the other hand, author of *Home Guard: A Handbook for the L.D.V.* (London,

1940), *A Home Guard Drill Book and Field Service Manual* (London, 1940), and *Advanced Training for the Home Guard* (London, 1941), submitted his manuscripts to the War Office [see *Advanced Training*, 9] and later authored a highly romanticized history of the Home Guard after the war (*Britain's Home Guard: A Character Study* (London, 1945)).

33. See LC, J. Walker Papers, YA 7517/5, 30 June 1940, encl. 79/HD/1299(TA1), 19 June 1940; 365 HC (Deb.) 5s, col. 1355; LHC, Liddell Hart Papers, 1/112, Brophy–Liddell Hart correspondence, 1940–2, *passim*; H. Slater, *Home Guard for Victory!* (London, 1941); Orwell's review of Slater, *New Statesman* 21 (1941), 168; *Sunday Pictorial*, Home Guard Parade column, *passim*.

34. See LHC, Liddell Hart Papers, 1/112/73, Brophy to Liddell Hart, 18 Nov. 1941; ibid., 1/112/77, Brophy to Liddell Hart, 31 Mar. 1942.

35. *Daily Mirror*, 21 Sept. 1941, 1; *Sunday Pictorial*, 17 Aug. 1941, 14; PRO, WO 199/3248, HG Instruction No. 26, Mar. 1941.

36. LHC, Pownall Diary, 19 Aug. 1940; PRO, WO 199/3237, encl. 303, circular to all officers Inspectorate HG, 3 Aug. 1940; see J. H. Levey, *Home Guard Training: Some Lessons to Teach and Learn* (London, 1940), foreword and preface.

37. LHC, Pownall Diary, 29 Sept. 1940; PRO, CAB 69/1, DO(40)30, 3 Sept. 1940.

38. PRO, WO 163/414, Report of a Sub-Committee of the AC convened to consider questions relating to the HG, Oct. 1940.

39. Bod. L., E. Grigg Papers, reel 14, Grigg to Bracken, 2 Nov. 1940.

40. PRO, T 162/864/E41628/1, Bovenschen to Barlow, 1 Nov. 1941, encl. Churchill minute, 20 Oct. 1940.

41. Bod. L., E. Grigg Papers, reel 14, Churchill to Grigg, 5 Nov. 1940; ibid., 4 Nov. 1940.

42. 365 HC (Deb.) 5s, cols. 1347–53.

43. *Punch* 169 (1940), 481.

44. *The Times*, 21 Aug. 1940, 5; see H. Gough, *Soldiering On* (London, 1954), 224–5.

45. See H. J. Wiltsher, 'Ever Faithful': The 1st (Loyal City of Exeter) Battalion, Devon Home Guard, 1940–1945 (Exeter, 1946), 39; *British Legion Journal*, 20 (1940), 147; PRO, INF 1/264, Public Opinion on the Present Crisis: Points from Regions, Eastern, 21 June 1940; 364 HC (Deb.) 5s, col. 1489; 365 HC (Deb.) 5s, cols. 88–9, 1353–4.

46. See Berks. RO, Glyn Papers, D/EGL/0149, Bisgood circular, 21 Aug. 1940, encl. to Glyn to Grigg, 4 Sept. 1940; Wiltsher, 'Ever Faithful', 42; *A History of the 44th London (London Transport) Battalion of the Home Guard 1940–1946* (London, 1948), 19; J. Lee, 'Early Days in the Home

Guard', *The Back Badge*, 1 (1946), 62; *British Legion Journal* 20 (1940), 147; *Daily Herald*: 29 Aug. 1940, 3; 7 Sept. 1940, 3.

47. D. Brownrigg, *Unexpected: A Book of Memories* (London, 1942), 161–2; see LC, J. Walker Papers, Group Cmdrs, Upper Agbrigg Group to West Riding Zone HQ, 29 Jan. 1941; *Defence* [incorporating *Home Guard Monthly*] 3 (6) (1941), 9.

48. *Tribune*, 20 Dec. 1940, 8; see also A. Albu, 'The Place of the Home Guard', *Tribune*, 16 Oct. 1940, 10–11; Hants RO, 268 M87/3, loose sheet, 'I have viewed with distrust . . .', n/d [c. early 1941].

49. Berks. RO, Glyn Papers, D/EGL/0149, E. Grigg to Glyn, 12 Sept. 1940; see *Sunday Graphic*, 2 Mar. 1941, 5; *Daily Herald*, 3 Sept. 1940, 2; *Sunday Pictorial*, 22 Sept. 1940, 17; Hants RO, 268 M87/3, loose sheet, 'I have viewed with distrust . . .'; 'Home Guardsmen Demand Efficient Leadership', *Millgate* 36 (1940), 96–9.

50. *The Times*, 15 Jan. 1941, 7.

51. 367 HC (Deb.) 5s, cols. 304–5.

52. See, e.g., H. L. Wilson, *Four Years: The Story of the 5th Battalion (Caernarvonshire) Home Guard* (Conway, 1945), 83.

53. 369 HC (Deb.) 5s, cols. 348–9, 578, 1129.

54. See PRO, T 162/864/E41628/1, DUS to PUS, 5 Nov. 1940.

55. 369 HC (Deb.) 5s, col. 1129; see 371 HC (Deb.) 5s, col. 578, 713.

56. 365 HC (Deb.) 5s, col. 1245.

57. See, e.g., BUL, Avon Papers, AP 20/8/198, Churchill to Dill, 20 Oct. 1940.

58. PRO, PREM 3/223/4, Churchill to Dill, 19 Oct. 1940.

59. Ibid., Dill to Churchill, 21 Oct. 1940.

60. Ibid., Eden to Churchill, 22 Oct. 1940.

61. Ibid., Churchill to Dill, 6 Nov. 1940.

62. Ibid., Eden to Churchill, 16 Nov. 1940.

63. IWM, J. K. Howard and H. W. Endicott, *Summary Report, British Home Guard* (1941), 12.

64. J. Leutze (ed.), *The London Observer: The Journal of General Raymond E. Lee 1940–1941* (London, 1971), 429.

65. See MRC, MSS. 292/881.423/5, Con. Cttee. M.O.L. 22/4, 14 May 1941.

66. E. Summerskill, *A Woman's World* (London, 1967), 73; D. Lampe, *The Last Ditch* (London, 1968), 5–6; R. Minns, *Bombers and Mash: The Domestic Front 1939–45* (London, 1980), 55; see Brownrigg, *Unexpected*, 158; Berks. RO, Glyn Papers, D/EGL/0152, Ross to Glyn, 10 July 1940; F. and J. Shaw (comps.), *We Remember the Home Guard* (Oxford, 1990), Mrs L. V. Baker recollection, 103–5.

67. E. R. Murrow, *This is London* (New York, 1941), 108.

68. Wilson, *Four Years*, 30; Glos. RO, D2095/1, Bn Order 3, para. 6, 24 June 1940.
69. Summerskill, *Woman's World*, 74.
70. See PRO, CAB 123/204, Grigg to Anderson, 3 Oct. 1942.
71. PRONI, CAB 4/439/4, Cabinet conclusions, 25 May 1940.
72. See Parliament of Northern Ireland, *House of Commons Debates* 23, cols. 1256–7, 1447–8, 1510–11, 1683–4, 1792, 1801–3.
73. Ibid. 24, col. 193; see cols. 20, 25, 174–5; ibid. 23, cols. 2315–16, 2388–90, 2608–9.
74. See PRO, CAB 123/197, Maxwell to Brook, 13 Feb. 1941.
75. Ibid., Morrison to Margesson, 1 Dec. 1940.
76. Ibid., Margesson to Morrison, 15 Jan. 1941.
77. Ibid., Maxwell to Brook, 13 Feb. 1941.
78. Ibid.; see ibid., Morton to Allen, 8 Feb. 1941.
79. *Northern Ireland House of Commons Debates* 24, col. 597; see PRONI, CAB 4/467/5, Cabinet conclusions, 25 Mar. 1941; PRO, CAB 123/197, Anderson to Churchill, 28 Mar. 1941.
80. LC, J. Walker Papers, Notes on conference held at Zone HQ, 8 Nov. 1940.

Chapter 6

1. J. Lee, 'Early Days in the Home Guard', *The Back Badge*, Dec. 1946, 62.
2. As reported in *New York Times*, 7 Feb. 1942, 1.
3. *Evening News*, 11 Feb. 1942, 3.
4. See PRO, INF 1/264, Daily Report on Morale: 23 July 1940; 1 Aug. 1940; 5 Aug. 1940; INF 1/292, Home Intelligence Weekly Report: 2–9 Apr. 1941; 19–26 Mar. 1941; 6–13 Apr. 1941; see also G. Beardmore, *Civilians at War: Journals 1938–1946* (London, 1984), 79; W. P. Crozier, *Off the Record: Political Interviews 1933–1943*, ed. A. J. P. Taylor (London, 1973), 178.
5. PRO, CAB 79/8, COS(41)24, 20 Jan. 1941.
6. See GLRO, HG1, Oswald to Symonds, 13 Nov. 1940; Northants RO, HGb5, 6th Northants (Corby Works) Bn, Bn Orders, Part II, *passim*; Glos. RO, D2095/1, Bn Orders, 5th Glos. Bn, 47, 8 May 1941. HLRO, HG/1, *passim*.
7. See, e.g., GLRO, HG1, Coy CO, Parks Bn to OC, LCC Bn, 25 Oct. 1940; LC, J. Walker Papers, OC 3 Bn to Group Cmdr, 31 Oct. 1940.
8. Northants RO, HGb12, letter to CO, Wellingborough HG, 9 Dec. 1940; see PRO, WO 199/361, encl. 276C, Report on Parade and Training HG, F Coy, 3rd Bedford Bn HG, 18 Aug. 1941; WO 199/3201, War Diary of

22nd (Tunbridge Wells) Bn, Kent HG, July 1940–Mar. 1941; N. R. Bishop, *'An Honour to Serve': A Short History of the 8th Surrey (Reigate) Battalion Home Guard, May 1940–December 1944* (n/d), 29.

9. L. W. Kentish, *Bux 4: Records and Reminiscences of the 4th Buckingham-shire Battalion Home Guard* (1945), 23; see also LC, J. Walker Papers, Northern Cmd circular, 30 May 1941; IWM, Ingram Papers, Notes for 22 June 1941; F. and J. Shaw (comps.), *We Remember the Home Guard* (Oxford, 1990), R. J. Warner recollection, 65–7. To be fair, it should be added that when Rudolf Hess bailed out over Renfrewshire on the night of 10 May 1941, the local Home Guard arrested him promptly—but had some difficulty in convincing the nearest Army unit to take Hess (then posing as a Luftwaffe officer) into custody that night. [PRO, WO 199/32881, Report by OC 3rd Bn Renfrewshire HG of the Incidents of the Night 10/11th May 1941.]

10. See B. Collier, *The Defence of the United Kingdom* (HMSO, 1957), 231–2, 229; PRO, CAB 69/2, DO(41)3, 10 Jan. 1941; IWM, MI4/14/68, OKW Nr. 44349/41, Gk. Chefs. WFst/Abt.L (I Op.), Chief of OKW to C-in-C Netherlands, 26 Mar. 1941; Alan F. Wilt, ' "Sharle" and "Harpoon": German Cover Operations Against Great Britain in 1941', *Military Affairs* 38 (1974), 1–4; J. Farquharson, 'After Sealion: A German Channel Tunnel?', *Journal of Contemporary History* 25 (1990), 411–12, *passim*; see also J. P. Campbell, 'A British Plan to Invade England, 1941', *Journal of Military History* 58 (1994), 663–84.

11. PRO, CAB 79/10, COS(41)102, 18 Mar. 1941; CAB 79/7, COS(40)354, 21 Oct. 1940; see also T 162/864/E41628/2, Humphreys-Davies to Crombie, 14 Jan. 1941.

12. See J. Colville, *The Fringes of Power: Downing Street Diaries 1939–1955* (London, 1985), 178; C. Andrew, 'Churchill and Intelligence', *Intelligence and National Security* 3 (1988), 185; Farquharson, 'After Sealion', 412; Crozier, *Off the Record*, 177; Campbell, 'British Plan', 671.

13. LHC, Alanbrooke Papers, 3A/4, 253.

14. Colville, *Fringes*, 192; see PRO, CAB 69/2, DO(41)3, 10 Jan. 1941. For an example of Churchill's technique in banging the invasion drum through into the autumn of 1941, see Crozier, *Off the Record*, 238.

15. *The Times*, 10 Feb. 1941, 3.

16. Bishop, *'An Honour'*, 25.

17. RA, GVI 5338 ARMY, special order encl. Hardinge to Margesson, 7 May 1941; see ibid., Hardinge–Margesson correspondence, Jan.–May 1941.

18. For a brief description of press censorship during the Hess episode, see A. Calder, *The People's War: Britain, 1939–1945* (London, 1969), 215. For

reactions to the Home Guard anniversary, see, e.g., *The Times*, 14 May 1941, 5; *Daily Mirror*, 14 May 1941, 3.

19. See R. Bint, *Record of Service: The 'Highland' Platoon, East Company, 6th Oxfordshire (Oxford City) Battalion* (Oxford, 1945), 9; S. W. Wayman, *With the Home Guard: The History of 'A' (Winchester City) Company 5th Hampshire Battalion* (Winchester, 1945), 22; G. D. S. Garrett, *The Hawker Platoon, 'E' Company, 53rd Surrey Battalion H. G. Service Record 1940–1944* (1945), 35; *'We Also Served': The Story of the Home Guard in Cambridgeshire and the Isle of Ely 1940–1943* (Cambridge, 1944), 20; *The Watch on the Braids: The Record of an Edinburgh Home Guard Company 1940–1944* (Edinburgh, 1945), 40.

20. See W. S. Churchill, *The Second World War, II: Their Finest Hour* (London, 1949), 573, 596; see n. 1, above.

21. PRO, WO 163/414, Home Guard: Weapons and Ammunition Position, 28 Sept. 1940.

22. See Northants RO, HGb36, H. Banks, 'Jordan's Lot: A Saga of the Home Guard' (1945), 3; H. Smith, *Bureaucrats in Battledress: A History of the Ministry of Food Home Guard* (Conway, 1945), 32; B. G. Holloway (ed.), *The Northamptonshire Home Guard 1940–1945* (Northampton, 1949), 108; K. R. Gulvin, *Kent Home Guard: A History* (Tonbridge, 1980), 22–8; T. Holman, 'Looking Back', *Choughs Annual Register* 2 (1945); J. Brophy, *Britain's Home Guard: A Character Study* (London, 1945), 33.

23. See PRO, WO 163/85, ECAC/P(41)70, 30 Aug. 1941; WO 163/85, ECAC/P(41)45, 19 June 1941.

24. H. P. Croft, *My Life of Strife* (London, 1948), 332; see also, e.g., BUL, Avon Papers, AP 13/2/11F, radio speech by Eden, summer 1940; Kentish, *Bux 4*, 15.

25. M. M. Rostan, D. Hay, J. D. Scott, *Design and Development of Weapons: Studies in Government and Industrial Organization* (HMSO, 1964), 264, 269.

26. See N. Longmate, *The Real Dad's Army* (London, 1974), 80; Collier, *Defence*, 133–4.

27. PRO, WO 199/1891, app. B, C; see also WO 199/1889, encl. 1198A; see R. S. Macrae, *Winston Churchill's Toyshop* (Kineton, 1971), 120.

28. PRO, WO 199/1891, encl. 1A, note; see ibid., encl. 13B, Training and Use of the Anti-Tank Petrol [*sic*] Bomb.

29. See, e.g., Chester City RO, Western Cmd HG Orders, series 3, 14 May 1941.

30. *The Story of No. 2 Company of the 7th Battn. Somerset Home Guard* (1944), 29.

31. B. L. Davis (ed.), *The British Army in WWII: A Handbook on the Organization, Armament, Equipment, Ranks, Uniforms, etc. 1942* (London, 1990), 143; E. D. Barclay, *The History of the 45th Warwickshire (B'Ham) Battalion Home Guard* (Birmingham, 1945), 92.
32. Brophy, *Britain's Home Guard*, 30.
33. PRO, WO 185/1, minute 7, 18 June 1940.
34. See BUL, Avon Papers, AP 20/8/228, Eden to Churchill, Nov. 1940; ibid., AP 20/8/227, Churchill to Eden, 10 Nov. 1940; PRO, CAB 69/1, DO(40)17, 19 June 1940; Rostan *et al.*, *Design*, 268; Macrae, *Toyshop*, 84.
35. I. V. Hogg, *The Encyclopedia of Infantry Weapons of World War II* (London, 1977), 161–2; see Davis, *British Army in War II*, 143; H. L. Wilson, *Four Years: The Story of the 5th Battalion (Caernarvonshire) Home Guard* (Conway, 1945), 108–9.
36. Macrae, *Toyshop*, 125.
37. Barclay, *45th Warwickshire*, 94; see Brophy, *Britain's Home Guard*, 30.
38. *Watch on the Braids*, 17; see Shaw, *We Remember*, B. Cooper recollection, 126.
39. Berks. RO, Glyn Papers, D/EGl/0155, Whitehead to Glyn, 4 July 1941.
40. PRO, WO 163/85, ECAC/P(41)45, app.; WO 185/23, encl. 1A, 44A.
41. Ibid., encl. 1, 1A; HLRO, HG/6(8), Northover Projector: Report, 23 Nov. 1941; PRO, WO 199/1889, encl. 1235D, 11th (Cornwall) Bn CO to Group Commander, 26 Sept. 1941; LC, J. Walker Papers, Weekly Letter, 1 Dec. 1941, para. 484 issued by HGSO, Yorks Area HQ; Wilts RO, 299/4, OC 'A' Coy to OC 3rd Bn, 12 Nov. 1941; T. Holman, 'Looking Back', *Choughs Annual Register* 2 (1945); Smith, *Bureaucrats*, 46; IWM, Baker Papers, Box P251, '46 Years in the Royal Arsenal', 242; Shaw, *We Remember*, E. Gregory recollection, 181; ibid., R. Tredget recollection, 95.
42. West Country, 'The Greatest Bluff in History', *Fighting Forces* 21 (1945), 307.
43. See W. Heath Robinson, *Heath Robinson at War* (London, 1978), 44, *passim*; J. Lewis, *Heath Robinson: Artist and Comic Genius* (New York, 1973), 199, *passim*; 'We Also Served', 79.
44. IWM, H. W. Endicott, *Confidential Supplementary Report re: British Home Guard* (1942), 31; see LC, J. Walker Papers, Weekly Letter, 22 Sept. 1941, para. 380, issued by SOHG (Yorks Area).
45. *North–West (London) Frontier, No. 6 Company, 23rd Middlesex Battalion: A Souvenir of Home Guard Training, Duties, and Other Activities during the World War of 1939–45* (London, 1946), 71; see Holman, 'Looking Back'; Brophy, *Britain's Home Guard*, 30; J. R. Williams, *A Record of Service, No. 1 Battalion (Denbighshire) Home Guard* (Conway,

1943), 43; Smith, *Bureaucrats*, 46; NLS, MS 3819, 3rd Stirlingshire Bn, f. 214; S. W. Wayman, *With the Home Guard: The History of 'A' (Winchester City) Company 5th Hampshire Battalion* (Winchester, 1945), 18; W. A. D. Englefield, *Limpsfield Home Guard 1940–1945* (London, 1946), 19; Kentish, *Bux 4*, 32; C. Browne, *12th Battalion Northumberland Home Guard, C Company, 1940–1944* (Gateshead-on-Tyne, 1946), 18.

46. Macrae, *Toyshop*, 86.

47. LHC, Alanbrooke Papers, 3A/IV, 307.

48. HLRO, Beaverbrook Papers, BBK/D/359, Margesson to Beaverbrook, 4 Dec. 1941.

49. Hogg, *Encyclopedia*, 148; see HLRO, Beaverbrook Papers, BBK/D/359, Beaverbrook to Margesson, 29 Nov. 1941.

50. Macrae, *Toyshop*, 85.

51. See *Ashford Home Guard O.C.A. Magazine* 2 (1946), Mar. 1948, 9; PRO, WO 199/351, encl. 1B, Report on visit of GSO1, HG Trg, to Home Guard school, Dorking, and East Sussex Sub-District HQ, 10–11 Aug. 1943; Holman, 'Looking Back'; Endicott, *Supplementary Report*, 32; Hogg, *Encyclopedia*, 104; *North-West (London) Frontier*, 71.

52. HLRO, Beaverbrook Papers, BBK/D/359, Margesson to Beaverbrook, 4 Dec. 1941.

53. See IWM, *West Sussex Group Home Guard Diary 1941–1945*, app. 16; Holman, 'Looking Back'; D. C. Crombie, *History of the 5th (Bideford) Battalion Devon Home Guard* (Bristol, 1946), 78; Holloway, *Northamptonshire Home Guard*, 194. The same process of adaptation to weaknesses occurred with the less common Home Guard flame weapons, especially the unwieldly Harvey flame thrower. [See LC, J. Walker Papers, Weekly Letter, 7 Apr. 1941, para 28, issued by SOHG (Yorks Area).]

54. Smith, *Bureaucrats*, 78; see, e.g., Wiltsher, '*Ever Faithful*', 50; '*We Also Served*', 60; see also Berks. RO, Glyn Papers, D/EGI/0155, Whitehead to Glyn, 4 July 1940.

55. Berks. RO, Glyn Papers, D/EGL/0153, Group Commander UTP to Deputy Group Commander UTP, 1 July 1940; see LC, J. Walker Papers, Walker to Eastwood [c. 1941]; GLRO, HG/5, Ham to Lomas, 7 Aug. 1941; ibid., Lomas to Ham, 20 Aug. 1941; NLS, MS 3816, Record of Scottish HG 1940–45, iv.

56. Lee, 'Early Days', 62; Crombie, *5th (Bideford) Battalion*, 52; see NLS, MS 3819, 3rd Stirlingshire Bn, f. 214; *The Watch on the Braids*, 2.

57. 376 HC (Deb.) 5s, col. 1032.

58. PRO, WO 216/141, Churchill to Dill, Margesson, 29 June 1940.

59. See, e.g., LHC, Adam Papers, VIII, ch. 8, 2.

60. See T. Wintringham, 'What's the Good of All This Bayonet Practice?', *Picture Post*, 24 Aug. 1940, 28–9; G. Orwell, 'The Home Guard and You', *Tribune*, 20 Dec. 1940, 8–9; F. Jones, 'Home Guard—and Old Guard', *National Review*, July 1942, 53–7; id., 'Home Guard Problems', *Spectator*, 17 July 1942, 55–6; *Defence* 3 (1941), 32, 34; 365 HC (Deb.) 5s, col. 1308; see also D. Wheatley, *Stranger Than Fiction* (London, 1976), 187.

61. CCRO, CR 528/1, Memo on dress, W. T. Polkinghome, 20 Oct. 1940; see Shaw, *We Remember*, J. Bevis recollection; WYAS(H), KC113/12, Routine Orders, 2nd (West Riding) Bn, nos. 69, 100.

62. NLS, MS 3819, Training Instruction No. 3, 30 Aug. 1943, f. 133; J. Cameron, 'The Spirit of the Bayonet', *Night Hawk Magazine* 1 (2), Feb. 1941, 6.

63. HLRO, Beaverbrook Papers, BBK/D/359, Beaverbrook to Margesson, 4 Aug. 1941.

64. Ibid., Margesson to Beaverbrook, 11 Aug. 1940.

65. See PRO, WO 199/1918, encl. 13A, Army Cmdr's Conference with HG, 25 Aug. 1941.

66. See J. Brady, *The History and Record of 'B' Company 10th (Torbay) Battn. Devonshire Home Guard* (Torquay, 1944), 16; Crombie, *5th (Bideford) Battalion*, 78; NLS, MS 3818, 3rd Lanarkshire Bn, f. 46; ibid., 4th Lanarkshire Bn, f. 57; ibid., MS 3820, 1st Bn, City of Edinburgh HG, f. 25; P. Finch, *Warmen Courageous: The Story of the Essex Home Guard* (Southend-on-Sea, 1951), 34; Holloway, *Northamptonshire Home Guard*, 180; LHC, Burnett Stuart Papers, unpublished memoir, 181.

67. Quoted in *New York Times*, 7 Feb. 1942, 1; see *The Times*, 12 Feb. 1942, 2.

68. Ibid.; see D. Krause (ed.), *The Letters of Sean O'Casey 1942–1954*, II (New York, 1980), 16; C. Mackenzie, *My Life and Times, Octave 8, 1938–1946* (London, 1969), 228.

69. 378 HC (Deb.) 5s, col. 1129.

70. 122 HL (Deb.) 5s, cols. 278–9, 274.

71. 121 HL (Deb.) 5s, col. 702.

72. Croft, *Life of Strife*, 333–4; PRO, INF 1/292, Home Intelligence Weekly Report No. 73, 16–23 Feb. 1942; ibid., No. 72, 9–16 Feb. 1942.

73. PRO, WO 199/363, encl. 78B.

74. See Collier, *Defence* 296; LHC, Alanbrooke Papers, 5/4/1, diary, 4 Feb. 1941, 7 Mar. 1941. See also D. Lindsay, *Forgotten General: A Life of Andrew Thorne* (London, 1987), 151; NLS, MS 3816, HG Branch, HQ Scottish Cmd, May 1940–Mar. 1945: Brief Account, iv; Wiltsher, *'Ever Faithful'*, 56.

75. See Collier, see Berks. RO, Glyn Papers, D/EGL/0153, Report on South Midland Area HG Conference, 30 June 1941; *The Times*: 8 Jan. 1942, 8; 17 Jan. 1942, 5; 'We Also Served', 31.

76. Brophy, *Britain's Home Guard*, 36; see LC, J. Walker Papers, Group Cmdrs, Upper Agbrigg to West Riding Zone HQ, 3 Apr. 1941; *The Times*: 6 Jan. 1942, 8; 17 Jan. 1942, 5; Barclay, *45th Warwickshire*, 2; Wayman, *With the Home Guard*, 11; Holloway, *Northamptonshire Home Guard*, 173–4; 'We Also Served', 18; Brady, *History and Record*, 17; Williams, *Record of Service*, 66; Kentish, *Bux 4*, 30; Mackenzie, *Life and Times*, 103.

77. Kentish, *Bux 4*, 23.

78. J. Marshall-Cornwall, *Wars and Rumours of Wars: A Memoir* (London, 1984), 196.

79. F. Morgan, *Peace and War: A Soldier's Life* (London, 1961), 141.

80. 'We Also Served', 19; see Kentish, *Bux 4*, 58–9; Shaw, *We Remember*, A. Lawrie recollection, 83.

81. Mackenzie, *Life and Times*, 102.

82. PRO, WO 216/141, HF 3010/Ops, GHQ HF to Cmd HQs, 30 June 1941.

83. Lord Bridgeman, 'The Home Guard', *Journal of the Royal United Services Institute*, May 1942, 144; see LC, J. Walker Papers, SOHG (Yorks) to County Cmdrs, 3 Jan. 1941.

84. *Sunday Graphic*, 18 May 1941, 7.

85. 371 HC (Deb.) 5s, col. 778; see 371 HC (Deb.) 5s, col. 1052; see also 373 HC (Deb.) 5s, col. 432.

86. *Sunday Graphic*, 8 June 1941, 7.

87. See PRO, WO 199/363, encl. 91A GS(Ops) to DGHG, 13 May 1942; ibid., CGS to Cmds, 20 Dec. 1941; *Night Hawk Magazine* 1 (1941), 8; Maj. Yeats-Brown article, *Sunday Graphic*, 10 Nov. 1940; *The Times*, 13 May 1941, 5.

88. PRO, WO 199/2489, encl. 47A.

89. PRO, WO 199/362, Paget to Fisher, 15 Dec. 1941.

90. PRO, PREM 3/223/9, DO(41)68, 21 Oct. 1941; see D. Fraser, *Alanbrooke* (London, 1982), 181.

91. PRO, PREM 3/223/9, Margesson to Churchill, 19 Nov. 1941.

92. Ibid., Churchill to Margesson, 23 Nov. 1941.

93. Ibid., Margesson to Churchill, 22 Jan. 1942.

94. See, e.g., Military Correspondent, 'Guerrilla Warfare and its Lessons', *Tribune*, 15 Aug. 1941, 6–7; Bridgeman, 'Home Guard', 144; F. Crisp, 'Sabotage behind the Enemy Lines', *Defence* 3 (1941), 27–9.

95. T. Wintringham, 'The Truth about "Guerrilla" War', *Tribune*, 19 Sept. 1941, 8.

96. Military Correspondent, 'Guerrilla Warfare and its Lessons', 6; see Smith, *Bureaucrats*, 44.

97. *New Statesman and Nation* 21 (1941), 168; see H. Slater, *Home Guard for Victory!* (London, 1941); LHC, Liddell Hart Papers, 10/1941/24a, 2.

98. Ibid., 10/1942/10b, 10/1942/11b, 10/1942/12b.

99. Dalgleish, *Rutland Home Guard*, 28.

100. *Watch on the Braids*, 17; see Finch, *Warmen Courageous*, 29–30; Lt. Col. C. B. Costin-Nian, 'Home Guard Notes', *Daily Express*, 12 Feb. 1941.

101. PRO, WO 199/363, encl. 14B, Petherick to Grigg, 7 Mar. 1942; see also ibid., encl. 16B.

102. *The Times*, 15 Aug. 1941, 2.

103. Bridgeman, 'Home Guard', 144.

104. PRO, WO 199/363, encl. 72B, minute to DCGS, 30 Apr. 1942.

105. See Lampe, *Last Ditch, passim*; PRO, PREM 3/223/5.

106. For comments on Paget's character, see J. B. Holmes (ed.), *Like It Was: The Diaries of Malcolm Muggeridge* (New York, 1982), 340; Marshall-Cornwall, *Wars and Rumours*, 196.

107. PRO, WO 199/387, encl. 9A [WO 199/363, encl. 72C], 'Guerrilla Warfare and the Home Guard', 30 Apr. 1942; see WO 199/364, encl. 7A, GS, G(OPs) to G(Trg), 7 June 1942; WO 199/361, encl. 209A, note for C-in-C *re* proposed instruction on guerrilla warfare (encl. 209B), 14 Aug. 1941.

108. PRO, WO 199/363, encl. 72A.

109. PRO, WO 199/3271, HG Directorate meeting 63, 3 Mar. 1942; see 378 HC (Deb.) 5s, col. 1813; 121 HL (Deb.) 5s, col. 708.

110. PRO, WO 199/1869, GOC to Corps Cmdrs, Operational Role of HG, June 1942.

111. F. Pile, *Ack-Ack: Britain's Defence against Air Attack during the Second World War* (London, 1949), 222.

112. PRO, CAB 80/31, COS(41)667; CAB 79/15, COS(41)385.

113. See PRO, WO 199/1847, encl. 1A, 8 Corps to Southern Cmd, 30 June 1941; WO 199/364, encl. 11A.

114. See PRO, WO 163/72, ECAC/M(41)17, 27 June 1941.

115. Central Statistical Office, *Statistical Digest of the War* (HMSO, 1951), 13.

116. See PRO, WO 163/72, ECAC/M(41)30, 24 Oct. 1941.

117. See ibid., ECAC/M(41)17, 27 June 1941; e.g., *The Times*, 13 Oct. 1941, 5; *Sunday Graphic*, 22 June 1941, 7.

118. PRO, CAB 65/20, 121(41)1, 28 Nov. 1941.

119. 376 HC (Deb.) 5s, col. 1032.

120. Ibid., col. 2120.

121. 376 HC (Deb.) 5s, cols. 2120–89; HL (Deb.) 5s, col. 492; *The Times*, 18 Dec. 1941.

122. See PRO, INF 1/292, Weekly Report 65, 29 Dec. 1941; WO 199/363, encl. 90A, C-in-C to US of S, 12 May 1942, report on visits by Maj. P. Crosthwaite to Southern Cmd, 3–5 May 1942; Bucks RO, Basden Papers, D113/77, 'The Home Guard of Farnham Royal', 11; *Watch on the Braids*, 40.

123. See Parliament of Northern Ireland, *House of Commons Debates* 24, cols. 1125, 1404–5.

124. PRO, WO 199/363, HG Progress Report No. 2, Apr. 1942, 8.

Chapter 7

1. S. Fine, *With the Home Guard* (London, 1943), 62.

2. J. G. Mountford, *Halesowen Home Guard* (Shrewsbury, 1944), 17.

3. E. Summerskill, *A Woman's World* (London, 1967), 74.

4. PRO, WO 199/2687, encl. 5A, Army Cmdr's Directive on the Role of the HG in Scotland, 7 July 1942.

5. PRO, WO 199/1869, GOC to Corps Cmdrs, 3 June 1942.

6. PRO, WO 199/363, encl. 60A, Marshall-Cornwall to Swayne, 27 Apr. 1942; see WO 199/366, encl. 5B.

7. PRO, WO 199/364, encl. 10A, CGS HF to Eastern Cmd, 10 June 1942.

8. IWM, West Sussex Group HG War Diary 1941–1945, app. 9; see G. D. S. Garrett, *The Hawker Platoon, 'E' Company, 53rd Surrey Battalion H. G. Service Record 1940–1944* (Claremont, 1945), 38; N. Hamilton, *Monty: The Making of a General* (London, 1981), 444, 496.

9. PRO, WO 199/364, encl. 64A, HQ Aux. Units to DCGS, HF, 10 Oct. 1942; see ibid., encl. 7A, GS, G(OPs) to G(Trg), 7 June 1942; HLRO, HG/ 18, Notes on a Lecture at Curzon Theatre, 2 Oct. 1942.

10. See PRO, WO 199/2487, encl. 1A; WO 199/2687, encl. 5A; H. J. Wiltsher, *'Ever Faithful': The 1st (Loyal City of Exeter) Battalion, Devon Home Guard, 1940–1945* (Exeter, 1946), 56; West Country, 'The Greatest Bluff in History', *Fighting Forces* 21 (1945), 308; LHC, Burnett-Stuart Papers, unpublished memoir, 181; Shropshire. RO, 3974/173, Official History of 'D' Coy, 1 Bn Shropshire HG, 5.

11. P. Finch, *Warmen Courageous: The Story of the Essex Home Guard* (Southend-on-Sea, 1951); see also B. G. Holloway (ed.), *The Northamptonshire Home Guard 1940–1945* (Northampton, 1949), 175–6.

12. See IWM, Baker Papers, Box P251, Folder 3, '46 Years in the Royal Arsenal', 254; PRO, WO 199/2487, encl. 52B, GHQ questionnaire, 8 HG Cambridge Bn (UTC); WO 199/363, encl. 41A, GOC Western Cmd to

GHQ HF, 16 Apr. 1942; see also WO 199/1889, encl. 1188A; WO 199/363, encl. 62A.

13. PRO, WO 199/363, Swayne to Marshall-Cornwall, 1 May 1942; see WO 199/3255, Meeting of House of Commons HG Committee, 9 June 1942.

14. PRO, WO 199/2487, encl. 28A, Lecture given at HG Coy Cmdrs Course, 29 Aug. 1942; see IWM, West Sussex Group HG War Diary 1941–1945, 12.

15. PRO, WO 199/364, encl. 74A CGS to Cmds, 2 Nov. 1942.

16. See, e.g., IWM, Sutton Papers, Box 72/59/5, Canadian Corps District, Plans to Defeat Invasion, 1943; ibid., Address to HG Cmdrs by GOC South Eastern Cmd, Jan. 1943; Holloway, *Northamptonshire Home Guard*, 247–8.

17. H. G., 'War Aims of the Home Guard', *Tribune*, 7 Aug. 1942, 11.

18. S. Orwell and I. Angus (eds.), *The Collected Essays, Journalism and Letters of George Orwell, III: As I Please, 1943–1945* (New York, 1968), 194–5.

19. PRO, CAB 79/23, JIC(42)392(0) (Final); CAB 79/13, COS(41)377, JIC(41)426; see CAB 65/28, 160(42)5.

20. F. Morgan, *Peace and War: A Soldier's Life* (London, 1961), 147.

21. Central Statistical Office, *Statistical Digest of the War* (HMSO, 1951), 13.

22. J. Marshall-Cornwall, *Wars and Rumours of Wars: A Memoir* (London, 1984), 197.

23. B. Collier, *The Defence of the United Kingdom* (HMSO, 1957), 298–9.

24. See CCC, Croft Papers, CRFT 1/5, Croft to Bridgeman, 7 March 1942.

25. See, e.g., IWM, West Sussex Group HG War Diary, app. 13, Montgomery Special Order of the Day, 27 June 1942; ibid., Sutton Papers, Box 72/59/5, *passim*; W. A. D. Englefield, *Limpsfield Home Guard* (London, 1946), 36; Hamilton, *Monty*, 496.

26. D. Lindsay, *Forgotten General: A Life of Andrew Thorne* (London, 1987), 151.

27. F. Pile, *Ack-Ack: Britain's Defence against Air Attack during the Second World War* (London, 1949), 255–6; IWM, Hawes Papers, 87/41/2, Short Note on the HG in AA Cmd, Jan. 1945, 36.

28. PRO, HO 186/1947, The HG and Civil Defence, 1.

29. Ibid., app. B, C.

30. See PRO, WO 163/73, ECAC M(42)23, 6 June 1942; 378 HC (Deb.) 5s, col. 21.

31. IWM, West Sussex Group HG War Diary, app. 11: see *The Times*: 15 May 1942, 2; 11 May 1942, 2.

32. *Mass-Observation Bulletin*, July 1943, 1. For discussion of Churchill's political difficulties at this stage, see K. Jeffreys, *The Churchill Coalition and Wartime Politics, 1940–1945* (Manchester, 1991), ch. 4.

33. *The Times*, 13 May 1942, 2.

34. PRO, WO 199/363, encl. 11A, Paget to Bridgeman, 14 Mar. 1942; ibid., encl. 10A, Bridgeman to Paget, 12 Mar. 1942.

35. RA, GVI 5338 ARMY, Hardinge to Grigg, 24 Mar. 1942; see ibid., Grigg to Hardinge, 23 Mar. 1942.

36. *The Times*, 14 May 1942, 4; see RA, GVI 5338 ARMY, Hardinge–Grigg correspondence, Mar.–Apr. 1942.

37. Holloway, *Northamptonshire Home Guard*, 192–3; I. V. Hogg, *The Encyclopedia of Infantry Weapons of World War II* (London, 1977), 52–3.

38. PRO, WO 199/3237, Meeting to discuss the HG weapon situation, 25 June 1942; see Holloway, *Northamptonshire Home Guard* 193; J. Brophy, *Britain's Home Guard: A Character Study* (London, 1945), 34; West Country, 'Greatest Bluff', 307; J. R. Williams, *A Record of Service, No. 1 Battalion (Denbighshire) Home Guard* (Conway, 1943), 43; D. C. Crombie, *History of the 5th (Bideford) Battalion Devon Home Guard* (Bristol, 1946), 79; F. and J. Shaw (comps.), *We Remember the Home Guard* (Oxford, 1990), R. Tredget recollection, 95–6.

39. Holloway, *Northamptonshire Home Guard*, 127; H. Smith, *Bureaucrats in Battledress: A History of the Ministry of Food Home Guard* (Conway, 1945), 46; see also Glos RO, D2095/1, Bn order 114, 20 Aug. 1942; IWM, Sutton Papers, Box 72/59/5, Sussex District HG General Notes No. 9, 27 June 1944; Shaw, *We Remember*, R. Tredget recollection, 95.

40. LC, J. Walker Papers, Weekly Letter, 18 Aug. 1941, para. 293, issued by SOHG (Yorks Area).

41. IWM, Baker Papers, Box P251, '46 Years in the Royal Arsenal', folder 3, 271.

42. *The Times*, 27 Sept. 1944, 2; Holloway, *Northamptonshire Home Guard*, 211–12; R. S. Macrae, *Winston Churchill's Toyshop* (Kineton, 1971), 120.

43. Wilts. RO, 2099/8, ADOS S.P. District to OC 3 Bn, 6 July 1943; Finch, *Warmen Courageous*, 168; IWM, Sutton Papers, Box 72/59/5, Sussex District HG General Notes No. 1, 25 June 1943; Shaw, *We Remember*, T. Wilkinson recollection, 303.

44. T. Holman, 'Looking Back', *Choughs Annual Register* 2 (1945); K. R. Gulvin, *Kent Home Guard: A History* (Tonbridge, 1980), 30–1. See also S. W. Wayman, *With the Home Guard: The History of 'A' (Winchester City) Company 5th Hampshire Battalion* (Winchester, 1945), 13; *North-West (London) Frontier, No. 6 Company, 23rd Middlesex Battalion: A Souvenir*

of Home Guard Training Duties and Other Activities during the World War of 1939–45 (London, 1946), 45.

45. Wilts. RO, 2099/8, 'Tactical Employment of the Smith Gun', encl. to OC 3rd Bn to Coy Cmdrs, 2 Dec. 1942.

46. *The Times*: 27 Sept. 1944, 2; 18 Sept. 1944, 5; 15 Sept. 1944, 5; see also West Country, 'Greatest Bluff', 307.

47. PRO, WO 199/382, GOC AA Cmd to US of S, 9 Dec. 1942; WO 166/173, Future of the HG, app. 3; WO 199/363, app. A to ECAC/P(42)27; WO 199/3237, Minutes of meeting to discuss the issue of new weapons to the HG, 21 Apr. 1943.

48. PRO, WO 199/382, encl. 11A, HG AA Progress Report, 11 June 1943.

49. PRO, WO 199/1918, encl. 94A, Notes of Army Commander's HG Conferences, 28 Apr., 1 May, 6 May 1943; WO 199/2687, encl. 10A, GHQ to Cmds, 8 July 1942.

50. See, e.g., Smith, *Bureaucrats*, ch. 7; see also PRO, WO 199/347, encl. 9A, DGHG to C-in-C HF, 1 Nov. 1942; ibid., encl. 5A GOC London District to GHQ HF, 11 Sept. 1942.

51. See *The Times*, 7 May 1943, 2; C. Graves, *The Home Guard of Britain* (London, 1943), ch. 19, *passim*; PRO, WO 199/2487, encls. 3A, 4A, *passim*; WO 199/3238, encl. 725.

52. See J. Radnor, *It All Happened Before: The Home Guard through the Centuries* (London, 1945), 120; E. H. Glasson, '"G" Company's Finest Hour', *Choughs Annual Register* 1 (1944); A. G. Street, *From Dusk Till Dawn* (London, 1942), 47; LC, J. Walker Papers, Group Commander (Wakefield) to Sector Commander, 13 Aug. 1941; IWM, White Papers, 83/4/1, 'Wartime Farming in the County of Berkshire', 16–18; Northants RO, HGb36, H. Banks, 'Jordan's Lot: A Saga of the Home Guard', ch. 5; see also Wayman, *With the Home Guard*, 27; 'We Also Served', 36, 28; WO 199/361, encl. 146A; Shaw, *We Remember*, P. Carter recollection, 13; ibid., J. Frewin recollection, 24; ibid., W. Mayhew recollection, 26; ibid., L. O. Allen recollection, 74.

53. Morgan, *Peace and War*, 142.

54. LC, J. Walker Papers, General Instructions for Exercise 'Wool', 23 Nov. 1942.

55. PRO, WO 199/3202, War Diary, app. 13; ibid., entry for 28 Aug. 1942; see NIRO, D3803/3/1, Toner Papers, Notes on paratroop landing exercise, *c.* 1942.

56. *The Watch on the Braids: The Record of an Edinburgh Home Guard Company 1940–1944* (Edinburgh, 1945), 36; see C. Mackenzie, *My Life and Times, Octave 8, 1938–1946* (London, 1969), 124–5; Shaw, *We*

Remember, A. H. Bush recollection, 13; ibid., H. McCraken recollection, 76–7.

57. Glos RO, D5023/3/3, Painswick Platoon range results, 1941.

58. CPL, Slack Papers, LOC 319, Memo to Coy Cmdrs, 6th Derbyshire Bn (Chesterfield Borough), 11 May 1942; see Shaw, *We Remember*: J. Slawson recollection, 64; L. O. Allen recollection, 73–4; P. C. Vigor recollection, 282; WYAS(H), KC 113/13, B Coy, 2 (West Riding) B HG, memo on Range Discipline, 22 June 1944.

59. See *The Times*: 19 May 1942, 2; 14 Oct. 1942, 4; H. L. Wilson, *Four Years: The Story of the 5th Battalion (Caernarvonshire) Home Guard* (Conway, 1945), 108–9; *'We Also Served': The Story of the Home Guard in Cambridgeshire and the Isle of Ely 1940–1943* (Cambridge, 1944), 35; L. W. Kentish, *Bux 4: Records and Reminiscences of the 4th Buckinghamshire Battalion Home Guard* (Buckingham, 1945), 13; GLRO, HG/18, *passim*; HLRO, HG/6(8), Northover Projector: Report on the practice with live bottles fired at Hounslow, 23 Nov. 1941; Shaw, *We Remember*, J. Goodwin recollection, 32; see also nn. 36, 37, above.

60. W. F. Mellor (ed.), *Casualties and Medical Statistics* (HMSO, 1972), 836; PRO, WO 199/3270, encl. 95.

61. Mellor, *Casualties*, 138, 836; *Statistical Digest of the War*, 13. In all probability, however, death from natural causes (strokes, heart-attacks, and so forth) was far more common than death from accidents with weapons in the Home Guard. In November 1942, for instance, at a time when the average age of Army personnel was in the low twenties, a far from atypical platoon in Cleekheaton was reporting that fully 36% of its officers and men were over 30 (and of them, 10% were over 45). WYAS(H), KC 113/8, OC 'B' Coy to OC 2 (West Riding) Bn HG, 6 Nov. 1942. It is suggestive that, while the mortality rate in the Home Guard was much higher than among regular troops, the number of those suffering non-fatal injuries on duty appears to have been much lower. See Mellor, *Casualties*, 836, 136, 148–9; *Statistical Digest*, 13.

62. The Canadian industrial czar C. D. Howe reported in October 1942 that the public mood in Britain could be characterized as '"business as usual", taking it for granted that there would be no invasion'. [PAC, Mackenzie King Diary, 21 Oct. 1942.]

63. See GLRO, HG/34, LD4/67005/HG/7, 8 Apr. 1942; ibid., Wade sub-file; *'We Also Served'*, 21; Smith, *Bureaucrats*, 146.

64. 386 HC (Deb.) 5s, cols. 1450, 1566; *The Times*, 8 Feb. 1943; see Shaw, *We Remember*, T. Wilkinson recollection, 305.

65. Pile, *Ack Ack*, 258; see PRO, WO 163/74, ECAC/M(43)17, 24 Apr. 1943; WO 199/402, Minutes of Army Commander's Conferences of Home Guard Commanders, 2–5 Nov. 1943; Shaw, *We Remember*; J. S. Davidson recollection, 154ff.; *History of the Cheshire Home Guard: From L.D.V. Formation to Stand-Down 1940–1944* (Aldershot, 1950), 63; E. D. Barclay, *The History of the 45th Warwickshire (B'Ham) Battalion Home Guard* (Birmingham, 1945), 26.

66. See PRO, WO 199/402, Minutes of Army Commander's Conference of HG, 7–10 July 1943; WO 199/1918, encl. 51A, Army Commander's Conference of Zone and Group Cmdrs HG, 5 Feb. 1943; *'We Also Served'*, 60.

67. Suffolk RO (Ipswich), IA2/1205/1, Suffolk TA Assoc. minutes, 5 Dec. 1941 and resolution; see PRO, WO 199/1918, encl. 94A, Notes of Army Commander's HG Conferences, 28 Apr., 1 May, 6 May 1942; WO 163/52, AC/M(43)4; Berks. RO, P/TA1/1/2, Berkshire TA Assoc. minutes, 2 July 1943, item 8; NLS, MS 3820, f. 256; 383 HC (Deb.) 5s, col. 1210; 391 HC (Deb.) 5s, cols. 369–70, 1384.

68. Summerskill, *Woman's World*, 74.

69. PRO, CAB 123/204, Grigg to Anderson, 3 Oct. 1942; M. Izzard, *A Heroine in Her Time: A Life of Dame Helen Gwynne-Vaughan 1879–1967* (London, 1969), 343–4; see C. Graves, *Women in Green (The Story of the W.V.S.)* (London, 1948), 55, 164; WYAS(B), ID83/5, General Shear's Orders, 4 May 1942.

70. PRO, LAB 8/112, Glen to Bridgeman, 8 May 1942; LAB 8/113, Civil Defence and the Home Guard, 27 Oct. 1942.

71. PRO, PREM 3/223/7, Note by PM on Manpower, 28 Nov. 1942.

72. PRO, WO 166/173, Future of the HG: Appreciation by DGHG prepared by direction of the S of S.

73. PRO, CAB 123/204, Grant to Redman, 15 Feb. 1943.

74. Ibid., Morrison to Anderson, 10 Oct. 1942.

75. Ibid., Morrison to Grigg, 6 Jan. 1943; ibid., 19 Dec. 1942; ibid., Grigg to Morrison, 22 Dec. 1942.

76. See ibid., Record of an informal meeting, Lord President's room, 1 Feb. 1943; ibid., Note of a meeting of Ministers held on 22 Feb. 1943, to discuss the Draft Paper on HG Questions to the PM.

77. PRO, WO 166/173 [also PREM 3/223/7, HO 186/1513], Minute to the PM on the future of the HG; PREM 3/223/7, Grigg to Churchill, 23 Feb. 1943.

78. Ibid.

79. See PRO, WO 163/52, AC/M(43)4; T 162/864/E41628/2–5, *passim*.

80. PRO, PREM 3/223/7, Cherwell to Churchill, 4 Mar. 1943.

81. Ibid., Churchill to Grigg, Bevin, Anderson, 5 Mar. 1942.

82. See PRO, WO 199/382, encl. 11A.

Chapter 8

1. PRO, WO 199/3240, encl. 76.

2. Marquis of Donegall, 'A Tribute!', *Sunday Dispatch*, 28 Mar. 1943, quoted in J. R. Williams, *A Record of Service, No. 1 Battalion (Denbighshire) Home Guard* (Conway, 1943), 141–2.

3. *Glasgow Herald*, 8 Nov. 1943, 2.

4. N. R. Bishop, *'An Honour to Serve': A Short History of the 8th Surrey (Reigate) Battalion Home Guard, May 1940–December 1944* (n/d), 55.

5. *The Times*, 8 Feb. 1943, 2.

6. 387 HC (Deb.) 5s, col. 339.

7. *Mass-Observation Bulletin*, July 1943, 1.

8. See J. Richards and A. Aldgate, *Best of British: Cinema and Society 1930– 1970* (Oxford, 1983), ch. 5; N. Pronay and J. Croft, 'British Film Censorship and Propaganda in the Second World War', in J. Curran and V. Porter (eds.), *British Cinema History* (London, 1983), 159. Churchill's fears that the film would send the wrong message were exaggerated, at least as far as the Home Guard was concerned. The historical consultant for the film was General Sir Douglas Brownrigg, a London Home Guard Zone Commander who modelled the career of the film's protagonist, General Clive 'Sugar' Candy (a.k.a. Colonel Blimp), after his own. Richards and Aldgate, *Best of British*, 64–5.

9. W. S. Churchill, *The Second World War, III: The Grand Alliance* (London, 1950), 840.

10. PRO, CAB 65/34, 52(43)4.

11. PRO, PREM 3/223/7, Note by S of S for War, 20 Jan. 1944, encl. C-in-C to GOCs, 2 Mar. 1942.

12. PRO, WO 199/350, encl. 1A, GHQ to Cmds, 13 Apr. 1943.

13. See PRO, CAB 65/34, 57(43)3.

14. RA, GVI PS 5338 ARMY, Grigg to Hardinge, 28 Apr. 1943.

15. PRO, WO 199/350, encl. 14B, DCGS to C-in-C HF, 15 Apr. 1943; ibid., encl. 2A, G(Ops) to DCGS, 14 Apr. 1943.

16. Ibid., encl. 15A G(Ops) to G1, 1 May 1943; ibid., encl. 19A, Order for Parade, 16 May 1943; RA, GVI PS 5338 ARMY, Grigg to Hardinge, 28 Apr. 1943.

17. PRO, CAB 66/36, WP(43)172.

18. PRO, WO 199/3240, encl. 76; see RA, GVI PS 5338 ARMY, Grigg to

Hardinge, 28 Apr. 1943 and encl.; ibid., Lascelles to Grigg, 1 May 1943; ibid., Hardinge to Grigg, 6 May 1943 and encl.

19. *The Times*, 15 May 1940, 5.

20. Ibid.; see *Daily Mirror*, 14 May 1943; *Daily Express*, 15 May 1943; M. Panter-Downes, *London War Notes, 1939–1945* (New York, 1971), 280–1; *'We Also Served': The Story of the Home Guard in Cambridgeshire and the Isle of Ely 1940–1943* (Cambridge, 1944), 85, 87; H. Smith, *Bureaucrats in Battledress: A History of the Ministry of Food Home Guard* (Conway, 1945), 85–6.

21. See PRO, WO 199/363, encl. 5B, Notes on a conference between MGGS and DGHG, Aug. 1943; W. S. Churchill, *The Second World War, IV: The Hinge of Fate* (London, 1951), 843.

22. See PRO, WO 199/3237, DGHG and MGGS meeting, 2 Sept. 1943; ibid., Minutes of meeting to discuss the issue of new weapons to the HG, 21 Apr. 1943; WO 199/366, encl. 5B, Notes on a conference between MGGS and DGHG, Aug. 1943.

23. K. R. Gulliver, *Kent Home Guard: A History* (Tonbridge, 1980), 32; PRO, WO 199/366, HF/636/Q(0), GS minute, 2 Aug. 1943, encl. HF2107/1/G(HG).

24. See PRO, WO 199/3237, Minutes of meeting to discuss the issue of new weapons to the HG, 21 Apr. 1943.

25. Churchill, *Second World War, IV*, 843; see ibid., 844.

26. M. Howard, *British Intelligence in the Second World War, 5: Strategic Deception* (HMSO, 1990), 75–6.

27. PRO, WO 199/366, encl. 5B, Notes on a conference between MGGS and DGHG, Aug. 1943.

28. PRO, WO 199/1869, encl. 1A, GHQ HF to Cmds, 31 Aug. 1943.

29. Ibid., encl. 4A, SOHG to G(Ops), 6 Sept. 1943.

30. See L. W. Kentish, *Bux 4: Records and Reminiscences of the 4th Buckinghamshire Battalion Home Guard* (1945), 33–4; WO 199/3248, HG Trg. Instructions No. 51, 56.

31. WO 199/402, Army Cmdr's Conferences of HG Commanders, 2–5 Nov. 1943; see WO 163/51, AC/G(42)3, AC/G(42)7, AC/G(42)10, AC/G(42)13, AC/G(42)19, *et al.*; WO 199/3237, Minutes of meeting to discuss the issue of new weapons to the HG, 21 Apr. 1943.

32. WO 199/366, encl. 1A, HF2107/1/G(HG), 2 Aug. 1943; ibid., encl. 5B, Notes on conference between MGGS and DGHG, Aug. 1943; ibid., encls. 6A-C; WO 199/402, Army Cmdr's Conferences of HG Commanders, 7–10 July, 2–5 Nov. 1943; WO 199/1869, encls. 14A, 22A.

33. 396 HC (Deb.) 5s, col. 57. Grigg pointed out in reply that many members

of the Home Guard were engaged in work of national importance and could not be spared unless the home base was attacked.

34. See I. F. W. Beckett, *The Amateur Military Tradition 1558–1945* (Manchester, 1991), 269; HLRO, HG/1, Record of Service Book, Civil Service Bn; GLRO, B/WHF/228, OC 2 Platoon to OC 'C' Coy, 26 Jan., 28 Jan. 1944; NLS, MS 3818, ff. 43, 47, 71; ibid., MS 3820, ff. 133, 211; Wilts RO, 2099/2, nominal rolls, 3 Bn Wilts HG; *History of the Cheshire Home Guard: From L.D.V. Formation to Stand-Down 1940–1944* (Aldershot, 1950), 2; J. W. Ogilvy-Dalgleish, *The Rutland Home Guard of 1940–1944* (Oakham, 1955), 52; N. Longmate, *How We Lived Then: A History of Everyday Life during the Second World War* (London, 1971), 113; E. Raymond, *Please You, Draw Near: Autobiography 1922–1968* (London, 1968), 89.

35. MRC, MSS. 292/881.423/5, Harries to Citrine, 13 Jan. 1943; see ibid., NAC Eng. & Ship. Industries 6/2, 5 Feb. 1943; ibid., TUC circular no. 56 (1942–43), 25 Feb. 1943; ibid., Memo EPH/JH/1274, 18 Apr. 1944.

36. MRC, MSS. 75/3/2/2, 6–7.

37. *Daily Worker*, 14 May 1943; see MRC, MSS. 292/881.423/5, Perry to Grant, 10 May 1943; Berks. RO, Glyn Papers, D/EGL/0160, Grigg to Glyn, 10 March 1944; *Mass-Observation Bulletin, April 1944*, 1; PRO, HO 186/1513, *passim*; WO 199/3261, Bridgeman to Lascelles, 15 Feb. 1944; 395 HC (Deb.) 5s, cols. 176–7.

38. PRO, CAB 65/33, WM(43)34; see CAB 66/54, WP(43)74.

39. See PRO, CAB 66/35, WP(43)116; CAB 65/35, WM(43)46, ref to LP(43)18.

40. PRO, PREM 3/223/6, Uniforms for Part-Time Services: Brief for Meeting of the Lord President's Committee on 19 July 1943.

41. Ibid., Anderson to Churchill, 29 June 1943.

42. Ibid., Grigg to Churchill, 21 July 1943.

43. Those responsible for the civil defence services thought that the real problem lay with the Home Guard taking a rather superior attitude to civil defence. See HO 186/1513, *passim*.

44. Ibid., Churchill to Anderson, 23 July 1943; see Grigg to Churchill, 21 July 1943; PREM 3/223/11, Memo from Lt. Col. G. H. Crump, 26 June 1943; ibid., Churchill to Grigg, 11 July 1943.

45. PREM 3/223/6, Anderson to Churchill, 29 July 1943.

46. Ibid., Churchill to Anderson, 1 Aug. 1943.

47. Ibid., Grigg to Churchill, 2 Aug. 1943.

48. See ibid., Churchill to Dalton, 3 Aug. 1943.

49. Ibid., Dalton to Churchill, 3 Aug. 1943; see ibid., Churchill to Dalton, 3 Aug. 1943; *Sunday Express*, 1 Aug. 1943; B. Pimlott (ed.), *The Second World War Diary of Hugh Dalton* (London, 1986), 619.

50. 391 HC (Deb.) 5s, col. 2457.

51. PRO, PREM 3/223/6, LP(43)54.

52. See, e.g., West Country, 'The Greatest Bluff in History', *Fighting Forces* 21 (1945), 308.

53. 395 HC (Deb.) 5s, cols. 176–7; PRO, INF 1/291, Weekly Report 147, 29 July 1943; see Bucks. RO, Basden Papers, D113/77, 'The Home Guard of Farnham Royal', 25; GLRO, B/WHF/232, *Fighting Fulham!: The Bulletin of the 3rd County of London (Fulham) Bn, Home Guard* 2, Nov. 1943, 1–2; R. Bint, *Record of Service: The 'Highland' Platoon (East Company), 6th Oxfordshire (Oxford City) Battalion* (Oxford, 1945), 19; B. G. Holloway (ed.), *The Northamptonshire Home Guard 1940–1945* (Northampton, 1949), 289.

54. PRO, WO 163/52, AC/M(43)22; NLS, MS 3822, 35–6, 54–5, 67; IWM, Hawes Papers, 87/41/2, Short Note on the HG in AA Cmd, Jan. 1945, 29; see Smith, *Bureaucrats*, 146; GLRO, HG/34, *passim*; 'We Also Served', 21; *The Watch on the Braids: The Record of an Edinburgh Home Guard Company 1940–1944* (Edinburgh, 1945), 40.

55. PRO, WO 163/52, AC/M(43)20.

56. Ibid., AC/P(43)17.

57. Ibid., AC/M(43)21; PREM 3/223/7, Grigg to Churchill, 5 Nov. 1943.

58. IWM, Hawes Papers, 87/41/2, Short Note on the HG in AA Cmd, Jan. 1945, 30.

59. See MRC, MSS. 292/881.423/5, *passim*.

60. *Sunday Express*, 7 Nov. 1943.

61. PRO, WO 199/402, Minutes of Army Cmdr's Conference of HG Cmdrs, 2–5 Nov. 1943.

62. PRO, PREM 3/223/7, Churchill to Grigg, 7 Nov. 1943.

63. PRO, WO 199/3270, encl. 47, DGHG to Cmds, 11 Nov. 1943, enclosing extract from PM's Mansion House speech, 8 Nov. 1943. See Churchill, *Second World War*, IV, 844; M. Gilbert, *Road to Victory: Winston S. Churchill 1941–1945* (London, 1986), 548.

65. 393 HC (Deb.) 5s, col. 1284.

65. PRO, WO 163/52, AC/M(43)22; WO 199/3270, encl. 47; see IWM, West Sussex Group HG War Diary 1941–1945, app. 31.

66. PRO, WO 199/1869, GOC to HG Bn Cmdrs, 13 Nov. 1943.

67. PRO, PREM 3/223/7, Churchill to Grigg, 7 Jan. 1944; see ibid., Cherwell to Churchill, 8 Dec. 1943; ibid., Cherwell to Churchill, 6 Jan. 1944.

68. Ibid., Churchill to Cherwell, 27 Jan. 1944; ibid., Grigg to Churchill, and encl., 20 Jan. 1944.

69. Berks. RO, Glyn Papers, D/EGL/0610, Glyn to Bridgeman, 3 Mar. 1944; see NLS, MS 3822, 6; PRO, INF 1/292, Weekly Report 166, 9 Dec. 1943; ibid. 170, 6 Jan. 1944; ibid. 174, 3 Feb. 1944; ibid. 178, 2 Mar. 1944.

70. Central Statistical Office, *Statistical Digest of the War* (HMSO, 1951), 13.

71. NLS, MS 3822, 101 Glasgow HG Rocket AA Battery, 35–6.

72. Holloway, *Northamptonshire Home Guard*, 278.

73. PRO, WO 163/75, ECAC/M(44)7.

74. Ibid., ECAC/M(44)18.

75. PRO, WO 199/350, encl. 29A, GOC Western Cmd to GHQ HF, 28 Nov. 1943.

76. PRO, WO 163/53, AC/M(44)4.

77. See PRO, WO 199/350, encl. 32A, MGGS to C-in-C, 28 Feb. 1944; ibid., encl. 34A, MGGS to Cmds, 15 Mar. 1944; ibid., encl. 35B, Parade Orders for London, 14 May 1944; *35th City of London Battalion Home Guard* (London, 1946), Part II, 5–6.

78. *The Times*, 15 May 1944. For the King's involvement in the celebrations and modifications to the War Office draft message, see RA, GVI PS 5338 ARMY, Grigg–Lascelles correspondence, Mar.–May 1944.

79. *The Times*, 15 May 1944.

80. PRO, WO 199/3202, Special Order of the Day from HQ, SE Cmd, 15 May 1944; see WO 199/2487, encl. 258.

81. See *The Times*, 20 Sept. 1944, 2.

82. See PRO, WO 199/3202, entries for 19 June and 17 July 1944; WO 199/1856, encl. 54A, GHQ HF to Cmds, 6 June 1944; B. Collier, *The Defence of the United Kingdom* (HMSO, 1957), 396, 323; F. and J. Shaw (comps.), *We Remember the Home Guard* (Oxford, 1990), F. Taylor recollection, 46.

83. See V. Kuhn, *German Paratroops in World War II* (London, 1978), ch. 15 *et al.*

84. Panter-Downes, *London War Notes*, 323.

85. See *The Times*, 25 Apr. 1944, 2; W. S. Churchill, *The Second World War, V: Closing the Ring* (London, 1952), 527; Kentish, *Bux 4*, 39; Wiltsher, '*Ever Faithful*', 97–8.

86. PRO, INF 1/292, Weekly Report 202, 17 Aug. 1944; see ibid. 194, 22 June 1944; ibid. 198, 20 July 1944; Holloway, *Northamptonshire Home Guard*, 281; Kentish, *Bux 4*, 41; *North-West (London) Frontier*, 66.

87. PRO, WO 163/75, ECAC/M(43)47.

88. P. Finch, *Warmen Courageous: The Story of the Essex Home Guard* (Southend-on-Sea, 1951), 280.

89. PRO, WO 199/2495, encl. 38A, SO1(L) to BGS, Eastern Cmd, 26 June 1944; see Holloway, *Northamptonshire Home Guard*, 284–5.

90. PRO, PREM 3/223/12, Grigg to Churchill, 25 Aug. 1944; see *Daily Mail*, 30 Aug. 1944.

91. PRO, WO 199/354, Drew to Callander, 21 Aug. 1944.

92. PRO, PREM 3/223/12, Churchill minute, 28 Aug. 1944.

93. PRO, WO 163/53, AC/M(44)9.

94. See *The Times*: 7 Sept. 1944, 2, 5; 24 Sept. 1944, 5; 25 Sept. 1944, 5; PRO, INF 1/292, Weekly Report 206, 14 Sept. 1944; ibid. 207, 21 Sept. 1944; ibid. 208, 28 Sept. 1944.

95. Kentish, *Bux 4*, 45.

96. Wiltsher, '*Ever Faithful*', 104; see *The Times*: 18 Sept. 1944, 5; 20 Sept. 1944, 2; 24 Sept. 1944, 5; 403 HC (Deb.) 5s, cols. 739–40.

97. *News of the World*, 30 Jan. 1944, 2; see ibid., 16 Jan. 1944, 2; PRO, WO 199/3261, Bridgeman to Lascelles, 15 Feb. 1944; Finch, *Warmen Courageous*, 281.

98. IWM, J. K. Howard and H. W. Endicott, *Summary Report, British Home Guard* (1941), 14; see H. Gough, *Soldiering On* (London, 1954), 248; *The Times*, 14 May 1943, 5.

99. Berks. RO, Glyn Papers, D/EGL/0161, GOC S.M. District to Southern Cmd, 17 July 1944; see ibid., Glyn to Bracken, 23 July 1944, Future of the HG and Demobilization of the Services.

100. *The Times*, 30 Oct. 1944, 2.

101. Ibid., 27 Oct. 1944, 2; see Finch, *Warmen Courageous*, 281; *Choughs Annual Register* 2 (1945), Morgan to Holman, 8 Nov. 1944.

102. PRO, PREM 3/223/12, Churchill to Grigg, 19 Sept. 1944; see ibid., 16 Sept. 1944.

103. PRO, CAB 65/44, WM(44)129.

104. 403 HC (Deb.) 5s, cols. 1570, 1574–5; see *The Times*: 3 Oct. 1944, 5; 6 Oct. 1944, 5; West Country, 'Greatest Bluff', 308.

105. See *The Times*, 4 Dec. 1944, 2; IWM, *West Sussex*, app. 43; PRO, WO 199/350, encl. 56A, Stand-down parade orders, 3 Dec. 1944; PREM 3/223/12, Grigg to Churchill, 16 Sept. 1944.

106. IWM, *West Sussex*, app. 45; see PRO, PREM 3/223/12, Grigg to Churchill, 16 Sept. 1944, app. A.

107. J. W. Wheeler-Bennett, *King George VI: His Life and Reign* (London, 1958), 615.

108. PRO, INF 1/292, Weekly Report 218, 7 Dec. 1944.

109. Ibid. 219, 14 Dec. 1944; see ibid. 218, 7 Dec. 1944; *The Times*, 4 Dec. 1944, 2; Holloway, *Northamptonshire Home Guard*, 294–5; S. W. Wayman, *With the Home Guard: The History of 'A' (Winchester City) Company 5th Hampshire Battalion* (Winchester, 1945), 33.

110. PRO, WO 163/75, ECAC/M(44)52.

111. IWM, Sutton Papers, Box 72/59/5, Address to 26th Sussex HG, Crawley, 3 Dec. 1944.

112. MRC, MSS. 292/881.423/5, Citrine to Lawson, 3 Sept. 1945.

113. Ibid., Extract from minutes of the Finance and General Purposes Committee, 26 Nov. 1945.

114. 417 HC (Deb.) 5s, cols. 418–20.

Chapter 9

1. *Home Guard News*, national edition, May 1954, 8.

2. See P. Dixon, *Double Diploma: The Life of Sir Pierson Dixon* (London, 1968), 245–6; H. Cantrel (ed.), *Public Opinion 1935–1946* (Princeton, NJ, 1951), 276; Mass-Observation, *Peace and the Public* (London, 1947), 23.

3. For Cabinet concern over the Communist threat to industry and its response, see: PRO, CAB 21/2554, DO(47)25; K. O. Morgan, *Labour in Power 1945–1951* (Oxford, 1984), 295–6, 374–7; D. Childs, 'The Cold War and the "British Road", 1946–53', *Journal of Contemporary History* 23 (1988), 557–8.

4. PRO, DEFE 7/597, HGWP/P(50)5; see PRO, WO 163/108, ECAC/M(49)9; ibid., ECAC/P(49)30.

5. 480 HC (Deb.) 5s, col. 1714; PRO, DEFE 7/597, encl. 20, DO(50)164; ibid., encl. 9, HGWP/P(50)5; see PRO, WO 163/111, ECAC/M(50)2; ibid., ECAC/P(50)2.

6. 465 HC (Deb.) 5s, cols. 40–1; 478 HC (Deb.) 5s, col. 1871; 480 HC (Deb.) 5s, cols. 743, 1714.

7. See PRO, DEFE 7/597, encl. 26B, DO(51)18.

8. Ibid., encl. 26B, 'Home Guard' memo by COS.

9. See A. Boyle, *The Climate of Treason: Five who Spied for Russia* (London, 1979), 378 ff.

10. PRO, WO 163/58, AC/P(51)6; see ibid., DEFE 7/597, encl. 41.

11. Ibid., encl. 45, extract from SM/M(51)12; ibid., SM/P(51)49.

12. PRO, HO 45/25009, ref.700.169/62, minutes of 18 and 11 Sep. 1951.

13. A. Seldon, *Churchill's Indian Summer: The Conservative Government, 1951–55* (London, 1981), 311.

14. Churchill to Trenchard, 5 Mar. 1951, cited in M. Gilbert, *Never Despair: Winston S. Churchill, 1945–1965* (London, 1988), 598. For the views of Liddell Hart, see B. H. Liddell Hart, *Defence in the West: Some Riddles of War and Peace* (London, 1950), ch. 17.
15. *The Times*, 19 June 1951, 3.
16. Conservative Research Department, *General Election 1951: The Campaign Guide Supplement* (Conservative and Unionist Central Office, Oct. 1951), 73; see id., *Campaign Guide 1951: An Encyclopedia of Politics* (Conservative and Unionist Central Office, Jan. 1951). This change in emphasis was in the context of the much higher public concern over defence matters after the outbreak of the Korean War. In the 1950 General Election, only 28% of Tory candidates had mentioned defence issues in their addresses. In the 1951 General Election, that figure had risen to 72%. D. Capitanchik, 'Public Opinion and Popular Attitudes Towards Defence', in J. Baylis (ed.), *British Defence Policy in a Changing World* (London, 1977), 266–7. See also W. P. Snyder, *The Politics of British Defence Policy, 1945–1962* (London, 1965), 56–7. For Eden's involvement on the Home Guard question, see 485 HC (Deb.) 5s, cols. 718, 734, 750, 828–9, 885.
17. K. Student, 'Airborne Forces', in B. H. Liddell Hart (ed.), *The Soviet Army* (London, 1956), 380–1. Soviet airborne capabilities—as with the offensive capabilities of the Soviet armed forces as a whole in the post-war years—were in all likelihood greatly overestimated in the West. See M. A. Evangelista, 'Stalin's Postwar Army Reappraised', *International Security* 7 (1982/3), 110–38.
18. PRO, WO 163/58, app. A to AC/P(51)22.
19. Ibid., AC/M(51)10.
20. PRO, CAB 123/23, CC(51)10; see 494 HC (Deb.) 5s, cols. 580–1; PRO, WO 163/58, AC/M(51)10; see also F. W. S. Craig (ed.), *British General Election Manifestos, 1918–1966* (London, 1970), 145.
21. 494 HC (Deb.) 5s, cols. 578–695; see 493 HC (Deb.) 5s, col. 562; Chatham House Study Group, *Defence in the Cold War: The Task for the Free World* (London, 1950), 120; see also Cmd. 8475/52, 7.
22. *The Times*, 22 Nov. 1951, 5; see *Glasgow Herald*, 8 Nov. 1951, 4.
23. See 494 HC (Deb.) 5s, cols. 1126–475.
24. WO 163/362, HG Co-ordinating Conference, 13 Dec. 1951.
25. See *The Times*: 26 Jan. 1952, 3; 19 Jan. 1952, 3.
26. PRO, HO 45/25009, minutes, 3 Jan. 1952, 19 Jan. 1952.
27. Ibid., Maxwell Fyfe to Head, 24 Jan. 1952.
28. 496 HC (Deb.) 5s, cols. 8–9.

29. Ibid., col. 9; see *The Times*: 11 Nov. 1952, 3; 28 Apr. 1952, 2.

30. 497 HC (Deb.) 5s, cols. 80, 2462.

31. Lord Moran, *Winston Churchill: The Struggle for Survival 1940–65* (London, 1966), 366; see also ibid., 310, 315, 361.

32. *The Times*, 28 Apr. 1952, 2; see PRO, CAB 128/24, CC(52)30.

33. See, e.g., *The Services and Territorial Magazine*, May/June 1952, comment by Lt.-Col. T. A. Lowe, 1.

34. *The Times*: 28 Apr. 1952, 2; 11 Nov. 1952, 3; 507 HC (Deb.) 5s, col. 258; see PRO, WO 163/362.

35. PRO, WO 163/119, ECAC/P(52)86.

36. Ibid., ECAC/M(52)24; see Cmd. 8770/53, 12.

37. 507 H.C. (Deb.) 5s, col. 426.

38. See 505 HC (Deb.) 5s, cols. 187–8; 507 HC (Deb.) 5s, cols. 389–90; 501 HC (Deb.) 5s, col. 1127.

39. PRO, WO 163/119, ECAC/M(52)26; ibid., WO 163/59, AC/M(52)10.

40. 507 HC (Deb.) 5s, col. 949.

41. 512 HC (Deb.) 5s, cols. 576, 993.

42. Ibid., col. 576; see Moran, 7 Mar. 1953, 403.

43. MRC, MSS. 292/881.423/6, Butter to Tewson, 15 May 1953; see ibid., *passim*.

44. See 512 HC (Deb.) 5s, cols. 953, 993, 1018–19; 513 HC (Deb.) 5s, col. 270.

45. PRO, CAB 129/63, CC(53)258.

46. PRO, CAB 129/26, CC(53)62.

47. 520 H.C. (Deb.) 5s, col. 784.

48. PRO, CAB 129/26, CC(53)62.

49. 520 HC (Deb.) 5s, col. 784.

50. 524 HC (Deb.) 5s, col. 2745; 520 HC (Deb.) 5s, col. 784. The Conservative government suffered from a similar political problem—how to avoid allowing the Opposition to say 'I told you so'—in its later efforts to come to a decision about the termination of National Service. [See M. S. Navias, 'Terminating Conscription? The British National Service Controversy', *Journal of Contemporary History* 24 (1989), 195–208.]

51. 524 HC (Deb.) 5s, col. 2662.

52. *The Times*, 6 Apr. 1954, 6; Cmd. 9075/54, 13.

53. *Home Guard News* (National Edition): Aug. 1954, 7; June 1954, 5; May 1954, 7; *The Times*: 4 June 1954, 4; 29 Apr. 1954, 8; 524 HC (Deb.) 5s, col. 2745; *Army Estimates 1954–55* (HMSO, 1954), 38.

54. *The Times*, 13 Dec. 1954, 5.

55. 546 HC (Deb.) 5s, col. 1245; Cmd. 9395/55, 14.

56. See Craig, *General Election Manifestos*, 160, 177–8; *Army Estimates 1955–56* (HMSO, 1955), 38.

57. C. J. Bartlett, *The Long Retreat: A Short History of British Defence Policy, 1945–70* (London, 1972), 107; see Cmd. 9391/55, *passim*.

58. 547 HC (Deb.) 5s, col. 1847; Cmd. 9688/56, 9.

59. *The Times*, 21 Dec. 1955, 9; see F. J. B. Atkinson letter, ibid., 9 Dec. 1955, 11; *The Dunovarian: The Journal of the 2nd Dorset Home Guard Battalion* 1 (1) 5 Jan. 1956, 12.

60. 572 HC (Deb.) 5s, col. 210; *Manchester Guardian*, 27 June 1957; see Cmnd. 124/57.

61. SRO, HH51/61, 9/HG/172(DTA), 26 July 1957.

Conclusion

1. Vt. Bridgeman, 'When we had 1,700,000 Home Guards', *Home Guard News*, May 1954, 14.

2. R. Harrison, *Rex: An Autobiography* (London, 1974), 66.

3. H. Greiner, 'Operation Seeloewe and Intensified Airwarfare against England up to 30 Oct. 1940', 11, MS C-059a Supplementary, reprinted in D. S. Detwiler (ed.), *World War II German Military Studies: A collection of 213 special reports prepared by former officers of the Wehrmacht for the United States Army* 7 (New York, 1979), 11.

4. J. Wedgwood, *Memoirs of a Fighting Life* (London, 1941), 248.

5. I. F. W. Beckett, *Riflemen Form: A Study of the Rifle Volunteer Movement 1859–1908* (Aldershot, 1982), 85.

6. See P. Simpkins, *Kitchener's Army: The Raising of the New Armies, 1914–16* (Manchester, 1988).

7. Central Statistical Office, *Statistical Digest of the War* (HMSO, 1951), 1, 8–9, 13; Beckett, *Riflemen Form*, 85; B. R. Mitchell, *British Historical Statistics* (Cambridge, 1988), 9; PRO, WO 32/5048, Volunteer Force Return of Strength, 31 Mar. 1917.

8. See P. Grafton (ed.), *You, You & You! The People Out of Step with World War II* (London, 1981), 28.

9. See Bridgeman, '1,700,000 Home Guards', 14.

10. See P. Morton, 'Another Victorian Paradox: Anti-Militarism in a Jingoistic Society', *Historical Reflections* 8 (1981), 170 ff.; J. M. Osborne, 'Defining Their Own Patriotism: British Volunteer Training Corps in the First World War', *Journal of Contemporary History* 23 (1988), 64 ff.

11. S. Orwell and I. Angus (eds.), *The Collected Essays, Journalism and Letters of George Orwell, III: As I Please, 1943–1945* (New York, 1968), 201.

12. LHC, Pownall Diary, 29 Sept. 1940.

13. IWM, J. K. Howard and H. W. Endicott, *Summary Report, British Home Guard* (1941), 16.

14. PRO, HO 186/1513, minute to Secretary, 19 May 1942.

15. H. Smith, *Bureaucrats in Battledress: A History of the Ministry of Food Home Guard* (Conway, 1945), foreword by Lord Bridgeman.

16. IWM, H. W. Endicott, *Confidential Supplementary Report re: British Home Guard* (1941), 10. A sense of Bridgeman's style can be gathered from the record of a talk he gave at the RUSI in January 1942. See Bridgeman, 'The Home Guard', *Journal of the Royal United Services Institution*, May 1942, 140–9.

17. P. J. Grigg, *Prejudice and Judgement* (London, 1948), 352; see, e.g., E. Summerskill, *A Woman's World* (London, 1967), 74.

18. See, e.g., PRO, WO 199/3202, War Diary, 19 Bn Kent HG, 5 Dec. 1940; P. J. Grigg foreword, J. Brophy, *Britain's Home Guard: A Character Study* (London, 1945), 5; J. R. Williams, *A Record of Service, No. 1 Battalion (Denbighshire) Home Guard* (Conway, 1943), 121; S. W. Wayman, *With the Home Guard: The History of 'A' (Winchester City) Company 5th Hampshire Battalion* (Winchester, 1945), 9.

19. For the planning of Sealion, see: W. Ansel, *Hitler Confronts England* (Durham, NC, 1960); R. Wheatley, *Operation Sea Lion: German Plans for the Invasion of England, 1939–1942* (Oxford, 1958). See also Greiner, 'Operation Seeloewe'; and G. Blumentritt, 'Operation "Sealion"', and 'Herr Warlimont's Opinion on Operation "Seeloewe"', C-059, in Detwiler, *German Military Studies*. On the problem of transport aircraft, see A. Ausems, 'The Luftwaffe's Airborne Losses in May 1940: An Interpretation', *Aerospace Historian* 32 (1985), 184–8.

20. See IWM, RFSS files, H/5/157, Brandt to Berger returning survey of Home Guard, 21 Oct. 1944. Nor, despite assertions made in many unit histories, did the Home Guard serve as an example for the Germans in setting up the *Volkssturm* in 1944. Though similar in aims amd makeup, this German 'Home Guard' was linked in its creators' minds with the Prussian *Landsturm* of 1813–14 rather than anything the enemy had done earlier in the war. F. W. Seidler, *Deutscher Volkssturm: Das letzte Aufgebot 1944/45* (Munich, 1989), 35, 372, *passim*.

21. See, e.g., Bundesarchiv-Militärarchiv, WK XIII/577, Nachrichtenblatt Nr. 33, 1 Aug. 1940; ibid., Nachrichtenblatt Nr. 39, 10 Aug. 1940; ibid., WK XIII/574, Britisches Heer (Bestimmt für den Gebrauch der Truppe im Felde), July 1940.

22. R. Cox, *Operation Sealion* (London, 1975); D. G. Chandler, 'Fire Over

England: Threats of Invasion that Never Came', *Consortium on Revolutionary Europe Proceedings* 16 (1986), 444. Norman Longmate, in imagining the consequences of a successful September 1940 invasion in his book *If Britain Had Fallen* (London, 1972), found it necessary to give the Germans not only a vastly more successful campaign against the RAF, but also perfect invasion weather and opponents who possessed no strategic reserve (i.e. the Mobile Column) [chs. 5–7]. Kenneth Macksey has postulated that if an invasion attempt had been planned in late May and mounted in July 1940, in good weather, it probably would have succeeded. His scenario, however, depends heavily on Hitler taking a far greater interest in the idea of invasion than he actually did. [See K. Macksey, *Invasion: The German Invasion of England, July 1940* (New York, 1980).]

23. Ansel, *Hitler Confronts*, 227.
24. West Country, 'The Greatest Bluff in History', *Fighting Forces* 21 (1945), 306; see W. A. D. Englefield, *Limpsfield Home Guard 1940–1945* (London, 1946).
25. For the equipment and training of German airborne forces, see R. Edwards, *German Airborne Troops, 1936–45* (London, 1974), chs. 3, 5.
26. Jimmy Perry had been a member of the Home Guard, as the sometimes quite frightening accuracy of the series demonstrates. See J. Perry and D. Croft, *Dad's Army* (London, 1975), 8. Earlier comic treatments include *Keep the Home Guard Turning* (1943) by Compton Mackenzie, and *Home Guard Goings On* (1941) by Basil Boothroyd.
27. See M. Middlebrook, *The Nuremberg Raid: 30–31 March 1944* (London, 1973), 314.
28. LHC, Burnett-Stuart memoir, 181; see B. Horrocks, *A Full Life* (London, 1974), 96.
29. For the social aspects and class mixing of the Home Guard, see, e.g., F. and J. Shaw (comps.), *We Remember the Home Guard* (Oxford, 1990), J. Slawson recollection, 55, 61, J. O'Keefe recollection, 199, P. C. Vigor recollection, 284; E. Raymond, *Please You, Draw Near: Autobiography 1922–1968* (London, 1969), 82; IWM, Howard and Endicott, 14; H. Gough, *Soldiering On* (London, 1954), 248; Orwell and Angus, *As I Please*, 22–3. For the wearing of old uniforms by officers, see IWM, Baker Papers, Box P251, '46 Years in the Royal Arsenal', 25; *British Legion Journal* 20 (1940), 93. For the lack of awe displayed towards authority figures, see, e.g., *Ashford Home Guard O.C.A. Magazine* 2 (1948), 12; P. Mayhew (ed.), *One Family's War* (London, 1985), 65; D. Fernbach, 'Tom Wintringham and Socialist Defence Strategy', *History Workshop* 14

(1982), 74. For reflections generated through Home Guard duty, see C. S. Lewis, *Christian Reflections* (London, paperback edn., 1981), 80; C. Day Lewis, 'Watching Post', *Word Over All* (London, 1943), 27; Hants RO, 286M87/1, Binstead LDV Journal, H. V. Morgan entry, 6 July 1940.

30. See, e.g., Shaw, *We Remember*, J. Bevis recollection, 49–50.
31. PRO, WO 199/382, encl. 27A, AA Progress Report, 4 Oct. 1944.
32. See ibid.; Grigg, *Prejudice*, 362; F. Pile, *Ack Ack: Britain's Defence against Air Attack during the Second World War* (London, 1949), *passim*.
33. See Smith, *Bureaucrats*, title page; *'We Also Served': The Story of the Home Guard in Cambridgeshire and the Isle of Ely 1940–1943* (Cambridge, 1944); J. C. Spence, *'They Also Serve': The 39th Cheshire Battalion Home Guard* (London, 1945). John Milton, *Sonnet XVI, On His Blindness*.

Select Bibliography

MANUSCRIPT SOURCES

Public Record Office
AVIA 15; CAB 65, 66, 69, 79, 80, 106, 118, 128, 129, 131, 140; DEFE 7; FO
    371; HO 45, 186, 199; INF 1, 6; LAB 8; PREM 3; MEPO 2; WO 32, 161, 163,
    166, 185, 193, 197, 199, 216.
Public Record Office of Northern Ireland
CAB 3A; CAB 4; D 3803.
Scottish Record Office
HH 50, 51; MD 2, 4, 5.
Royal Archives
GVI PS 5338 ARMY
Bundesarchiv-Militärarchiv
WK XIII/577
Berkshire Record Office
P/TA1/1
Birmingham Reference Library
MS 1383/2
Carmarthen County Record Office
CDX/429/2; DX/26/27.
Cheshire Record Office
DDX 539, 445.
Chester City Record Office
CR 501, 528.
Gloucestershire Record Office
D 2078/3/1–7; D 2078, Box 57; D2095/1–2; D 2388/2/4.
Greater London Record Office
HG 1–81; B/WHF/232, 238.
Guildhall Library
MS 5919/1; MS 5924/6; MS 5926/1.
Hampshire Record Office
268 M 87.
Imperial War Museum
H/5/157; MI4/14/68.
Leicestershire Record Office
DE 3620; DE 3548; DE 819.

Modern Records Centre, Warwick University
MSS. 292/881.423/5–6; MSS. 75/2/3/2–3; MSS. 200/F/3/51/22/66.
Northamptonshire Record Office
ZB 75; 1964/12; 1968/138.
Shropshire Record Office
101/1; 1024/1; 2588/1.
Suffolk Record Office (Ipswich)
HD 1012/1; IA 1/411/15; IA 2/1205/9, 1, 3.
Tom Harrisson Mass-Observation Archive
TC 23, Box 7, files I, J.
West Yorkshire Archives Service (Bradford)
ID 83/5.
West Yorkshire Archives Service (Huddersfield)
KC 113.
Wiltshire Record Office
2099/1–21; 1292/1–8; 2435/1; 2585/8.

Private Papers

ALANBROOKE [A. Brooke, 1st Viscount] (Liddell Hart Centre for Military Archives).

ALTRINCHAM [E. Grigg. 1st Baron] (Bodleian Library/Queen's University, Ontario).

AVON [A. Eden, 1st Earl] (Birmingham University Library).

BARKER, H. A. (Imperial War Museum).

BASDEN, E. B. (Buckinghamshire Record Office).

CROFT [H. P., 1st Baron] (Churchill College, Cambridge).

DAWSON [G., 1st Viscount] (Bodleian Library).

FARLEY, J. (Imperial War Museum).

GLYN, R. (Berkshire Record Office).

GRIFFIN, F. J. (Imperial War Museum).

GRIGG, P. J. (Churchill College, Cambridge).

HAWES, L. A. (Imperial War Museum).

HAYES, L. T. (Imperial War Museum).

INGRAM, C. (Imperial War Museum).

KIRKE, W. (Liddell Hart Centre for Military Archives).

MACKENZIE KING, W. L. (Public Archives of Canada).

POWNALL, H. (Liddell Hart Centre for Military Archives).

ROE, W. C. (Imperial War Museum).

SLACK, A. E. (Chesterfield Public Library).

SPEARS, E. (Churchill College, Cambridge).

STUART, J. B. (Liddell Hart Centre for Military Archives).

SUTTON, G. W. (Imperial War Museum).

TAYLOR, M. J. (Public Archives of Newfoundland).

WALKER, J. (Liddle Collection).

WIMBERLEY, D. (Imperial War Museum).

WOOLTON [F. J. Marquis, 1st Earl] (Bodleian Library).

Theses

HALL, D. I., 'Peering Through the Veil of Uncertainty: British Anti-Invasion Planning, 1940', MA thesis (University of New Brunswick, 1987).

MOON, H. R., 'The Invasion of the United Kingdom: Public Controversy and Official Planning, 1888–1918', Ph.D. thesis (London, 1968).

NEWBOLD, D. J., 'British planning and preparations to resist invasion on land, September 1939–September 1940', Ph.D. thesis (London, 1988).

PRINTED SOURCES

Government and Service Publications

Army Estimates, 1952–53.

Army Estimates, 1953–54.

Cmd. 5381/1937; Cmd. 6325/1941; Cmd. 6326/1941; Cmd. 8475/1952; Cmd. 8477/1952; Cmd. 8770/1953; Cmd. 8763/1953; Cmd. 9075/1954; Cmd. 9391/ 1955; Cmd. 9395/1956; Cmd. 9688/1956; Cmnd. 124/1957.

Home Guard Lists, 1941–45, 1952–56.

House of Commons Debates, Fifth Series [H.C. (Deb.) 5s.].

House of Commons Paper 29, *Army Appropriation Account 1940* (HMSO, 1940).

House of Commons Paper 29, *Army Appropriation Account 1941* (HMSO, 1943).

House of Lords Debates, Fifth Series [H.L. (Deb.) 5s.].

Index to the Correspondence of the Foreign Office, 1940, Part IV (HMSO, 1971).

Parliament of Northern Ireland, *House of Commons Debates*, 23–7.

US Department of Defense Technical Manual 30–410, *Handbook on the British Army, with Supplement on the Royal Air Force and Civil Defense Organisation*, 30 Sept. 1942 [reprinted as: Brain L. Davis (ed.), *The British Army in WWII* (London, 1990)].

Memoirs, Diaries

ALLINGHAM, M., *The Oaken Heart* (London, 1941).

ARCHER, F., *When Village Bells were Silent* (London, 1975).

BEARDMORE, G., *Civilians at War: Journals 1938–1946* (London, 1984).

BELL, A. O. (ed.), *The Diary of Virginia Woolf: V, 1936–1941* (London, 1984).

BISHOP, A. and BENNETT, Y. A. (eds.), *Wartime Chronicle: Vera Brittain's Diary, 1939–1945* (London, 1989).

BOOTHROYD, B., *Home Guard Goings On* (London, 1941).

BROWNRIGG, D., *Unexpected: A Book of Memories* (London, 1942).

BRYANT, A., *The Lion & the Unicorn: A Historian's Testament* (London, 1969).

CHANDOS [O. Lyttelton, 1st Viscount], *The Memoirs of Lord Chandos* (London, 1972).

CHURCHILL, W. S., *The Second World War*, vols. II–IV (London, 1949–51).

COLVILLE, J., *The Fringes of Power: Downing Street Diaries, 1939–1955* (London, 1985).

CROFT, H. P., *My Life of Strife* (London, 1948).

CROZIER, W. P., *Off the Record: Political Interviews 1933–1943*, ed. A. J. P. Taylor (London, 1973).

DIXON, P., *Double Diploma: The Life of Sir Pierson Dixon* (London, 1968).

DONNELLY, P. (ed.), *Mrs Milburn's Dairies: An Englishwoman's Day-to-Day Reflections 1935–45* (London, 1979).

ECCLES, D. (ed.), *By Safe Hand: Letters of Sybil and David Eccles* (London, 1983).

AVON [A. Eden, 1st Earl], *Freedom and Order: Selected Speeches 1939–1946* (2nd edn. New York, 1971).

——*The Reckoning* (London, 1960).

GOUGH, H., *Soldiering On* (London, 1954).

GRAFTON, P. (ed.), *You, You & You! The People Out of Step with World War II* (London, 1981).

GRAVES, C., *Great Days* (London, 1944).

——*Off the Record* (London, 1942).

GRIGG, P. J., *Prejudice and Judgement* (London, 1948).

HARRISON, R., *Rex: An Autobiography* (London, 1974).

HODGSON, V., *Few Eggs and No Oranges: A Diary* (London, 1976).

HOLMES, J. B. (ed.), *Like It Was: The Diaries of Malcolm Muggeridge* (New York, 1982).

HOPKINSON, T., *Of This Our Time* (London, 1987).

HORROCKS, B., *A Full Life* (London, 1974).

ISMAY [H., 1st Baron] *The Memoirs of Lord Ismay* (London, 1960).

KRAUSE, D. (ed.), *The Letters of Sean O'Casey 1942–1954, II* (New York, 1980).

LAW, F., *A Man at Arms: Memoirs of Two World Wars* (London, 1983).

LEASOR, J. (comp.), *War at the Top: Based on the Experiences of General Sir Leslie Hollis* (London, 1959).

LEHMANN, J., *I am My Brother* (New York, 1960).

LEUTZE, J. (ed.), *The London Observer: The Journal of General Raymond E. Lee 1940–1941* (London, 1971).

LEWIS, C. D., *Word Over All* (London, 1943).

LEWIS, C. S., *Christian Reflections* (London, 1981 edn.).

LIDDELL HART, B. H., *The Memoirs of Captain Liddell Hart, I–II* (London, 1965).

MACKENZIE, C., *My Life and Times, Octave 8, 1938–1946* (London, 1949).

MACLEOD, R. and KELLY, D. (eds.), *The Ironside Diaries, 1937–1940* (London, 1962).

MACRAE, R. S., *Winston Churchill's Toyshop* (Kineton, 1971).

MARTIN, K., *Editor: A Second Volume of Autobiography* (London, 1968).

MILLIGAN, S., *Adolf Hitler: My Part in His Downfall* (London, 1971).

MORAN [C. M. Wilson, 1st Baron], *Winston Churchill: The Struggle for Survival 1940–1965* (London, 1966).

MARSHALL-CORNWALL, J., *Wars and Rumours of Wars: A Memoir* (London, 1984).

MAYHEW, P. (ed.), *One Family's War* (London, 1985).

MORGAN, F., *Peace and War: A Soldier's Life* (London, 1961).

MORRISON, H., *An Autobiography* (London, 1960).

MOSLEY, O., *My Life* (London, 1968).

MURROW, E. R., *This is London* (New York, 1941).

NICOLSON, N. (ed.), *Harold Nicolson: Diaries and Letters 1939–1945* (London, 1967).

ORWELL, S. and ANGUS, I. (eds.), *The Collected Essays, Journalism and Letters of George Orwell, III: As I Please, 1943–1945* (New York, 1968).

PANTER-DOWNES, M., *London War Notes, 1939–1945* (New York, 1971).

PILE, F., *Ack Ack: Britain's Defence against Air Attack during the Second World War* (London, 1949).

PIMLOTT, B., *The Second World War Diary of Hugh Dalton* (London, 1986).

RAYMOND, E., *Please You, Draw Near: Autobiography 1922–1968* (London, 1969).

SCHIMINSKI, S. and TREECE, H. (eds.), *Leaves in the Storm: A Book of Diaries* (London, 1947).

SCOTT, H., *Your Obedient Servant* (London, 1959).

SHAW, F. and J. (comps.), *We Remember the Home Guard* (Oxford, 1990).

SHINWELL, E., *Lead with the Left: My First Ninety-Six Years* (London, 1981).

SILLITOE, P., *Cloak Without Dagger* (London, 1955).

STIRLING, W. F., *Safety Last* (London, 1953).

SUMMERSKILL, E., *A Woman's World* (London, 1967).

WARBURG, F., *All Authors are Equal* (London, 1973).

WEDGWOOD, J., *Memoirs of a Fighting Life* (London, 1941).

WHEATLEY, D., *Stranger Than Fiction* (London, 1976 edn.).

WHEELER-BENNETT, J. (ed.), *Action This Day: Working with Churchill* (London, 1968).

Local Home Guard Histories [MoD & British Library]

BARCLAY, E. D., *The History of the 45th Warwickshire (B'Ham) Battalion Home Guard* (Birmingham, 1945).

BINT, R., *Record of Service: The 'Highlands' Platoon (East Company), 6th Oxfordshire (Oxford City) Battalion* (Oxford, 1945).

BISHOP, N. R., *'An Honour to Serve': A Short History of the 8th Surrey (Reigate) Battalion Home Guard, May 1940–December 1944* (Reigate, n/d).

BOYD, A., *A Brief History of the 1st Moray Battalion Home Guard* (1945).

BOYLE, H. K., *History of the 9th West Riding (Leeds) Bn. Home Guard, 14th May 1940 to 15th August 1945* (typescript, 1945).

BRADY, J., *The History and Record of 'B' Company 10th (Torbay) Battn. Devonshire Home Guard* (Torquay, 1944).

BRADLEY, D. A., *History of the 6th Battalion Devonshire Home Guard* (typescript, 1944).

BROCK, A. St. H. (ed.), *7th Herefordshire Battalion Home Guard: A History of the Battalion, 1940–44* (1945).

BROWNE, C., *12th Battalion Northumberland Home Guard, 'C' Company 1940–1944* (Gateshead-on-Tyne, 1946).

CHURCHILL, A. W., *From 'Stand To' to 'Stand Down': or with the Seventh Batt. Shropshire Home Guard from May 1940 to December 1944* (Hereford, 1946).

COOKE, W. A., *The Story of the 101 Surrey Home Guard Rocket Anti-Aircraft Battery, Anerley 1942–1944* (1944).

CROMBIE, D. C., *History of the 5th (Bideford) Battalion Devon Home Guard* (Bristol, 1946).

DAVIES, J. and LLOYD, J. E. (eds.), *3rd Cards. Battalion Home Guard* (Lampeter, 1947).

ENGLEFIELD, W. A. D., *Limpsfield Home Guard 1940–1945* (London, 1946).

FINCH, P., *Warmen Courageous: The Story of the Essex Home Guard* (Southend-on-Sea, 1951).

FINE, S., *With the Home Guard* (London, 1943).

FISKIN, A. J., *Lauriston 1940–1944: The Story of 'A' Company of the 8th Battalion City of Edinburgh Home Guard* (Edinburgh, 1945).

GARRETT, G. D. S., *The Hawker Platoon, 'E' Company, 53rd Surrey Battalion H.G.: Service Record 1940–1944* (Claremont, 1945).

GREENSHIELDS, C. E., *55th Surrey (Sutton and Cheam) Home Guard: An Historical Survey* (Sutton, 1944).

HOLLOWAY, B. G. (ed.), *The Northamptonshire Home Guard 1940–1945: A History* (Northampton, 1949).

JAGER, H., *The Rise and Ascent of 'Number Two Platoon', 'A' Company, 17th Battalion, Cheshire Regiment (Home Guard)* (Liverpool, 1945).

KENTISH, L. W., *Bux 4: Records and Reminiscences of the 4th Buckinghamshire Battalion Home Guard* (1945).

McGEOCH, W. P., *The Triumphs and Tragedies of a Home Guard (Factory) Company: B Company 41st Warwickshire (Birmingham) Battalion Home Guard* (Birmingham, 1946).

MACKAY, E. A. (ed.), *The History of the Wiltshire Home Guard* (Lockbridge, 1946).

MOUNTFORD, J. G., *Halesowen Home Guard* (Shrewsbury, 1944).

NEAL, D. H., *The 9th Hertfordshire Battalion Home Guard: A History 1940–1945* (London, 1946).

OGILVY-DALGLEISH, J. W., *The Rutland Home Guard of 1940–44* (Oakham, 1955).

PARKES, A. J., *The Record of the 24th Staffs. (Tettenhall) Bn. HG* (Wolverhampton, 1946).

PATTERSON, W. M., *'One O' One Durham': Being the Short Life Story of 101 (Durham) Home Guard Rocket Anti Aircraft Battery* (n/d).

RAMSDEN, J. V., *A Note on the 19th (Seaton) Battalion Home Guard Devonshire Regiment* (1945).

SMITH, H., *Bureaucrats in Battledress: A History of the Ministry of Food Home Guard* (Conway, 1945).

SPENCE, J. C., *'They Also Serve': The 39th Cheshire Battalion Home Guard* (London, 1945).

WAYMAN, S. W., *With the Home Guard: The History of 'A' (Winchester City) Company 5th Hampshire Battalion* (Winchester, 1945).

WILLIAMS, J. R., *A Record of Service, No. 1 Battalion (Denbighshire) Home Guard* (Conway, 1943).

WILTSHER, H. J., *'Ever Faithful': The 1st (Loyal City of Exeter) Battalion, Devon Home Guard, 1940–1945* (Exeter, 1946).

LDV, *The Bromley Home Guard: A History of the 51st Kent Battalion* (n/d).

The Story of 'A' Company 4th Bucks Battalion Home Guard 1940–1944 (n/d).

35th City of London Battalion Home Guard (London, 1946).

Choughs Annual Register, 1 and 2 (Truro, 1944, 1945).

History of the Cheshire Home Guard: From L.D.V. Formation to Stand-Down 1940–1944 (Aldershot, 1950).

Seven Battalions: The Story of London Transport's Home Guard 1940–1946 (London, 1947).

The Story of the First Berkshire (Abingdon) Battalion Home Guard (Manchester, 1945).

The Story of 'C' Company, 14th (Moorside) Battalion Devon Home Guard (1945).

North-West (London) Frontier, No. 6 Company, 23rd Middlesex Battalion: A Souvenir of Home Guard Training and Other Activities during the War of 1939–45 (London, 1946).

The Story of No. 2 Company of the 7th Battn., Somerset Home Guard (1944).

A History of the 44th London (London Transport) Battalion of the Home Guard 1940–1946 (London, 1948).

The Watch on the Braids: The Record of an Edinburgh Home Guard Company 1940–1944 (Edinburgh, 1945).

'We Also Served': The Story of the Home Guard in Cambridgeshire and the Isle of Ely 1940–1943 (Cambridge, 1944).

The 29th Warwickshire (Birmingham) Battalion Home Guard, May 1940– December 1944 (Birmingham, 1946).

Other Primary Sources

BROPHY, J., *Home Guard: A Handbook for the L.D.V.* (London, 1940).

——*A Home Guard Drill Book and Field Service Manual* (London, 1940).

BURKE, J., *Rights and Powers of the Home Guard* (London, 1940).

Conservative Research Department, *General Election 1951: The Campaign Guide Supplement* (Oct. 1951).

——*The Campaign Guide 1951: An Encyclopedia of Politics* (Jan. 1951).

ELLIOT, A. G., *The Home Guard Encyclopedia* (London, 1942).

[IWM] ENDICOTT, H. W., *Confidential Supplementary Report re: British Home Guard* (1942).

[IWM] HOWARD, J. K. and ENDICOTT, H. W., *Summary Review, British Home Guard* (1941).

KERR, A., *The Home Guard Handbook* (London, 1941).

——*The Art of Guerrilla Fighting and Patrol: A Manual of Infantry Defensive Training* (London, 1940).

LANGDON-DAVIES, J., *Home Guard Warfare* (London, 1941).

——*The Home Guard Training Manual* (London, 1940).

LEVEY, J. H., *Home Guard Training: Some Lessons to Teach and Learn* (London, 1940).

LIDDELL HART, B. H., *Defence of the West* (New York, 1950).
——*The Defence of Britain* (London, 1939).
SHIRLAW, G. B. and TROKE, C., *Medicine versus Invasion: The Home Guard Medical Service in Action* (London, 1941).
SLATER, H., *Home Guard for Victory! An Essay on Strategy, Tactics and Training* (London, 1941).
WINTRINGHAM, T., *New Ways of War* (London, 1940).

Newspapers and Periodicals
Army Quarterly; Back Badge; British Legion Journal; Daily Express; Daily Herald; Daily Mail; Daily Mirror; Daily Record; Daily Sketch; Daily Telegraph; Defence; Edinburgh Evening News; Fighting Forces; Glasgow Herald; Home Guard News; The Home Guardian; Household Brigade Magazine; Journal of the Royal United Services Institution; London Illustrated News; Manchester Guardian; Mass-Observation Bulletin; The Millgate; National Review; New Statesman and Nation; New York Times; New Review; News of the World; Night Hawk Magazine; Punch; Round Table; Scottish Daily Express; Scottish Sunday Express; Scotsman; Spectator; Sphere; Sunday Chronicle; Sunday Dispatch; Sunday Express; Sunday Graphic; Sunday Pictorial; Sunday Post; The Times; Tribune; Volunteer for Liberty; Yorkshire Post.

Secondary Sources: Books
ABLEMAN, P., *Dad's Army: The Defence of a Front Line English Village* (London, 1989).
AGAR, H., *Britain Alone: June 1940–June 1941* (London, 1972).
ANDREW, C., *Secret Service: The Making of the British Intelligence Community* (London, 1985).
ANSEL, W., *Hitler Confronts England* (Durham, NC, 1960).
BABINGTON, A., *Military Intervention in Britain: From the Gordon Riots to the Gibraltar Incident* (London, 1990).
BAILER, U., *The Shadow of the Bomber: The Fear of Air Attack and British Politics, 1932–1939* (London, 1980).
BARKER, E., *Churchill and Eden at War* (London, 1978).
BARNETT, C., *Britain and Her Army 1509–1970* (London, 1970).
BARTLETT, C. J., *The Long Retreat: A Short History of British Defence Policy, 1945–70* (London, 1972).
BARTON, B., *The Blitz: Belfast in the War Years* (Belfast, 1989).
BAYLIS, J. (ed.) *British Defence Policy in a Changing World* (London, 1977).
BECKETT, I. F. W., *The Amateur Military Tradition 1558–1945* (Manchester, 1991).

BECKETT, I. F. W., *Call to Arms: The Story of Bucks Citizen Soldiers from their Origins to Date* (Buckingham, 1985).

——*Riflemen Form: A Study of the Rifle Volunteer Movement 1859–1908* (Aldershot, 1982).

——and GOOCH, J. (eds.), *Politicians and Defence: Studies in the Formulation of British Defence Policy 1845–1970* (Manchester, 1981).

BERLIN, I., *Mr Churchill in 1940* (Boston, 1950).

BOND, B., *British Military Policy Between the Two World Wars* (Oxford, 1980).

——*The Victorian Army and the Staff College, 1854–1914* (London, 1972).

BLAKE, R. and LOUIS, WM. R. (eds.), *Churchill* (New York, 1993).

BULLOCK, A., *Ernest Bevin: Foreign Secretary 1945–1951* (London, 1983).

CALDER, A., *The Myth of the Blitz* (London, 1991).

——*The People's War: Britain 1939–45* (London, 1969).

CARVER, M., *Tightrope Walking: British Defence Policy since 1945* (London, 1992).

Central Statistical Office, *Statistical Digest of the War* (HMSO, 1951).

CHAMBERLIN, E. R., *Life in Wartime Britain* (London, 1972).

COLLIER, B., *The Defence of the United Kingdom* (HMSO, 1957).

CLARKE, I. F., *Voices Prophesying War: Future Wars 1763–3749* (Oxford, 1992).

COLVILLE, J. R., *Man of Valour: The Life of Field-Marshal the Viscount Gort* (London, 1972).

CONNELL, J., *Auchinleck* (London, 1959).

COOK, D., *Forging the Alliance: NATO, 1945–1950* (New York, 1989).

COUSINS, G., *The Defenders: A History of the British Volunteer* (London, 1968).

COX, R., *Operation Sealion* (London, 1975).

CREVELD, M. VAN, *Technology and War: From 2000 BC to the Present* (New York, 1989).

——*Command in War* (Cambridge, Mass., 1985).

CUNNINGHAM, H., *The Volunteer Force: A Social and Political History* (Hamden, 1975).

DENNIS, P., *The Territorial Army 1906–1940* (Woodbridge, 1987).

DICKINSON, H. T. (ed.), *Britain and the French Revolution, 1789–1815* (London, 1989).

EDWARDS, R., *German Airborne Troops, 1936–45* (London, 1974).

EMSLEY, C., *British Society and the French Wars 1793–1815* (London, 1979).

FARRAR-HOCKLEY, A., *Goughie: The Life of General Sir Hubert Gough* (London, 1975).

FLEMING, P., *Operation Sea Lion* (New York, 1957).

FRASER, D., *Alanbrooke* (London, 1982).

FRASER, G. M., *The Hollywood History of the World* (London, 1988).

GALVIN, K. R., *Kent Home Guard: A History* (Tonbridge, 1980).

GELB, N., *Scramble: A Narrative History of the Battle of Britain* (London, 1985).

GILBERT, M., *Finest Hour: Winston S. Churchill, 1939–1940* (London, 1983).

——*Road to Victory: Winston S. Churchill, 1941–1945* (London, 1986).

——*Never Despair: Winston S. Churchill, 1945–1965* (London, 1988).

GILLETT, E. and MACMAHON, K. A., *A History of Hull* (Oxford, 1980).

GILLMAN, P. and L., *'Collar the Lot!': How Britain Interned and Expelled its Wartime Refugees* (London, 1980).

GLOVER, M., *Invasion Scare 1940* (London, 1990).

GLOVER, R., *Britain at Bay: Defence against Bonaparte, 1803–14* (London, 1973).

GOOCH, J., *The Prospect of War: Studies in British Defence Policy 1847–1942* (London, 1981).

GRAVES, C., *The Home Guard of Britain* (London, 1943).

——*Women in Green (The Story of the W.V.S.)* (London, 1948).

GRIFFEN, W., *Clive Staples Lewis: A Dramatic Life* (San Francisco, 1986).

HALL, H. D., *North American Supply* (HMSO, 1955).

HAMER, W. S., *The British Army: Civil–Military Relations 1885–1905* (Oxford, 1970).

HAMILTON, N., *Monty: The Making of a General 1887–1942* (London, 1981).

HEATH ROBINSON, W., *Heath Robinson at War* (London, 1978).

HEWISON, R., *Under Siege: Literary Life in London 1939–1945* (London, 1977).

HINSLEY, F. H. and SIMKINS, C. A. G., *British Intelligence in the Second World War, 4: Security and Counter-Intelligence* (HMSO, 1990).

HOUGH, R. and RICHARDS, D., *The Battle of Britain: The Jubilee History* (London, 1989).

HOGG, I. V., *The Encyclopedia of Infantry Weapons of World War II* (London, 1977).

HOWARD, M., *British Intelligence in the Second World War, 5: Strategic Deception* (HMSO, 1990).

IZZARD, M., *A Heroine in Her Time: A Life of Dame Helen Gwynne-Vaughan 1879–1967* (London, 1969).

JEFFREYS, K., *The Churchill Coalition and Wartime Politics, 1940–1945* (Manchester, 1991).

JOHNSON, D. E., *East Anglia at War 1939–1945* (Norwich, 1978).

KEEGAN, J. (ed.), *Churchill's Generals* (New York, 1991).

KUHN, V., *German Paratroopers in World War II* (London, 1978).

LAMPE, D., *The Last Ditch* (London, 1968).

LEWIS, J., *Heath Robinson: Artist and Comic Genius* (New York, 1973).

LEWIS, P., *A People's War* (London, 1986).

LIDDELL HART, B. (ed.), *The Soviet Army* (London, 1956).

LINDSAY, D., *Forgotten General: A Life of Andrew Thorne* (London, 1987).

LONGMATE, N., *How We Lived Then: A History of Everyday Life during the Second World War* (London, 1971).

——*If Britain Had Fallen* (London, 1972).

——*The Real Dad's Army* (London, 1974).

MACKSEY, K., *Armoured Crusader: A Biography of Major-General Sir Percy Hobart* (London, 1967).

——*Invasion: The German Invasion of England, July 1940* (New York, 1980).

McLYNN, F., *Invasion: From the Armada to Hitler, 1588–1945* (London, 1987).

McMILLAN, J., *The Way It Happened: Based on the Files of Express Newspapers* (London, 1980).

MARDER, A. J., *From Dreadnought to Scapa Flow, 1: The Road to War, 1904–1914* (London, 1961).

MELLOR, W. F. (ed.), *Casualties and Medical Statistics* (HMSO, 1972).

MINNS, R., *Bombers and Mash: The Domestic Front 1939–45* (London, 1980).

MITCHELL, B. R., *British Historical Statistics* (Cambridge, 1988).

MORGAN, K. O., *Labour in Power 1945–1951* (Oxford, 1984).

MOSLEY, L., *Backs to the Wall: London Under Fire 1939–45* (London, 1971).

MURPHY, J., *Dorset at War* (Sherborne, 1979).

PARKER, H. M. D., *Manpower: A Study in War-time Policy and Administration* (HMSO, 1957).

PARKINSON, R., *The Auk: Auchinleck, Victor at Alamein* (London, 1977).

PARTRIDGE, M. S., *Military Planning for the Defense of the United Kingdom, 1814–1870* (New York, 1989).

PERRY, J. and CROFT, D., *Dad's Army* (London, 1975).

PONTING, C., *1940: Myth and Reality* (London, 1990).

PORTER, B., *Plots and Paranoia: A History of Political Espionage in Britain, 1790–1988* (London, 1989).

POSTAN, M. M., HAY, D., SCOTT, J. D., *Design and Development of Weapons: Studies in Government and Industrial Organization* (HMSO, 1964).

RHODES JAMES, R., *Anthony Eden* (London, 1986).

RICHARDS, J. and ALDGATE, A., *Best of British: Cinema and Society 1930–1970* (Oxford, 1983).

RICHMOND, H. W., *The Invasion of Britain: An Account of Plans, Attempts & Counter-Measures from 1586 to 1918* (London, 1941).

RITTER, G., *The Sword and the Sceptre, II: The European Great Powers and the Wilhelmian Empire, 1890–1914* (Miami, 1970).

ROOTES, A., *Front Line Country* (London, 1980).

ROWLANDS, M. B., *The West Midlands from* AD *1000* (London, 1987).

SAINSBURY, J. D., *Hazardous Work* (Welwyn, 1985).

SCHWOERER, L. G., *'No Standing Armies!': The Anti-Army Ideology in Seventeenth-Century England* (Baltimore, 1974).

SCOTT, L. V., *Conscription and the Attlee Governments: The Politics and Policy of National Service 1945–1951* (Oxford, 1993).

SEIDLER, F. W., *Deutscher Volkssturm: Das Letzte Aufgebot 1944/45* (Munich, 1989).

SELDON, A., *Churchill's Indian Summer: The Conservative Government, 1951–55* (London, 1981).

SHELDEN, M., *Orwell: The Authorized Biography* (New York, 1991).

SHERMAN, A. J., *Island Refuge: Britain and Refugees from the Third Reich, 1933–1939* (Berkeley, Calif., 1973).

SIMPSON, A. W., *In the Highest Degree Odious: Detention without Trial in Wartime Britain* (Oxford, 1992).

SNYDER, W. P., *The Politics of British Defence Policy, 1945–1962* (London, 1965).

SPIERS, E. M., *The Army and Society 1815–1914* (London, 1980).

——*Haldane: An Army Reformer* (Edinburgh, 1980).

——*The Late Victorian Army, 1868–1902* (Manchester, 1992).

STACEY, C. P., *A Date with History* (Ottawa, 1983).

STRACHAN, H., *The Reform of the British Army, 1830–54* (Manchester, 1984).

STREET, A. G., *From Dusk Till Dawn* (London, 1947).

THOMAS, H., *John Strachey* (London, 1973).

THOMPSON, L., *1940: Year of Legend, Year of History* (London, 1966).

THOMPSON, R. W., *Churchill and Morton* (London, 1976).

THORPE, F. and PRONAY, N., *British Official Films in the Second World War: A Descriptive Catalogue* (Oxford, 1980).

TURNER, E. S., *The Phoney War on the Home Front* (London, 1969).

WARD, S., *War in the Countryside 1939–45* (London, 1988).

WARNER, P., *Invasion Road* (London, 1980).

WHEATLEY, R., *Operation Sea Lion: German Plans for the Invasion of England, 1939–1942* (Oxford, 1958).

WHEELER-BENNETT, J. W., *John Anderson: Viscount Waverley* (New York, 1962).

——*King George VI: His Life and Reign* (London, 1958).

WHITTAKER, L. B., *Stand Down: Orders of Battle for the Units of the Home Guard of the United Kingdom, November 1944* (Newport, 1990).

WOOTON, G., *The Official History of the British Legion* (London, 1956).

Secondary Sources: Articles

ANDREW, C., 'Churchill and Intelligence', *Intelligence and National Security 3* (1988), 181–93.

AUSEMS, A., 'The Luftwaffe's Airborne Losses in May 1940: An Interpretation', *Aerospace Historian* 32 (1985), 184–8.

BECKETT, I. F. W., 'Aspects of a Nation in Arms: Britain's Volunteer Training Corps in the Great War', *Revue Internationale d'Histoire Militaire* (1985), 27–39.

——'H. O. Arnold-Forster and the Volunteers', in I. Beckett and J. Gooch (eds.), *Politicians and Defence: Studies in the Formulation of British Defence Policy 1845–1970* (Manchester, 1981), ch. 3.

BRAZIER, J., 'The Home Guard—and Charles Graves', *The Military Historical Society Bulletin* 43 (1992), 65–6.

CAMPBELL, J. P., 'A British Plan to Invade England, 1941', *Journal of Military History* 58 (1994), 663–84.

CAPITANCHIK, D., 'Public Opinion and Popular Attitudes Towards Defence', in J. Baylis (ed.), *British Defence Policy in a Changing World* (London, 1977), ch. 10.

CHANDLER, D. G., 'Fire Over England: Threats of Invasion that Never Came', *Consortium on Revolutionary Europe Proceedings* 16 (1986), 432–47.

CHILDS, D., 'The Cold War and the "British Road", 1946–53', *Journal of Contemporary History* 23 (1988), 551–72.

DICKINSON, H. T., 'Popular Conservatism and Militant Loyalism 1789–1815', in H. T. Dickinson (ed.), *Britain and the French Revolution, 1789–1815* (London, 1989), ch. 5.

EVANGELISTA, M. A., 'Stalin's Postwar Army Reappraised', *International Security* 7 (1982/83), 110–38.

FARQUHARSON, J., 'After Sealion: A German Channel Tunnel?', *Journal of Contemporary History* 25 (1990), 409–30.

FERNBACH, D., 'Tom Wintringham and Socialist Defence Strategy', *History Workshop* 14 (1982), 63–91.

FRENCH, D., 'Spy Fever in Britain, 1900–1915', *Historical Journal* 21 (1978), 355–70.

GOLLIN, A. M., 'England is no longer an Island: The Phantom Airship Scare of 1909', *Albion* 13 (1981), 43–57.

GOOCH, J., 'Haldane and the "National Army"', in I. Beckett and J. Gooch (eds.), *Politicians and Defence: Studies in the Formulation of British Defence Policy 1845–1970* (Manchester, 1981), ch. 4.

GORST, A., ' "We must cut our coat according to our cloth": the making of British defence policy, 1945–8', in R. J. Aldrich (ed.), *British Intelligence, Strategy and the Cold War, 1945–51* (London, 1992), ch. 6.

GREENWOOD, D., 'Defence and National Priorities Since 1945', in J. Baylis, (ed.), *British Defence Policy in a Changing World* (London, 1977).

MACKENZIE, S. P., 'Citizens in Arms: The Home Guard and the Internal Security of the United Kingdom, 1940–41', *Intelligence and National Security* 6 (1991), 548–72.

MEISEL, J. S., 'The Germans are Coming! British Fiction of a German Invasion 1871–1913', *War, Literature and the Arts* 2 (1990), 41–79.

MORTEN, P., 'Another Victorian Paradox: Anti-Militarism in a Jingoistic Society', *Historical Reflections* 8 (1981), 169–89.

NAVIAS, M. S., 'Terminating Conscription? The British National Service Controversy, 1955–56', *Journal of Contemporary History* 24 (1989), 195–208.

OSBORNE, J. M., 'Defining Their Own Patriotism: British Volunteer Training Corps in the First World War', *Journal of Contemporary History* 23 (1988), 59–79.

PRONAY, N. and CROFT, J., 'British Film Censorship and Propaganda Policy during the Second World War', in J. Curran and V. Porter (eds.), *British Cinema History* (London, 1983), ch. 9.

REES, W., 'Continuity and Change in British Threat Assessments, 1945–1960', *Sandhurst Journal of Military Studies* 1 (1990), 47–58.

REYNOLDS, D., 'Churchill in 1940: The Worst and Finest Hour', in R. Blake and Wm. R. Louis (eds.), *Churchill* (New York, 1993), 241–55.

SPIERS, S., 'Tom Wintringham and the Socialist Way of War' (unpublished paper).

STAFFORD, D. A. T., 'Spies and Gentlemen: The Birth of the British Spy Novel', *Victorian Studies* 24 (1981), 489–509.

WARNER, P., 'Auchinleck', in J. Keegan (ed.), *Churchill's Generals* (New York, 1991), ch. 7.

WILT, A. F., ' "Sharte" and "Harpoon": German Cover Operations Against Great Britain in 1941', *Military Affairs* 38 (1974), 1–4.

WOODHALL, R., 'Come if You Dare: The Origins of the Volunteer Force of 1859–1908', *Army Quarterly and Defence Journal* 120 (1990), 176–81.

YELTON, D. K., 'British Public Opinion, the Home Guard, and the Defense of Great Britain, 1940–1944', *Journal of Military History* 58 (1994), 461–80.

Index